Questions Catholics Ask

FATHER BILL O'SHEA

From *The Catholic Leader* Question Box series

DOVE COMMUNICATIONS

Published by DOVE COMMUNICATIONS
60-64 Railway Road, Blackburn, Victoria 3130

Reprinted 1986

Designed by Shane Conroy
Cover design by Shane Conroy
Typesetting by Bookset, North Melbourne
Printed in Australia by the Leader Press, Brisbane

National Library of Australia
card number and ISBN 0 85924 339 7

Nihil Obstat:
Maurice J. Duffy, S.T.L.,
Censor Deputatus.

Imprimatur:
✠ Francis R. Rush, D.D.,
Archbishop of Brisbane.

The Nihil Obstat and Imprimatur are official
declarations that a book or pamphlet is free of
doctrinal or moral error. No implication is
contained therein that those who have granted
the Nihil Obstat and Imprimatur agree with the
contents, opinion or statements expressed. They
do not necessarily signify that the work is
approved as a basic text for catechetical
instruction.

Contents

To my Mother
Stella
my first teacher in the ways of faith
and the best of teachers.

Foreword

It is now more than two years since the editor of the Brisbane *Catholic Leader* put to me the proposal that I might conduct a regular question-and-answer feature in this newspaper.

My initial reaction to his suggestion was a guarded one. My first reason was an awareness of how much time and energy such a project would consume and I had my reservations about whether parish commitments would enable me to meet constant, weekly editorial deadlines.

The second reason for my hesitation was more fundamental, namely a doubt that there was a need for this kind of ministry in the Australian Church of the 1980s.

To my knowledge, nothing comparable had been attempted since the days of the illustrious Dr Rumble MSC, whose radio replies and newspaper contributions made his name a household word among Australian Catholics in the 1940s and 1950s.

Facetiously, I suggested the title 'Rumble Revisited' as a possible title for the proposed column. Ultimately, we were to settle for the more prosaic 'Question Box'.

Two years on, the success of the feature has proved that the editor's instincts were right and that my apprehensions, at least on the latter score, were unfounded.

In retrospect, I realise it was foolish to query the need for such a forum in the first place, and particularly in this period of the Church's history.

The rapid and widespread changes that have occurred in the Church in the twenty years since the Second Vatican Council have left many Catholics suffering from that psychological condition known as 'future shock'.

I believe that much of this could (and should) have been averted if more attention had been paid to the need for educating people to prepare them for the changes that took place. I am thinking particularly about changes in the liturgy and especially the way the celebration of Mass in the vernacular replaced the old Latin Mass with almost brutal suddenness.

In one of my 'Question Box' replies, I remarked that previous generations grew up with the idea that the Latin Mass was sacrosanct. People were not sufficiently aware that the Church's liturgy had undergone many developments in the course of its long history and that the standardisation of the celebration of the Eucharist which followed the Council of Trent in the 16th century represented just one more development in the 2000 year life-span of the Church.

Other new directions initiated by the Second Vatican Council which have caused much heartburn among traditionalist Catholics have been the Council's insistence on the primacy of conscience and its teaching about the nature of biblical truth.

The nature of biblical truth is perhaps the more sensitive area. The Council broke new ground with its definition of biblical truth as 'the truth which God willed to be put into the Scriptures for the sake of our salvation'.

This important principle was intended to free people from an over-preoccupation with historical and/or scientific truth which had shackled Catholic biblical study for many generations. The Council's aim was to teach that 'truth' should not be restricted to such a narrow understanding.

To some extent, this was simply an extension of the principles enunciated by Pius XII in an encyclical letter in 1943 that in our interpretation of the Bible we must take account of 'literary forms' — those forms of expression common and acceptable to the people of the time when the biblical books were written.

The clear implication of these principles is that God's saving truth can be communicated by means other than historical (or literally true) narratives.

It is apparent from the many questions on biblical topics I have received that this way of understanding the Scriptures has still not permeated through to the grass roots of Catholicism. Questions about Adam and Eve, the Flood, the Gospel miracles; the biblical accounts of the activity of angels and devils; the resurrection of Jesus and the nature of his risen body — these are all indications that these basic principles of biblical interpretation have not been fully grasped. Fundamentalism is still alive and well in the Church.

The answer to the problem lies in convincing those who see new theological insights and changes in the Church's practices as a betrayal of our heritage. I would hope that 'Question Box' has made its own small contribution.

When 'Question Box' was launched, we began the feature in a 'Dorothy Dix' fashion, with members of the *Catholic Leader's* staff invited to submit questions which they or their acquaintances had been discussing and wanted to have answered. This procedure lasted for only the first two weeks of the life of the column. After that the questions began to flow in.

Many readers have informed me that it has been their practice to keep a scrap-book of the weekly replies, and I have been particularly gratified to hear religion teachers, especially at secondary level, say how helpful these have proved with high school children. Several have suggested the collection and publication of these questions and answers in book form.

It is in response to these requests that this book makes its appearance under the title *Questions Catholics Ask*. As the title indicates, it is not intended by any means to be a comprehensive presentation of the Catholic faith. It is no more than what it claims to be, a collection of the questions and answers which have appeared in the column over the first eighteen months or so of its existence.

I am aware of the debt of thanks which I owe to many people for the success of this enterprise. I should like to express my thanks to Mr John Coleman, the editor of the *Catholic Leader*, whose brain-child the feature was originally, and who has subsequently given me his full support; to members of the *Leader* staff, especially Miss Joan Hannan and Miss Patricia Butler, whose skills and patience have ensured the accurate reporting of my telephoned replies; to Mr Garry Eastman, the Managing Director of Dove Communications, who approached me very early in the piece with a view to publishing, and has guided the complex transitional process from newspaper column to book form; to Archbishop Rush of Brisbane and his auxiliaries, Bishops Gerry and Cuskelly, for their constant support and encouragement, and at times valuable advice.

I wish also to thank a number of people who have assisted me from time to time in the compilation of answers in areas of specialisation which are outside my own competence: Bishop Wallace of Rockhampton; Monsignor Roberts, former Rector of Banyo Seminary; Father Jim Spence, Director of the Brisbane Matrimonial Tribunal; Fathers Peter Casey and Kevin Caldwell of the Catholic Family Welfare Bureau; Father Frank Douglas, Chancellor of the Archdiocese of Brisbane; Fathers Morgan Howe, Barry Copley, Michael McClure and Peter Gillam; as well as any I might have overlooked.

I thank the people of the parish of Beenleigh — fellow priests, religious and laity — for their encouragement and support, and for their patient understanding and tolerance of any pastoral neglect of them that the hours spent in working on 'Question Box' might have entailed.

And finally, my thanks to all those who contributed with their written questions and comments. Without them, of course, the whole enterprise would have been stillborn. I am grateful not only to those who have agreed with me, but also to the many who dissented from my own approach. Their reactions often challenged me to re-examine my own position and helped to sharpen my thinking. Though we may not have arrived at any 'consensus', it might at least be hoped that overall the promotion of the cause of truth has been served.

Father Bill O'Shea
Beenleigh, Qld.

Angels

Question 1:
This verse is in response to Fr Bill O'Shea's suggestion that Mary's angelic visitor at the Annunciation was 'all in her mind'.

It's all in the mind.
No angel? Next no Mary?
Is this the teaching now we find?
Perhaps we have no loving Mother,
She is only 'in the mind'?
Mary was a Jewish girl,
the flower of her race.
Mary was 'for real'
A living person with a face.
She was of the House of David
A princess of her line.
Would she bring it disgrace and scandal
Without a heavenly sign?
Would she risk death by stoning,
Destroy St Joseph's faith and love
Without heavenly reassurance
Brought by an angel from above?
Beyond this world's scheme and plan
I believe in angel visitants
To the family of man.
And holy eyes may see them,
Though other eyes are blind,
Yes there are truly angels
They are not only 'in the mind'
St Gabriel, St Raphael,
St Michael of the Sword,
Archangel of the Legions
The champion of the Lord.

Please leave me my Guardian Angel
Who walks with me day by day
And who so often guards me
From the perils of the way.
When the bridge is quaking
Through the storm at sea
When the bushfire threatens
Guardian Angel stay by me!
For when the cliff edge crumbles
Do we really wish to find
We have no Guardian Angel
It was only 'in the mind'?

Question 2:

'*If theologians are uncertain about the existence of good and evil spirits . . .*' *was the initial sentence of Fr Bill O'Shea. The question should have been labelled:* '*Why are some theologians and Scripture scholars uncertain about the existence of good and evil spirits?*'

Perhaps the answer might be somewhere between intellectual pride and a loss of faith in the teachings of the Catholic Church.

The second question might read: '*What is the teaching of the Catholic Church on the existence of good and evil spirits?*' *To this question, only, I will attempt to give an answer.*

When, on 11 October 1962, Pope John XXIII, of saintly memory, opened the 21st Ecumenical Council, he mentioned in his address:

'*The salient point of this council is not, therefore, a discussion of one article or another of the fundamental doctrine of the Church, which has repeatedly been taught by the Fathers and the ancient and modern theologians, and which is presumed to be well known and familiar to all.*

'*For this the council was not necessary. But from the renewed, serene and tranquil adherence to all the teachings of the Church, in its entirety and preciseness, as it still stands resplendent in the acts of the Councils of Trent and Vatican I, the Christian, Catholic and apostolic spirit of the whole world expects a step forward toward a doctrinal penetration and a formation of consciences, in faithful and perfect conformity with the authentic doctrine : . .*'

Angels, the name given to pure spirits that were all created good, of whom some chose to be evil, are part of the 'authentic doctrine' of the Church.

This is found explicitly in the Fourth Lateran General Council, in 1215 AD, Chapter 1, On the Catholic Faith: 'We firmly believe and confess that . . . (the Trinity) by his almighty power from the beginning of time made at once (simul) out of nothing both orders of creatures, the spiritual and the corporeal, that is, the angelic and the earthly, and then (deinde) the human creature, who, as it were, shares in both orders, being composed of spirit and body . . .'*

In our times, preoccupied by 'the disquiet which at the present time agitates certain quarters with regard to the faith', Pope Paul VI considered it his duty to 'fulfil the mandate entrusted by Christ to Peter, whose successor he is, to confirm his brothers in the faith'.

He accordingly expressly declared his profession of faith which repeats in substance the Creed of Nicaea, *with some developments called for by the spiritual condition of our times: 'We believe in one God . . . creator of things visible . . . and of things invisible such as pure spirits which are also called angels . . .' (June 30 1968).*

Although the Pope expressly declared that his Credo was not 'properly speaking a dogmatic definition,' it is a development of the Creed of Nicaea *and the* Dogmatic Constitution Dei Filius *on the Catholic faith of the First Vatican Council (1870). It is sadly noticeable, of late, that some are more infallible and dogmatic than the Pope, while denying the Pope these faculties, questioning his power to 'bind' in Heaven as on earth!*

Turning to Scripture, we find 109 direct references throughout the Old Testament to angels, with verbs ranging from: said; found; called; sent; spoke; redeemed; went before; stood in the way; came up; appeared; his countenance shone; ascended; stretched out; smote; touched; commended; persecuted; talked; answered.

In the New Testament, the references cover 171 occasions, of which the Book of Revelations is 65 times only. Thus, again, more than 100 references to angels! Many other references refer to the casting out of devils who called out; shouted; threw the boy down. We believe that the Bible is divinely inspired, the instruments differing.

When we pray, Lex Orandi, Lex Credendi, *is a famous and universal maxim! (The law of my prayer is the law of my faith — or — as I pray, so I believe.)*

The Church, at every preface of every Mass throughout the liturgical year, mentions angels directly. *The Angelus is an ancient prayer recited thrice daily at 6 am, noon and 6 pm and is hardly a prayer to a literary form. There are two specific feast days of angels: Michael, Gabriel and Raphael on 29 September; and the Guardian Angels on 2 October.*

When we talk of theologians, there is St Thomas Aquinas who was the only theologian quoted at the Councils of Trent, Vatican I, and Vatican II. His section from the Summa on Angels *is one of the finest pieces of literary logic that has been penned on the subject and yet 'both angels and men bow down in humble union in matters of faith.'*

In conclusion, I quote the famous words of Pope Pius XII when answering Josef Stalin on military strength: 'One day you will be dead and I will be dead. Then you may/can ask that question again.'

For my part, I am most happy with that special angel friend whom God, in his love, has confided to my earthly existence giving me that intensive care that I have seen epitomised in hospitals.

Question 3:

After reading Fr O'Shea's definition of an angel I browsed through my Bible to fit it to the angels mentioned in its pages.

It seemed odd to have 'one of God's channels of comunication' stating indignantly that 'I am Gabriel, who stand in the presence of God . . . you will be silent and unable to speak until the day that these things come to pass because you did not believe my words' (Luke 1:19-20). Is a communication channel able to stand in God's presence and know it?

And then there was Peter who was twice released from prison (Acts 5:19 and 12:5) by a channel of communication — one he in fact called by the name 'angel'.

Fr O'Shea is not only denying the existence of an enormous crowd of angels (a crowd so vast that John in his book of Revelation computes their number at at least

100,000,000 (Revelation 5:11) but also takes from all members of the human family their Guardian Angels of whom Christ said 'See that you do not despise one of these little ones for I tell you that in Heaven their angels always behold the face of God' (Matthew 18:10).

Answer:

The question of the existence of angels is one that is open to discussion on many different levels.

On the philosophical level, there should be no difficulty about accepting the existence of a category of purely spiritual beings, with a higher form of life than man, but still infinitely below God.

In the ascending hierarchy of God's creation we begin at the level of inanimate material beings. Above them come lower forms of life, plant life and merely animal life.

We human beings are at the highest level of material/ spiritual being. We are distinct from Nature but also at one with Nature, in that we, too, are part of God's created order.

Next in the hierarchy of beings would come those spiritual beings that we call angels.

The word itself is derived from the Greek word *angelos* which in turn is the translation of the Hebrew *mal'ak*, which means 'messenger'.

The existence of angels reminds us that there is more to the created order than we can apprehend by sense knowledge, that is what we can actually see, hear, taste, smell and feel.

The existence of angelic creatures serves to bridge the gap between God and ourselves and reminds us of unseen spiritual realities, as well as of God's ever-present help.

In our space age, man has become more aware than ever before that he is only a small part of a vast universe.

When we face the almost limitless possibilities of rational life in other parts of the universe, references to angels remind us of how little we really know about God's creation.

I am at a loss to know how one correspondent could have concluded that I am 'denying the existence of an enormous crowd of angels', though I do believe that the numbers and varieties of angels mentioned in Scripture are probably mythological exaggerations.

I am aware, as another correspondent points out, that the existence of angels is firmly rooted in the long tradition and liturgy of the Church.

The official teaching that angels exist as creatures of God is given by the Fourth Lateran Council in 1215 and by the First Vatican Council in 1869-1870.

There are many scholars, however, who question whether the existence of angels and devils is part of the strictly dogmatic teaching of the Church.

It is for this reason that — as I stated in an earlier reply — some theologians feel the freedom to re-study the whole question of angels and demons.

My own view, for what it is worth, is that it is difficult to dismiss the reality of angels, both for philosophical reasons (the hierarchy of created beings) and for their long and firmly established position in the Church's tradition and liturgy.

However, the questions that have been posed to me and my answers to these questions have not been on the level of philosophy or the Church's official teaching.

They have concerned rather the biblical account of the *functions* or *activities* of angels in particular instances and events of salvation history — like the Annunciation, the temptation of Jesus, and the story of Job, and how we are to understand these reports.

This is a different question entirely.

I have to say that the comments and observations made by some correspondents suggest a good deal of mis-understanding.

There are a variety of issues to be distinguished and they should not be confused.

Some of the questions and comments reflect a refusal or an inability to accept the whole principle of literary form. This reaction is a sobering reminder of the urgent need that many Catholics have for adult education in the faith.

It is not surprising that this principle might have raised some eyebrows in 1943 when it was proposed by Pius XII as one of the main factors to be taken into account when interpreting the Scriptures. But that was 40 years ago!

The principle that Pius XII emphasised was that when interpreting the Bible, modern readers should take account of those forms of expression which were commonly accepted by people at the time the accounts were written.

His point was that we should not always be 'hung up' on the historical truth of the events thus described, but that we should look for the real truth, the deeper truth, which God inspired the human authors to convey via the contemporary forms of communication which they used.

In the Bible, angels generally function — as their names suggest — as messengers of God. They are portrayed as intermediaries or channels of communication between God and man; they are conceived of as moving with swiftness of thought and are therefore often pictured as winged (cf. Revelation 12:11-12; Psalm 103:20).

Other functions attributed to them in the Bible are those of worshipping God, and of guarding and praying for human beings.

Visitations by an 'Angel of the Lord' and 'birth announcements' are two standard biblical literary forms.

The announcement by an angel to Mary of the conception of Jesus has numerous earlier literary parallels in the Old Testament.

Often even the details are reproduced: an appearance of an angel in human form; his delivery of God's message; the surprise and questioning reaction from the receiver of the message; a further assurance from God's messenger, sometimes with a sign (like Zechariah's loss of speech); acceptance finally of God's will.

On several occasions in the Old Testament, such messages conveyed by angels concerned the future birth of an illustrious person in sacred history.

In the case of the Annunciation story, the event is historical in the sense that God did reveal to Mary her crucial part in his plan of salvation, that she was the one chosen by him to be the Mother of his Son, who was to be the long-awaited Messiah.

But the nature of biblical truth does not demand that we accept literally Luke's account of *how* God revealed his will to Mary.

The fact that there are numerous accounts of such angelic visitations in Scripture does not constitute any argument in favour of their literal historical truth. Rather they serve to show how prevalent was this literary form in Jewish religious thought.

Nor does the identification of angels by name, such as Raphael, Gabriel or Michael (all derived from the divine name *El*) give to the accounts any more literal historical veracity.

Similarly the report that the angel 'speaks' in no way infringes the principle of literary form.

How else could a communication of God's will be presented except by human words which people could read and understand?

A comparison between the first two chapters of the Gospels of Matthew and Luke should illustrate how different biblical authors employed different literary forms to report God's communication of his will to human beings.

Luke employs the standard biblical model of angelic visitation: 'There appeared to him (Zechariah) an angel of the Lord' (1:11), who later identified himself as 'Gabriel who stands in the presence of the Lord' (1:19); the same 'Angel Gabriel was sent from God ... to a virgin ... and the virgin's name was Mary. And he came to her and said ...' (1:26-28).

Matthew prefers a different literary form, the dream, as the means of communication, with sometimes an angel (unidentified) as the messenger. 'An angel of the Lord appeared to him (Joseph) in a dream' (1:20); 'And being warned in a dream not to return to Herod, they (the wise men) departed to their own country by another way' (2:12); 'The angel of the Lord appeared to Joseph in a dream and said, 'Rise, take the child and his mother, and flee to Egypt' (2:13); 'But when Herod died, behold, an angel of the Lord appeared in a dream to Joseph in Egypt' (2:19).

The literary form is different: the truth is the same.

God revealed his will to Mary (Luke) and to Joseph (Matthew). Indeed it was in the minds of Mary and Joseph that these divine communications were received.

The poetess (Q1) questions this assertion, though it is difficult to understand her inference that I might question the existence of Mary herself!

This would appear to be the result of a total misunderstanding of what the Church means by 'literary form' — which I referred to earlier.

Incidentally, although it is peripheral to the question, there is absolutely no biblical evidence to suggest that Mary was 'of the house of David' or 'a princess of her line'.

The whole point of Matthew 1:18-25 is that the fulfilment of the prophecy of Jesus' descent from David depended on Joseph consenting to be the legal father of the child.

It was Joseph, not Mary, who was 'of the house of David' (Matthew 1:20), and his acceptance of legal paternity ensured that Jesus was descended from David.

There is nothing in Scripture or valid tradition to suggest that Mary was descended from David. Even if she were, it would have cut no ice in the Jewish genealogical system, because family descent was calculated only from the male line.

That is why Matthew is so insistent that Joseph, a son of David, agreed to accept Jesus legally as his son.

If I have disturbed some people by my interpretation of these biblical passages, I am afraid I can make no apology for having done so.

If it should lead some to question their fundamentalist approach to Scripture and move them to find out what the Church has been saying for a long time about how we should interpret the Bible, then the exercise has been well worthwhile.

Again I should like to stress that my interpretation of these biblical passages concerning the physical or visible appearance of angels and the functions that they performed is not intended to deny the existence of angels as such.

That is another question, as I pointed out earlier in this article.

Finally, although it is not my intention to undermine faith in the existence of personal Guardian Angels, it should be pointed out that the text of Matthew 18:10 'See that you do not despise one of these little ones; for I tell you that in Heaven their angels always behold the face of God', is probably simply a way of saying that God himself has a very special care and concern for those 'little ones'.

Question 4:
Thank you for writing a further account of your beliefs

regarding angels. Our criticisms at least show your column is read and appreciated.

New thoughts, new ideas can be candles to lighten our darkness — or they can be 'min min' lights.

For the sake of those young people coming after us on life's road we must, I think, establish what are verities — universal everlasting truths.

I am an old woman who has travelled the world, lived Outback through drought and Depression, participated in a war, seen the overthrow of a country's ruling system, survived a shoot-out or two, been through floods, bushfires, cyclones and a few perils at sea.

During some of these experiences I had no belief in the existence of God or an after-life. I was shaping my life by Plato's creed: 'It is best to do good and avoid evil'.

I would like to assure young people choosing a creed for their lives that this one is not sustaining when bullets are flying, and you feel your time to live and do anything is about to be cut short.

About midway through this life of mine I was granted the grace of the Catholic faith. I found belief in God, his teaching Church, in our Blessed Mother and her Rosary, and in my guardian angel. All these have been very sustaining to me.

As for your comment about the 'urgent need some Catholics have for adult education' surely if the Church's teaching has become so complex that one needs education to understand it, perhaps the time has come to simplify the teaching!

Our Lord managed to put the plan of salvation in one sentence: 'Believe on the Lord Jesus Christ and you shall be saved'. Devotion to Mary he put in three words: 'Behold your Mother'.

Now about those angels: A cheering thought — if no angels, no Lucifer, no Evil One, no sin; no sin equals no Ten Commandments — and sin is 'probably' only in the mind anyway.

I'm afraid it's too late for me to indulge in any of the more interesting sins, but you just watch what I might get up to next pension day!

As for 'what Christ probably meant when speaking of

guardian angels', if you are going to introduce 'probablies'
into the debate, there can be no debate.
　　And may I break forth into verse again:

Probably, that 'probably'.
Now I grew up Outback
And I distrust all 'probablies'
Strewn along the track.

Sure the river's running high,
And there's a cyclone coming too,
But I wouldn't let it worry me
You'll probably get through.

When you get beyond the signposts
You'll probably find a track.
Other folks have been that way,
And they've never yet come back.

So they've probably got through,
Though it's desert there you see
And they took no water with them.
Rain? Oh, it may quite probably.

Now Father you think probably this,
And I think probably that,
But only the One up there
Can tell us where certainties are at.

So let's have a friendly cuppa
In the good old Australian way,
And we'll probably reach agreement
On what we probably meant to say!

　　PS: There are *still angels and Mary* was *of the House of*
David, the ruling house of Israel. In the Old Testament era
women were ranked as inferior to men. Christ made it clear
that in the new dispensation this would not be so. It would
be 'one soul, one value'.
　　Therefore a woman's genealogy would count as Mary's
must have done. As St Joseph was not *the father of Jesus and*

*if Mary was not of the House of David, how could Christ
claim to be of the House of David?*

Under a false passport in the name of Joseph?

*I think that is hardly worthy of the truth-filled Holy
Spirit, the just Joseph, or the virtuous Mary.*

*Perhaps you may say my 'ifs' are no better than your
'probablies' and now I've introduced a 'perhaps' as well!*

*Ah well — why talk of scheme and plan? The Lord is
God: he needeth not the poor device of man.*

Answer:

Thank you for your letter. I enjoyed the beautiful auto-
biographical section and the humour and compassion that
ran through your whole letter.

I cannot, however, let pass some of the observations you
make, because I believe that some of your statements —
while they have a plausibility about them — could mislead
readers.

I agree with you completely that we must establish and
hold on to what are 'the verities — universal everlasting
truths', the truths we must believe and live by. However, we
must be very careful not to erect any probable opinions or
theological theories into dogmas of faith.

You seem to regard 'probably' as almost a dirty word —
or a least a term that should have no place in any discussion
on religious matters.

With this I must disagree. It would appear to me to be no
more than an attitude of honesty and humility to admit that
there *are* questions about which we do not and cannot have
certainty.

This is especially true as regards our knowledge of the
Scriptures, the area which is my special field of interest and
expertise.

I agree with you that one does not need to be an expert to
appreciate the Bible as a whole. It contains spiritual food
which provides nourishment for even the most simple and
uneducated reader.

However, it would be folly to suggest that the Bible as a
whole is a simple book. After half a lifetime of studying it in
depth, I cannot profess to claim certainty about the meaning
of every passage and verse.

You might say that if one's faith is sufficiently strong, then there should be no need to be concerned about such difficulties.

While this is true, it is also true that God does not demand of us blind faith. Our human intelligence is one of his greatest gifts and we are surely justified in using it to arrive at a rational basis for what we believe.

This is not to confuse reason and faith. I am well aware that an uneducated, even an illiterate, person could have a greater depth of faith than the most brilliant theologian or biblical scholar.

Indeed it is possible to know the Bible from back to front and have a thorough understanding of the teachings of the Church — and not believe a word of either.

But I reaffirm very strongly the need for adult education in the faith for those who are capable of it.

It is important that we Catholics should understand clearly what are the eternal verities, the universal everlasting truths, and what on the other hand are those areas where we are free to speculate.

In fact the Church has made dogmatic pronouncements on the meaning of only two or three passages of Scripture.

For the rest she has left people free to find their own meanings, provided these interpretations do not conflict with the fundamentals of the Catholic faith.

In the light of all I have said I fail to see why you should be so impatient about my use of the word 'probable'. Nor can I understand what you mean when you say that if we introduce probablies into the debate there can be no debate.

I should have thought that this provides the most fertile grounds for debate and your own letter would seem to prove my point.

From what I have said it follows that there are parts of Scripture which contain and teach eternal truths and others which do not.

Nobody should pretend that the existence of angels is as important a truth as the saving value of the death and Resurrection of Christ.

I am not going to say any more on the question of angels, but I certainly would challenge your false assumption that the reality of sin depends on the existence of angels and demons.

Even if there were no mention of good and evil spirits in the Bible, the biblical teaching on sin and redemption would remain intact.

Sin is the violation of the law of God — expressed in the Ten Commandments and, on a much higher level, in the moral teaching of Jesus — such as we find it expressed in the Sermon on the Mount.

In neither case is there any reference to the activities of good or evil spirits.

Finally you raise again the question of Mary being of the House of David, and argue that this was necessary for Jesus to fulfil the prophecy of his being a descendant of David.

Evidently you must have access to sources about Mary's family tree which are not available to me.

Luke's genealogy of Jesus begins in 3:23. There is no mention of Mary. It is said that Jesus was 'the son (as was supposed) of *Joseph*' whose family descent is then traced back to David (v.31).

Matthew also has a genealogy of Jesus. He, too, respects the virginal conception of Jesus in 1:16. He speaks of 'Joseph, the husband of Mary, of whom Jesus was born, who is called Christ'.

He is careful not to say that Joseph was the natural father of Jesus, but obviously — if you read Matthew 1:1-17, it is Joseph's family tree that the evangelist is interested in.

As I said in my earlier reply, the whole point of Matthew 1:18-25 is to show that Joseph consented to be the legal father of Mary's child.

Since Joseph was descended from David, his acceptance of legal paternity made Jesus a descendant of David in Jewish law, in exactly the same way as if he had been his natural father.

So Jesus was a descendant of David because of Joseph, not because of Mary.

With all due respect, your comments about 'the truth-filled Holy Spirit, the just Joseph and the virtuous Mary' betray a misunderstanding of the biblical evidence.

It is precisely because of such misinterpretations that I emphasise the need for adult education in the faith — a need that the Second Vatican Council insists on more than once.

Despite this, as I said, I really appreciated your letter and I admiré the faith which evidently shines through. I am even beginning to appreciate your poetry but I would like to declare a moratorium on angels. I feel my knowledge of the subject is just about exhausted.

In conclusion I would just like to repeat: Let us not confuse the area of universal everlasting truths with matters that are legitimate areas for investigation for theologians and biblical scholars.

Bible Problems

Question 5:

What is the historical background to the choosing of the Old Testament books included in the Catholic Bible, but not in Protestant versions, that is, the Deutero-canonical books? In the light of modern biblical scholarship, how are they viewed today by both traditions?

Answer:

By the time of Jesus, the Jews had in their possession a collection of books which they held to be sacred and inspired by God. There had never been any official decision about the contents of their Scriptures. They simply came to be accepted in practice as sacred.

It would not be correct to say that there was complete unanimity among all Jews on the subject. For example, the Sadducees accepted only the Law, the first five books of the Bible as the word of God.

But by Jesus' day, orthodox Judaism in Palestine, as represented by the party of the Pharisees, had come to accept as sacred those books which now make up the Old Testament as it appears in Protestant versions of the Bible.

On the other hand, among the Greek-speaking Jews living outside of Palestine, the collection of sacred books was not yet regarded as closed. They believed that there were some other books which also had divine authority.

Consequently, when the Greek language edition of the Old Testament (the Jewish Scriptures) was produced, it included seven additional books, which are found also in Catholic versions of the Bible today. These are: Tobit (or Tobias), Judith, 1 and 2 Maccabees, Wisdom, Sirach (or Ecclesiasticus) and Baruch. We call them the 'Deutero-canonical' books, but Protestants give them the name 'Apocryphal'.

About the year 90 AD, some 60 years after the death of Christ, a group of Jewish scribes in Palestine moved to determine officially a canon of Scripture. They met and formally adopted the strict Pharisaic canon (that is, the shorter list of books) and rejected the seven Deutero-canonical books which were included in the Greek Bible.

Christianity prospered and grew outside Palestine in the Greek-speaking world and so in practice the Greek Bible became the Church's Bible. Most of the Fathers of the Church accepted the Old Testament as they found it in the Greek Bible, but in the East there was a certain amount of hesitation.

We find some big names in early Christianity who followed the shorter Palestinian catalogue of books.

In the Western Church, however, no distinction was made between the books. St. Augustine (c.400) certainly accepted the larger canon, and his influence had a lot to do with the position of the later Church.

The Eastern Church ultimately came around to the Western view, and today the Greek Orthodox Church accepts the same Old Testament canon as do Roman Catholics (46 books rather than 39).

Apart from isolated local and personal doubts, the traditional New Testament canon was accepted up until the 16th century. Then the Protestant reformers rejected the seven Old Testament books in question as later additions, and accepted only those contained in the Hebrew Bible.

They believed that in doing so they were returning to a purer and more primitive faith.

The most Martin Luther would admit was that these books were useful and good to read, but he denied their equality with the rest of sacred Scripture.

Even at the Council of Trent, summoned to combat the Protestant Reformation, some Bishops wanted the seven Duetero-canonical books rejected, or at least their acceptance qualified in some way. But Trent's final decision in 1546 was to define formally the traditional canon of sacred Scripture, as it now appears in our Catholic Bibles.

The reformed Churches, on the other hand, have stuck to the Jewish Old Testament canon — even though many Protestants admit the spiritual value of the books in question.

In more recent times, some ecumenical or 'common' versions of the Bible, published under Protestant auspices, have included these seven books in a separate section at the end of the Old Testament. But they do not acknowledge them as the inspired word of God, carrying the same authority as the rest of Scripture.

Question 6:

Would you help me to answer a question that one of my children put to me, which I was unable to answer?

We had watched the movie, The Ten Commandments. *Later we were reading parts of the Bible and discussing some of its mysteries. One of my sons who is interested in the Bible was reading again about the Commandments, and I was explaining the way I had learned them.*

When we came to the Commandment 'Thou shalt not kill', my son argued that God had broken his own Commandment. He gave as an example all the people who were killed because they did not believe at the site of the holy rock when Moses was receiving the Commandments.

Then there was the time when Moses was trying to make all the others accept the God he believed in. I could not explain it, and I would like to be able to do so, as I have always abided by the Commandments and I would like my children to do the same.

The way my son put it to me, it seems indeed that God did break his own Commandment.

Answer:

I suppose the first thing to note is that the Ten Commandments are a statement of a person's obligations towards God and his fellow human beings.

As they are formulated, they can hardly be seen as binding on God himself. If we take them one by one, we can see that several of them can have no relevance to God's conduct in dealing with his creatures.

Nevertheless, the God of Israel and of Christians is conceived of as a moral being, whose conduct is taken as the model for human behaviour. He is not an arbitrary dictator who acts according to whims or caprice. There is always a moral motivation behind his actions.

When we come to the Commandment 'Thou shalt not

kill' we must remember that God's relationship to human life is quite different from the relationship which exists between human beings themselves. God is the giver of life, and he alone has the right to decide when life should be forfeited.

There is a sense, therefore, in which we can hold him responsible for every human life which is lost, and accuse God of taking the life of every person who dies.

Indeed, this is often the anguished complaint in cases where young people die prematurely. Frequently we can only acknowledge humbly our inability to comprehend God's plan, and say 'the Lord gives, and the Lord takes away'. What our human criteria might evaluate as injustice is not necessarily so in the sight of God.

When we come to some biblical incidents which refer to God destroying people who are unfaithful or disobedient there is a further consideration which comes into play.

The Hebrews did not have the same appreciation of secondary or natural causes that we do. For them, because God was in complete control of all events, everything that happened was attributed to him.

In the mentality of the biblical authors it was God who caused storms and famines and plagues; it was God who was responsible for Israel's victories and defeats.

The prosperity of some and the destruction of others were seen as either his reward for their fidelity or his punishment for their sinfulness.

Another thing to note is that the biblical writers did not make the distinction, which later Christian theologians did, between God's positive will and his permissive will. God positively wills the good and permits the evil. This distinction enables us to explain some of those Old Testament incidents which might otherwise give the impression that God has acted unjustly or vindictively.

In other words, it must be acknowledged that some deaths which might well have been the result of what we would attribute to 'natural' causes, are stated by the biblical writers to be the direct result of God's intervention.

This stems from their strong conviction of God's overriding control of all human affairs.

Having said all this, we need to remember that God the Creator is the one who ultimately decides on matters of life and death, and no limited human intelligence may presume to judge on the rightness of his actions or otherwise.

Question 7:

St Paul makes me uneasy. Why was he so prominent in the early Church when the Apostles were alive? Why was a separate apostle to the Gentiles necessary? Christ had, after all, chosen the 12 and commissioned them to teach all nations.

It is almost as if St Paul were an after-thought. But why? Can God have after-thoughts? To me, Paul just does not seem to fit into the programme Christ had apparently worked out in calling the 12 and preparing them to teach others.

Answer:

In one sense your question, 'Why St Paul?' cannot be answered at all, because it is part of the mystery of God's plan of salvation. Why God chose Paul of Tarsus, persecutor of the Church, and commissioned him to be the Apostle to the Gentiles, is a question whose answer is hidden in the mind and purpose of God.

God does not have 'after-thoughts'. The conversion and vocation of Paul were an important part of the overall eternal, divine plan.

Jesus chose 12 to be the core group or nucleus of the community, the Church, which would be the continuing sign of his presence in the world.

According to the book of the *Acts of the Apostles*, they proceeded to carry out the mandate of the risen Lord to preach, teach and baptise. Acts 2:41 tells us that as a result of Peter's first sermon preached on Pentecost Day 3000 people came forward, confessed their faith and requested baptism.

The first six chapters of Acts chart the growth of the Jerusalem Church.

What is not so clear, however, is the extent of the awareness of the original disciples of Jesus, that their mandate included a mission to Gentiles or non-Jews.

It is true that there are passages in the Gospels (like Matthew 28:18-20) which report Jesus as explicitly commanding them 'to make disciples of all nations'. But we must remember that the Gospels were written between 30 and 60 years after the death of Jesus, when the successful mission to the Gentiles was already a fact of history.

It seems probable that in the light of the Church's later self-understanding, commands of Jesus to evangelise the Gentiles came to be formulated much more explicitly when the Gospels were written. This conclusion is unavoidable from a close reading of Acts.

In the early years, the Jerusalem Church showed no awareness of any commission to carry the Gospel beyond the Jewish people. The Christians continued to observe the Jewish law and to worship in the temple.

It was only the dispersal of some of the Jerusalem Christians as a result of the persecution that began with the killing of Stephen which led to the spread of the faith beyond Jerusalem and Judea.

Acts describes the missionary activity of Philip (not the Philip who was one of the original 12) and the action of Peter in baptising the Roman soldier Cornelius and his household.

But it was Paul who, under God, was the man most responsible for the Church coming to understand that it was to be a catholic or universal family, and not just a reformed Judaism.

By his background, of course, Paul had been providentially prepared for his vocation. He grew up in a Greek environment and was proficient in the Greek language. None of the original 12 possessed these qualifications.

Question 8:

I have a 1962 New Catholic Edition Bible, printed by the Catholic Book Publishing Company, New York, and would like you to inform me if I should continue to use this Bible, or is there a more modern Bible available. If so, where can it be purchased?

Answer:

I am not sure what version or translation of the Bible you have in your possession. I suspect that the *New Catholic Bible* published in 1962 is the American Confraternity version of the Scriptures. The title page of the book should indicate this.

Certainly there are more modern Catholic translations of the Bible available. In 1966, the *Jerusalem Bible* was translated from the French into English. More recently (1970) the *New American Bible* was published, the first complete Catholic translation into English from the original Greek and Hebrew languages.

Both these editions of the Bible are especially valuable because of the extensive and informative footnotes which explain difficult verses and passages.

In addition to these, we also have Catholic editions of the *Revised Standard Version* and *Today's English Version (The Good News Bible)*, both originally published under Protestant auspices. *The Good News Bible* is the most 'modern' of all translations, as far as the language which is employed.

None of this requires that you should discontinue using the Bible which you have. While those I have mentioned would be of a superior quality, the Confraternity version and even the old Douay version are perfectly acceptable.

Perhaps the purchase of one of the more modern translations mentioned above would be desirable, even for the purpose of comparing it with the copy that you have. Such comparison of different versions is an interesting exercise, and can often help to clarify the true meaning of a passage.

These versions of the Scriptures would be available in any Catholic book store. I suggest you ask your parish priest to refer you to the most convenient outlet in your own area.

Question 9:

A Seventh Day Adventist has told me that the Church has changed the Sabbath, or Saturday, to the first day, or Sunday. He says there is no place in the Bible which mentions this change. Is this true? What answer can I give him to help him see that there is a reason for observing Sunday as the Lord's day?

Answer:

In the Old Testament law the day of the week which was set aside for the Lord was the Sabbath or seventh day. This law of Sabbath observance is stated explicitly in the Third Commandment.

It is true that there is no single verse or text of Scripture in which God authorises any change in this practice.

Nevertheless, it is clear that the early Christians felt free to change the Lord's day from the seventh to the first day of the week. They realised that the essence of the Third Commandment was to set aside a day of the week to honour God in a special way. The actual day they considered to be of secondary importance.

The New Testament reveals that the change was made very early in the life of the Church. In Acts 20:7, St Luke reports the custom of the Christian community in the town of Troas. 'On the first day of the week when we were gathered together to break the bread, Paul talked with them . . .'

Probably a major reason for the change was the desire of the first Christians to distinguish themselves from the Jews. In the early days of the Church they tended to be identified as just another sect of Judaism and they wanted to establish their own distinctive identity.

By observing the first day rather than the seventh day, the leaders of the Church wished to make it clear that Christians were no longer obliged by the Jewish laws of Sabbath observance.

Some Jewish Christians wanted to impose the Sabbath observance on converts from paganism to the faith. St Paul strenuously opposed this. In Colossians 2:16, he wrote: 'So let no one make rules about what you eat or drink or about Holy Days or the New Moon Festivals or the Sabbath'. By these words he intended to set Christians free from the obligations of the Sabbath law.

No doubt the main reason Christians chose the first day of the week as their day for honouring the Lord was that Jesus rose from the dead on that day. (Matthew 28:1.)

The leaders of the Church felt free to make such a decision by virtue of the authority which Christ had vested in them: 'Whatever you bind on earth shall be bound in heaven; whatever you loose on earth shall be loosed in heaven'. (Matthew 18:18.)

Blessed Virgin Mary

Question 10:

I have been endeavouring to find scriptural support for the dogma of faith, the Immaculate Conception. My main cause of concern, however, is that Scripture seems to contradict the teaching. Therefore, I would be grateful if you could give me clarified answers on some scriptural texts.

Answer:

(The above question is a summary of a lengthy letter.) There is not really an explicit scriptural support for the dogma of the Immaculate Conception. As you say in your letter, the text of Genesis 3:15 does not refer to Mary.

It is, rather, a prophecy of continuing conflict between the descendants of the woman (Eve), that is, the human race, and the powers of evil.

Similarly, the words addressed to Mary in Luke's account of the Annunciation are best translated as 'Rejoice, highly favoured one'. (Luke 1:28.)

Nor, as you say again, is there any evidence that the Immaculate Conception was part of the oral preaching of the Gospel in the apostolic period. Indeed, it is highly unlikely, to say the least.

When you say that Scripture seems to contradict the teaching, I think you are on much more shaky ground. The words attributed to Mary in Luke 1:47, 'My spirit rejoices in God my Saviour', do not really pose a problem.

It has never been claimed that the Immaculate Conception exempted Mary from the need of a saviour. If Mary were immaculately conceived and lived a sinless life, this was precisely the effect of a gift received from her God and Saviour.

Paul's comment in Romans 3:23 that 'all have sinned' is a statement of a universal truth. Any privilege conferred by

God on an individual person, by way of exception, does not invalidate that statement. Paul could hardly have said, 'except Mary, the Mother of Jesus'. At any rate Paul knew nothing about any Immaculate Conception of Mary.

Nor can anything be inferred against the dogma by the fact that Mary and Joseph underwent the Jewish rite of purification (Luke 2:22). This law concerned legal or ritual cleanness: it was not a matter of morality.

Finally, when the Bible says that the wages of sin is death, the kind of death it has primarily in mind is spiritual or eternal death. Thus in Romans 5:17-21, Paul contrasts the death which is the effect of sin, with the life, obviously eternal life, won for us by Jesus Christ.

The Church has never felt it necessary to have to defend the dogmas it proclaims by citing scriptural texts which explicitly state those truths. Of course, it could not define something that was contradicted by Scripture. The Church claims to be guided by the same Holy Spirit who inspired the Scriptures. It can also be called the mother of the Scriptures, because the New Testament at least came out of the Church.

For this reason, it claims the right to propose for the belief of its members, truths which it gains from an insight into God's revelation of his plan contained in Scripture. In the case of Mary, it is because of the Church's assessment of her privileged role in the history of salvation, as the Mother of Jesus, the Son of God, that it has defined dogmas like the Immaculate Conception and the Assumption.

Question 11:

You say that the text of Genesis 3:15 does not refer to Mary. St Louis de Montfort for one would not agree with you. He had the understanding that it did refer to Mary.

Not as it is written in the bibles of today, but as it is in the Catholic Bible; 'I will put enmities between thee and the woman and thy seed and her seed; she shall crush thy head, and thou shalt lie in wait for her heel'.

Answer:

Your reference to 'the Catholic Bible' is misleading. There are several versions of the Bible in the English language which have been sponsored and/or approved by the Catholic Church.

Your quotation of Genesis 3:15 comes from the Douay-Rheims Version (published between 1582 and 1609), which was translated from the Latin Vulgate Edition of the Bible.

The Old Testament, of course, was written originally neither in Latin nor in English but in Hebrew.

A better understanding of ancient Hebrew since the 16th century has revealed that the Douay-Rheims English Version (and the Latin Vulgate, on which it was based) was defective at some points — including the text of Genesis 3:15 which you quote.

Some fundamentalist Protestant sects have such an exaggerated reverence for the King James or Authorised Version of Scripture that they regard all subsequent translations of the Bible into English as unacceptable — even blasphemous.

Let us Catholics not fall into the same trap. God did not verbally dictate either the King James or the Douay versions of the Bible.

Of the modern and more reliable Catholic versions of the Bible in English, the *Jerusalem Bible* describes God addressing the serpent in these words: 'I will make you enemies of each other, you and the woman, your offspring and her offspring. It will crush your head, and you will strike its heel'.

The *New American Bible*, the first complete Catholic version of the Bible to be translated into English directly from the original Hebrew, puts it this way: 'I will put enmity between you and the woman, and between your offspring and hers; he will strike at ycur head while you strike at his heel'.

The woman in the context is clearly Eve; her descendants (or offspring) are the whole human race. The offspring of the serpent-devil are the powers of evil. The passage is therefore a prediction of the continual and unending struggle which will occur between humanity and the forces of evil.

The literal sense of Genesis 3:15 contains no reference to Mary, the mother of Jesus.

The *Jerome Biblical Commentary*, widely accepted as an authoritative Catholic commentary on Holy Scripture, does not mention Mary in connection with this verse.

If St Louis de Montfort interpreted this passage primarily as a reference to Mary, then he was mistaken. Canonisation is an official declaration by the church of a person's sanctity, not of his proficiency as an interpreter of Scripture.

Question 12:

Could you please tell me why you think that the authors of the Jerome Biblical Commentary *were more inspired by the Holy Spirit in their interpretations of Scripture than St Louis de Montfort was?*
We were always taught that the book of Genesis referred to Mary, and I feel that way. It seems to me a direct message about our redemption, highlighting the place Mary was to take in it. Please, Father, if you could give us a further explanation I would be grateful.

Answer:

I presume that by now you have read my answer to a further question on the meaning of Genesis 3:15 about the descendants of the woman and the descendants of the serpent. I hope this answer has thrown further light on the subject for you.

The *Jerome Biblical Commentary* is a huge commentary on every book, chapter and verse of the Bible and was first published in 1968. It comprised at that time just about the best of Catholic biblical scholarship.

I do not believe that the editors or authors of this commentary were inspired by the Holy Spirit when they wrote, that is, in the sense that God directly enlightened them about the meaning of the biblical texts.

Nor do I have any reason to believe that Louis de Montfort was so inspired. It is not therefore a question of divine inspiration, but of human knowledge and expertise in the interpretation of the Bible.

Since the time of St Louis de Montfort, (1673-1716), great advances have been made in the science of biblical interpretation, as in every other field of science.

This is especially true of the last century. The rapid growth of knowledge in such fields as archaeology and literary and historical criticism has resulted in a much greater understanding of the history of the peoples who lived in ancient times.

At the same time, much more is now known of the ancient

languages which those people used. This includes biblical Hebrew which was the language in which the Old Testament, including the book of Genesis, was originally written.

Consequently, modern translations of the Bible are generally more accurate and reliable than the translations which were available in the 16th and 17th centuries.

To say this is by no means a criticism of the biblical scholars and spiritual writers of centuries past.

The knowledge and techniques which today's biblical scholars have at their disposal for interpreting the Scriptures were simply not available to their counterparts of those days.

My answer about the correct interpretation of Genesis 3:15 does not deny, or play down, Mary's role in God's saving plan. Her role does not depend on how we interpret Genesis 3:15.

If anything, modern biblical scholarship confirms and places on an even more secure base the important part which Mary plays in God's plan of redemption.

Question 13:

I feel compelled to protest about what I see as a direct contradiction of Catholic teaching down through the ages regarding the role of Mary in the plan of salvation (Q11). This teaching has been generally accepted in the orthodox Christian Churches, and was very positively confirmed at the Second Vatican Council.

To read the assertion (backed up by new interpretations/ translations of Scripture) that in Genesis 3:15, it was Eve, and her seed (not Mary!) who would 'crush the serpent's head' was to me staggering — the implications are quite mind boggling! If it had come from some supporter of the 'modernist' teachings of the last century, or some ardent enthusiast for the evolutionary theory, I would not have been surprised. In this particular context however, I repeat, I was amazed.

Regarding the writings of Simon de Montfort about Mary, people may be surprised to learn that they are officially accepted as nothing more or less than the actual teaching of the Church.

I also found disturbing the somewhat condescending

*reference to de Montfort's possible sanctity, with the infer-
ence that this would certainly have exceeded his intellectual
talents.*

Answer:

In no way does my answer regarding the interpretation of
Genesis 3:15 call into question the Catholic teaching on the
role of Mary in God's plan of salvation.

There are several New Testament passages (for example,
Luke 1:26-38; John 2:1-11; 19:25-27) which provide the
strongest evidence for Mary's important part in God's
saving plan. But this belief does not justify us in assigning to
texts like Genesis 3:15 meanings which are not contained
therein.

The whole of Genesis chapters two and three concerns
Adam and Eve. Eve is the only woman mentioned in the
text. It is against all the rules of logic and commonsense that
the author, who wrote many centuries before Christ, should
suddenly change course — without any warning — and give
to the word 'woman' an entirely different meaning, by
applying it to Mary, the mother of Jesus.

It is true that in some Church documents this text has
been applied to Mary. This is using Scripture in the 'accommodated' sense, because of a certain appropriateness or
aptness of the text to another person or event. In this case
the application has been made to Mary, because it is fitting
to see her as the 'new Eve', that is, as the mother of all the
faithful, the Mother of the Church.

But the primary literal sense of Genesis 3:15 refers to the
first woman, and to her alone. To conclude otherwise defies
all the basic laws of biblical exegesis.

Nor did my answer contain any 'condescending reference' to the 'possible sanctity' of Simon de Montfort (*sic*).
My words contained no such allusion.

Incidentally, you have your de Montforts confused.
Simon de Montfort was an English soldier and statesman of
the 13th century, and an important figure in the political
history of the period. He was the brother-in-law of King
Henry III of England.

The de Montfort under discussion was a French priest
who lived from 1673 to 1716, and was canonised in 1947.

His name was Louis Marie Grignion de Montfort, best known as the author of the spiritual classic, *True Devotion to the Blessed Virgin.*

Regarding the sanctity of St Louis de Montfort there is no question. What I queried was not his holiness but his interpretation of a scriptural text — which is hardly the same thing. At any rate, the value of St Louis de Montfort's spiritual treatise certainly does not stand or fall on the meaning of Genesis 3:15.

I repeat again that the primary meaning of that passage is that the powers of evil will continue the work of the tempter against mankind throughout human history. There is no indication in the New Testament that this text from Genesis was interpreted by the Church of the apostolic period as referring to Christ and Mary.

Only later in the history of Christianity did this application appear, and — as I have explained earlier — this is using the passage in an 'accommodated' sense, not a matter of drawing from it the sense which the author intended.

Question 14:

I am prepared to accept your explanation that the primary, literal sense of Genesis 3:15 concerning 'the woman' is a reference to Eve, and not to Mary. But I was under the impression that the Bible contained other real meanings besides the literal sense.

If we believe that the Bible is the word of God, then this surely means that God himself, or the Holy Spirit is the main author of Scripture.

Is it not possible therefore that God may have intended a passage like Genesis 3:15 to have another and deeper meaning that the human writer was not aware of?

You say that the only reference to Mary in this text is in an 'accommodated' sense, that is, finding in it a certain appropriateness to apply it to her. I suggest that it goes further than this.

I believe that the Holy Spirit meant this passage to refer also to Mary — perhaps not in the primary, literal sense — but in a real way nevertheless.

Answer:

Your query raises an important point in the overall problem

of how to interpret Scripture. For the reason that you mention — that God is the principal author of the Bible — we must at least consider the possibility of other meanings in the Bible besides the literal sense.

The literal sense is the meaning which the human writer intended. But the doctrine of divine inspiration raises the possibility that he may not always have grasped the full meaning which the Holy Spirit wanted to express.

Perhaps there are deeper, secondary meanings lying beneath the surface of parts of the Bible — meanings which do not destroy the literal sense, but extend it, amplify it and enrich it.

The big question is: how do we know when such a deeper meaning is present in a biblical passage? This is most important, for if we do not have some rule for discovering a fuller meaning in a text, then the imagination can run riot, and the way is left open to all sorts of weird and reckless interpretations.

Since the deeper meaning of a passage of Scripture is the meaning intended by God alone, then obviously only God can reveal this meaning to us. Only he can tell us what he intended when he inspired a particular passage.

The same God who inspired the Old Testament authors inspired also the New Testament writers. So when we find in the New Testament an assurance that there is a deeper meaning contained in an Old Testament passage, we can accept this as a fact.

Again the same Holy Spirit who inspired the Scriptures also guides the Church in interpreting these Scriptures, so the Church, too, can tell us when a meaning is present in the Bible deeper than the literal sense intended by the human author.

This, then, is one criterion for detecting a deeper meaning: an authoritative interpretation of the words of Scripture in a more-than-literal way either in the New Testament or in official Church pronouncements.

But there is still reason for caution. Because not every time the New Testament or Church documents suggest a more-than-literal sense of the words of Scripture is it a case of a deeper meaning in the words themselves.

Sometimes it may be no more than what is called 'accommodation' or loose association. 'Accommodation' is not really a sense of Scripture at all, but a sense which we give to Scripture; not a meaning taken from the words, so much as a meaning put into the words.

Let us take an example. In John's Gospel (1:6), it is said of John the Baptist: 'there was a man sent from God whose name was John'. A preacher may decide to apply this text to Pope John XXIII. There is nothing wrong with this procedure. It is not unbecoming to use a text like John 1:6 in reference to a beloved and saintly figure like Pope John.

But whatever the fittingness of the application, this is accommodation and not a sense of Scripture. Certainly it is not the literal sense. The author of St John's Gospel was referring to John the Baptist and to nobody else.

Nor is there any question of a deeper meaning contained in the words themselves. One could hardly suggest that God, when he inspired the author of the fourth Gospel, intended these words to refer to Pope John, or to any other John for that matter.

You have argued that Genesis 3:15, concerning the woman and the serpent and their descendants, is a passage which contains a deeper meaning intended by God himself. In this text God says to the serpent: 'I will put enmity between you and the woman, and between your seed and her seed; It (that is her seed, her descendants), will crush your head, and you will lie in wait for its heel'.

These words in their literal sense refer to Eve and her descendants, the whole human race. The seed or posterity of the serpent refers to the powers of evil with which the human race will always have to contend. God predicts perpetual struggle and hostility between humanity and the forces of evil.

This text has often been applied to Mary and her son, Jesus. It is thus seen by some to have a deeper biblical meaning. In this case, that meaning would be a reference beyond the literal sense to a future struggle between Christ, the son of Mary, and Satan, with the suggestion of Christ's ultimate victory in this contest.

The criteria are not always easy to apply. Some would see a deeper meaning in Genesis 3:15; others would not. Certainly, as several readers have pointed out, the text has been used in Church documents in reference to Mary.

All things considered, however, I do not believe that there

is conclusive evidence in either the New Testament or Church documents to say that Mary is intended as a deeper meaning of 'the woman' in Genesis 3:15.

This is not to deny that Mary plays a most important part in God's plan of salvation. Her role is clearly indicated in the New Testament.

Question 15:

Leader *readers could well be misled by your comments as to just what is the authentic teaching of the Catholic Church on the relationship of Mary, the mother of Jesus, to Genesis 3:15, as the following extracts from two official Church documents clearly show.*

The Dogmatic Constitution on the Church *issued by the Second Vatican Council states in section 55, chapter 8: 'The books of the Old Testament recount the period of salvation history during which the coming of Christ into the world was slowly prepared for.*

'*These earliest documents, as they are read in the Church and are understood in the light of a further and full revelation, bring the figure of a woman, mother of the Redeemer, into a gradually sharper focus.*

'*When looked at in this way, she is already prophetically foreshadowed in that victory over the serpent which was promised to our first parents after their fall into sin (cf. Genesis 3:15).*'

Pope Paul VI in his apostolic exhortation, Marialis Cultus, *stated: 'In its wonderful presentation of God's plan for man's salvation, the Bible is replete with the mystery of the Saviour, and from Genesis to the Book of Revelation also contains clear references to her who was the mother and associate of the Saviour'.*

Answer:

In my reply to a previous questioner I pointed out that, when the Church in its official documents quotes from, or refers to, biblical passages or texts it does not necessarily intend to define the primary, literal sense of those passages or texts.

In fact, the bishops of the Second Vatican Council choose their words very carefully. They say that the Old Testament books, 'as they are read in the Church and are understood in the light of a further and full revelation' (that is, the

Gospels), bring the figure of Mary 'into a gradually sharper focus'. It is 'when looked at in this way', says the Council document on the Church, that Mary is 'prophetically foreshadowed'.

The Council was very careful to avoid saying that Genesis 3:15 referred directly to Mary, the mother of Jesus, because those responsible for the formulation of the document knew that this was not the case.

I can only assume that Pope Paul VI, who presided over most of Vatican II, intended his words to be understood in the same way when he said that from Genesis to the Book of Revelation, the Bible contains 'clear references' to the mother of the Saviour.

What the Council is saying is this: in the light of the New Testament revelation, it can be seen that Mary, the mother of Jesus, plays a most important role in God's plan of salvation.

Looking back from this viewpoint of Christian faith one can then see Mary 'prophetically foreshadowed' (a very cautious statement) in the mention of the 'woman' of Genesis 3:15 and in some other Old Testament passages.

This association is reinforced by Jesus' strange way of addressing his mother both at Cana and from the Cross as 'woman' (John 2:4; 19:26).

This discovery of Mary 'prophetically foreshadowed' in Genesis 3:15 does not alter the fact that the person who wrote or edited the Book of Genesis did not intend any reference to Mary at all, but only to Eve, the first woman.

Whether the Holy Spirit who inspired him intended the words to contain a fuller or deeper sense is more difficult to determine.

Question 16:

The dogma concerning the perpetual virginity of Mary states that she was a virgin 'before, during and after the birth of Christ'.

The use of the word 'during' in this formula has led the Church for many centuries to believe that the birth of Our Lord was a miraculous event not following the ordinary laws of nature.

Is it permissible for a Catholic to reject this interpretation and hold that the rather unusual choice of words in the dogma is merely a very strong affirmation that Mary never had sexual intercourse in her life, but that the birth of Jesus was a perfectly normal one?

Answer:

It is permissible for a Catholic to hold that the birth of Jesus was a perfectly normal one, and to see the dogmatic formulation 'before, during and after the birth of Christ', as a very strong and comprehensive affirmation of Mary's perpetual virginity.

It is only the virginal conception of Jesus by Mary that is actually recorded in the Scriptures. Luke emphasises the virginal conception of Jesus by Mary's question: 'How can this be, since I have no husband?' (Luke 1:34) and in Matthew's Gospel we learn of how Joseph's doubts were resolved by a revelation from God that the conception was indeed a miraculous one (Matthew 1:18-25).

Although not found in Scripture, belief in the perpetual virginity of Mary is widely attested in early Christian writings.

St Basil, one of the great doctors of the early Church, sums up Christian teaching in these words: 'the friends of Christ do not tolerate hearing that the Mother of God ever ceased to be a virgin'.

The Protestant reformers continued to subscribe strongly to this traditional Christian belief.

It is often objected that the Gospels refer more than once to the 'brothers' of Jesus (for example Mark 6:3) but the word *brother* was commonly used among the Jews for any blood relation.

Nor can anything be proved by reference in the Scriptures to Jesus as Mary's 'first born' son. This title was always given to the first born male, even if he were an only child.

Similarly Matthew's statement that Joseph 'did not know her (Mary) *till* she brought forth her first born son' (Matthew 1:25) does not necessarily imply that there was any change in Mary's virginity after Jesus' birth.

In recent times, an increasing number of non-Catholic biblical scholars have questioned even the virginal conception of Jesus. They point to the wide use of symbols and story in the Gospel narratives, and argue that the story of the virginal conception, too, is but a symbolic way of expressing that the great event of the incarnation of the Son of God had taken place.

This viewpoint is not acceptable to the Catholic Church.

It can be said, however, that Mary's virginity should be seen as more than a mere physical phenomenon. Her virginity does symbolise something far greater, her perfect attitude of total openness to God alone. Her total consecration of herself to him before anyone or anything else.

Mary is a figure of the Church and her virginity is a prophetic sign of the Church's total dedication to Christ.

She is the ideal Christian, completely given only to God.

Having said all that, to return to your original question, there is nothing to be gained from attaching full force to the phrase, 'during birth' contained in the Church's dogmatic formula. It is a choice of words which is designed to leave no 'loop-holes'. But it really adds nothing to the meaning of Mary's virginity.

Question 17:

In your answer (Q16) to a question on the birth of Jesus you state that 'it is permissible for a Catholic to hold that the birth of Jesus was a perfectly normal one, and to see the dogmatic formulation "before, during and after the birth of Christ", as a very strong and comprehensive affirmation of Mary's perpetual virginity', and that 'there is nothing to be gained from attaching full force to the phrase "during birth" contained in the Church's dogmatic formula'.

This puzzles me because the catechism of the Council of Trent (part 1, article 3) has this to say on the point: 'but as the conception itself transcends the order of nature, so also the birth of Our Lord presents to our contemplation nothing but what is divine.

'Besides, what is admirable beyond the power of thoughts or words to express, he is born of his mother without any diminution of her maternal virginity just as he afterwards went forth from the sepulchre while it was closed and sealed and entered the room in which his disciples were assembled, the doors being shut; or, not to depart from every day examples, just as the rays of the sun penetrate without breaking or injuring in the least the solid substance of glass, so after a like but more exalted manner did Jesus Christ

come forth from his mother's womb without injury to her maternal viginity.'

My questions are: 1) In what sense could you call this birth perfectly normal? 2) In what sense could you call the affirmation of Christ's miraculous birth 'nothing to be gained'?

Answer:

Your letter demonstrates clearly that the authors of the catechism of the Council of Trent held a view of the virgin birth of Christ which is very different from that held by the majority of theologians today.

At that time some kind of miraculous emergence of Jesus from the womb of Mary was the prevailing theological opinion. Today, it is not. That is the simple fact.

If you find this change puzzling, it may help to realise that the contents of the catechism of the Council of Trent do not have the same authority as the decrees of the Council itself.

The catechism was commissioned by the bishops who took part in that 16th century Council, hence its name.

The need for such a manual of catechesis was raised at the very beginning of the Council, 1545, as a means of defence against the teachings of the Protestant reformers. But nothing was done about it until just before the conclusion of the Council 18 years later (1563).

Then a committee of bishops and theologians was formed to begin work on the project. The catechism was finally published in 1566, three years after the Council of Trent ended.

It was a most important work which had enormous influence for good in the post-Reformation period of Church history.

Not all of its teachings, however, are of equal value or authority. Like all catechisms, ancient and modern, it comprises statements of unchanging doctrines of faith, along with prevailing theological opinions and current interpretations of Church dogma.

Its explanation of the virgin birth of Christ which you quote is one theological view which is now very much out of favour.

It is more accurate to speak of the virginal *conception* of Jesus than of his virgin birth.

Catholics are not required to believe that Jesus, after being in Mary's womb for nine months, suddenly and miraculously appeared outside her womb, leaving the hymen intact! This is not the point of the Church's teaching on the perpetual virginity of Mary.

The remarkable passage which you quote from the Trent catechism reveals a mentality that insisted very strongly on the physical aspect of Mary's virginity.

Though resulting from a miraculous conception (well documented in Scripture) Mary's pregnancy was a physically normal one and Jesus' birth was a physically normal one in keeping with his real humanity.

Of course, there *is* a very real sense in which the birth of Jesus was no ordinary birth. Namely, because it was the Incarnation of the Son of God.

When Jesus was born, God Himself came to dwell among us as a human being. This is the sense in which the birth of Jesus was miraculous, not in the way he might have emerged from his mother's womb.

Question 18:

Some time ago you wrote something to the effect that one of the reasons why the virgin birth was called miraculous was that then the Word became flesh. Have I misunderstood, or was that your meaning?

My father-in-law, I remember, used to announce the third Joyful Mystery of the Rosary as 'the Incarnation', but I put this down to the slight confusion of age.

I have always believed, more from instinct than instruction, that the Incarnation took place nine months before the Nativity and that March 25, rather than December 25, is the feast of the Word becoming flesh.

I will accept wholeheartedly whatever is the teaching of the Church, but I should like the matter explained.

Answer:

I did not use precisely the words you quote, 'that the virgin birth was called miraculous (because) then the Word became flesh'.

What I wanted to convey was that the Incarnation of the Son of God, that is, that God should have become man, is the greatest miracle, whatever the actual manner of his birth.

I was commenting on whether the term 'virgin birth' necessarily requires our belief that Jesus' physical birth happened in a way different from the natural order of things.

I suggested that the term 'virgin birth' might be understood to mean that the birth of Jesus was the result of virginal conception, which is clearly attested in both the Gospels of Matthew and Luke.

Your father-in-law was not in doctrinal error in announcing the third Joyful Mystery of the Rosary as the Incarnation, because the term 'Incarnation' has commonly been associated and identified with the actual birth of Jesus.

As you say, the Feast of the Annunciation (March 25) is observed by the Church exactly nine months before the celebration of the birth of Jesus because the conception of Jesus by the Holy Spirit is presumed to have occurred at the moment when Mary was informed by God's messenger that she was to be the mother of the Messiah (Luke 1:26-38).

Question 19:

We (Catholics) and those gone before us have been accustomed to worship with prayer Mary the Mother of God within the Holy Trinity. The latest innovation gaining momentum is —

'Mary is a stumbling block hindering the cause of unity because of the word "worship". Let it be said absolutely and finally that Catholics do not give Mary the supreme honour (worship).'

'The words, "Hail Mary, full of grace; the Lord is with thee; blessed art thou among women and blessed is the fruit of thy womb, Jesus", should be abolished and the "Holy Mary, Mother of God" retained.'

In my opinion this line of reasoning is heresy ... I, for one, am not going to deny the Mother of God love, adoration, reverence, homage or worship. What do you believe?

Answer:

Devotion to Mary has always been and will continue to be an important part of our Catholic tradition. We honour her as mother of God because we believe that her Son Jesus is divine. We honour her also as Mother of the Church, spiritual mother of all believers.

We do *NOT* worship Mary. Only God may be worshipped. For all her greatness, Mary is a creature. To worship Mary would be to give to a creature the honour that is due to God alone and would therefore be idolatry.

This understanding of devotion is no 'innovation'. 'Worship' of Mary the Mother of God 'within the Holy Trinity' would have been considered heretical in any period of the Church. Love and reverence, yes; adoration and worship, definitely no!

The 'Hail Mary' is a popular Catholic prayer in honour of Mary. The first part is a combination of the words of Gabriel (Luke 1:28) and of Elizabeth (Luke 1:42).

The Church has added the second part of the prayer which praises Mary's holiness, her divine motherhood, and asks her special help in this life and at the hour of death.

There is no likelihood of any part of the prayer being abolished. It is an expression of legitimate Marian devotion.

Question 20:

An article has been sent to me by a reader, with the heading: Lourdes — Fatima — now Garabandal in Spain. God delivers his 'last warnings' to the world — through Mary.

The reader found this article in a Catholic church and asks for a comment on it.

Answer:

I might just summarise for readers who are not aware of the Garabandal apparitions, what it is all about.

It is alleged that in June 1961 the Archangel Michael appeared to four young girls, aged 11 and 12, at Garabandal in north-western Spain. This was the beginning of a series of appearances and messages that was to continue for the next four years.

The angel told them he had come to prepare them for the visitation of the Blessed Virgin Mary, who would make her first appearance in July. The apparition duly happened, and from then on Our Lady is claimed to have appeared to the girls hundreds of times until her final appearance in November 1965.

There were two 'formal messages'. The first, in July 1961,

was that people had to make sacrifices, do penance and visit the Blessed Sacrament often. If people did not change their ways a great punishment would come.

The second 'formal message', in January 1965, was 'that many cardinals, many bishops and many priests are on the road to perdition, and are taking many souls with them'.

The article which has been submitted to me carries with it the declaration that the events of Garabandal are under investigation by Rome.

As things stand, the apparitions have not been approved, nor have they been condemned.

My advice would be to follow Rome's lead and to suspend judgment on such alleged private revelations as Garabandal until the Church declares one way or the other. I think it unlikely that any official approval will be forthcoming in the foreseeable future.

Question 21:

A number of queries have been received on the subject of the dogma of the Assumption of Mary into Heaven. One reader asks: 'How can Fr Bill O'Shea so dogmatically assert that "Mary's earthly body is not in Heaven"? Surely it is a dogma of the Church — defined as an Article of Faith by Pope Pius X11 in the 1950 Apostolic Consitution Munificentissimus — that "the Immaculate Virgin was taken up body and soul into heavenly glory".'

Another reader refers to the misleading statement 'that Mary's earthly body is not in Heaven'.

She says this statement 'has caused great distress, indignation and even anxiety among many Catholics'. She, too, quotes from the 1950 Constitution in which the dogma was defined.

She quotes also from Chapter 8 of the Second Vatican Council Constitution on the Church, which re-affirms the doctrine, ard from The Credo of the People of God, *proclaimed by Pope Paul VI, in 1968, which states that 'the Blessed Virgin was at the end of her earthly life raised body and soul to heavenly glory and likened to her risen Son in anticipation of the future lot of all the just' and appeals to pictures which she has seen of the Assumption, showing Mary going up to Heaven on a cloud.*

Answer:

The sentence which seems to have caused the 'distress, indignation and anxiety' is that 'the earthly body of Mary is not in Heaven' (see Q.124).

This in no way amounts to a denial of the dogma of the Assumption. The earthly body, that is, the body we have on this earth, is physical, mortal and corruptible. It needs food, drink and sleep. It is prone to sickness, it ages, and ultimately dies and decays.

Mary's earthly body is not in Heaven, nor for that matter is the earthly body of Jesus himself. And that is certainly not a denial of the Ascension of Jesus!

There is a difference in kind between the earthly body and the heavenly, glorified body. St Paul teaches this in 1 Corinthians 15, which he wrote in 57 AD. At the same time, he emphasises the futility of speculating on the form of what he calls the 'spiritual body'.

Pope Paul VI captured the essential truth of the dogma of the Assumption when he said that Mary was 'raised body and soul to heavenly glory . . . in anticipation of the future lot of all the just'.

It is a dogma of faith that 'the resurrection of the body' is the destiny of all, and for the righteous this will lead to their glorification.

The Assumption of Mary means that she has been granted by God the privilege of enjoying already what awaits other mortals at the general resurrection.

When the dead are raised they will not possess the same kind of body as in this life and neither does Mary.

What has happened to her is meant to encourage us: as she was taken to Heaven and glorified, we have the assurance that one day we also will be, if we remain united to Christ in faith and love.

Those who think of Mary's heavenly existence in material, physical terms are missing the point of the dogma of the Assumption.

Question 22:

In repeated answers in 'Question Box', you have asserted: 'Mary's earthly body is not in heaven' (Q21). Opposed to this, correspondents have quoted the defined dogma of the

Church: 'the Immaculate Virgin was taken up body and soul into heavenly glory' (Pius XII, Munificentissimus, 1950).

Presumably this definition means what it says, and Mary's body is in heaven. Your answers do not face up to the evident contradiction here.

Further, in the answer to the question concerning the human body in heaven and in particular Christ's body — there is a danger from the context that readers might understand you to say that Christ's earthly body is not in heaven either. I hasten to affirm that you say no such thing. Rather you clearly and correctly state Catholic teaching 'that there has been a transformation from his physical, earthly body to his risen, glorified body'.

A transformation in no way implies a substitution — rather the reverse. Transformation implies that the original reality (body) is still there, but transformed. In other words, Christ's earthly body is in heaven but transformed (glorified).

Would it not be more helpful to Catholic enquirers to assert the same clear Catholic teaching in regard to Mary's earthly body and its assumption into heaven rather than seem to contradict Catholic dogma by asserting: 'Mary's earthly body is not in heaven'?

Answer:

First of all, let me say that I appreciate your attempt to reconcile my statements with the views of those who have obviously disagreed with me. However, while I acknowledge your efforts to achieve some sort of consensus, I am afraid I cannot accept your terminology. I hope our differences are more a matter of terminology that of doctrine.

You say that my answers do not 'face up to the evident contradiction' between my statement, 'Mary's *earthly* body is not in heaven', and the defined dogma of the Church, 'the Immaculate Virgin was taken up body and soul into heavenly glory'. I do not see any contradiction at all between these two statements.

The Church's dogma concerns Mary's heavenly, glorified 'body'. I am referring to her earthly, physical body.

You go on to say that there is a danger of readers understanding me to say that 'Christ's earthly body is not in heaven either'. That is precisely what I *am* saying: Christ's earthly body is not in heaven.

I appreciate your admission that I 'clearly and correctly state Catholic teaching' when I say that 'there has been a transformation from his physical, earthly body to his risen, glorified body'. If there has been a transformation (that is, change) from the earthly body, what else can this possibly mean than that the body of Jesus, as it was on earth, is no longer his mode of existence in his heavenly state?

Your concern rightly is to safeguard the continuity between the earthly and the glorified Jesus. This, of course, is of the essence of our faith.

There *is* an identity and continuity between the Jesus who died on the Cross, the Christ who rose, and the Lord who now 'sits at the right hand of the Father'.

But to assert the continuity and identity of the crucified, risen and glorified Lord is not the same thing as saying that Jesus' earthly body is in heaven. A close study of 1 Corinthians 15:35-54 reveals that there is an essential difference between the earthly, physical body and the risen, glorified body.

I am certain that St Paul would have considered the idea of a glorified earthly body as a contradiction in terms. Consequently I have real reservations about the theological accuracy of your statement that 'Christ's earthly body is in heaven, but transformed (glorified)'. Glorified humanity, yes; glorified earthly body, no!

Again, in regard to Mary I can see no apparent contradiction of Catholic dogma in the statement that 'Mary's earthly body is not in heaven'. I do not believe it would be 'more helpful to Catholic enquirers' to state otherwise. Mary has been fully glorified 'body and soul'. But she does not retain in heaven the body which she had on earth.

Underlying this whole debate is a misconception which I hoped I had corrected elsewhere. When the term 'body' occurs in the New Testament, especially in the context of resurrection, it does not mean the physical body as we understand it. To the biblical (Jewish) mentality, the 'body' is the equivalent of the whole person.

In defining its dogmas of faith, the Church has employed biblical language. In stating that the 'body' of Christ and the 'body' of Mary are in heaven, and that the 'bodies' of all believers will rise and be with Christ, the biblical authors and those who have formulated Church doctrines do not intend to teach that their physical earthly bodies are or will be in heaven.

Pius XII's statement that Mary was 'taken up body and soul into heavenly glory' means that she is already fully glorified, not just a disembodied spirit, but that her whole person is with the Lord — a condition that awaits all believers following on 'the resurrection of the body', in the biblical sense of the words.

Charismatics

Question 23:

I have struggled long and hard before formulating this question. I will try to do it with charity. If we regard the family as the core of Catholic community, and the parish as the meeting place of these communities, what role and place do Charismatic communities have in our parishes?

People belonging to these communities justify their existence by saying that they need the spiritual support they receive from them to live a fuller Christian life. Yet I find that, even though they certainly live a spirit-filled life, as far as the parish is concerned they are of little use.

Their commitment to community is so intense and strict that participation in parish activities is only token; and this, only after direction from their leadership for a specific task and for a limited time.

These communities claim they came into being because parishes were not catering for their needs. Maybe so, but how much did they cater for their parish's needs, or do they now?

I feel they have created division in our parishes and are a liability rather than an asset to the Church. We need these people to help us build Christ's Church, yet they are not available to us on our terms. 'Come and join us', they say, but apart from Sunday Mass two or three times a month (on other Sundays they have their own Mass elsewhere), they make no contribution to the life of the parish.

My frustration is showing. I try to love and understand them but . . .

Answer:

The question which you pose is a very difficult one for me to answer. Indeed, I suggest that those who might answer it satisfactorily would be members of the Charismatic communities themselves.

I presume that their degree of involvement in, and commitment to, the life of parishes varies from parish to parish, from Charismatic group to group, perhaps even from member to member.

In my own parish experience, I have usually found Charismatics to be very much to the fore in the activities of the parish. It may well be true that their contribution is restricted to those areas which fit in with their own interests and objectives.

But would not this also be true of most parishioners who become involved in one or other aspect of parish life?

There are, of course, Charismatics and Charismatics. I have no doubt that your negative evaluation of their parish commitment is verified in some instances. Personally, I do not have a lot of sympathy with the tightly-knit, hierarchical structure of some sections of the Charismatic renewal movement.

Charismatics may well answer your criticism by saying that some parishes, liturgically and pastorally, are not equipped to accommodate them; and that their efforts to act as catalysts for renewal have met with resistance and left them frustrated.

Sadly, in many instances, they would have good reason for feeling frustrated.

On the other hand, the Charismatic renewal movement, like all renewal movements in the Church today, must be humble enough to admit that it does not have a monopoly of the truth. The danger of being seen as an 'elitist' group is an ever present one.

Whenever this image is projected by any renewal movement, then it ceases to be an effective agent for building up the body of Christ.

Thus, Charismatic expectations of what a parish ought 'to be about' can sometimes be wrong. I am thinking, for example, of the kind of preaching and teaching they might expect from their pastors. In some cases they may have good cause for dissatisfaction.

But it must also be said that the fundamentalist approach to Scripture espoused by some Charismatic groups is far removed from the approach advocated by Pius XII, the

Second Vatican Council, and the Roman Biblical Commission.

Speaking as a parish priest — if I had in my parish a group of Charismatics who felt their needs were not being met, and who were therefore inclined to opt out of parish life, I should be most uncomfortable. Because they constitute an important movement in today's Church, I should want to discuss with them the reasons for their lack of participation.

Should I reasonably conclude that their expectations were not in line with the vision of the Church in the modern world which has evolved from the Second Vatican Council, then my hope would be that they would move on to other pastures and become some other pastor's headache.

I realise that my answer is not a satisfactory one. It is hedged with all sorts of exceptive clauses. But your question, as I said at the outset, is one which requires many 'ifs and buts'.

It would be interesting to hear what people in the Charismatic renewal movement might have to say.

Question 24:

I should like to try and answer the question (Q23) on Charismatics — from my point of view anyway.

I have been in a group since it began about 2 years ago. I have found it a great joy, and it has taught me a lot about my faith, and given me a better appreciation of the Mass.

This is what our prayer group is all about; to learn what is God's will for us, and to thank and praise him. We have a caring and sharing group and endeavour to help wherever possible in our parish.

I know also that other neighbouring parish groups run along the same lines as we meet together at different times and always finish up with a Mass or Benediction. We try and work in with our parish priests. Sunday Mass is most important to us all and we try to attend during the week when possible.

So, although the prayer group has been and is very important to me, I would not give up my faith in the Mass for it.

Answer:

Thank you for your letter. I am sure that charismatic prayer groups in many parishes could report in a similar vein.

Members of charismatic prayer groups perform a valuable prayer ministry, and so, in this sense, can play a big part in 'building up the body of Christ' at the local church level.

The true test of the Spirit's presence and activity will be that this 'upbuilding' is carried over into other areas of the life of the community.

Commandments of the Church

Question 25:

We once had seven Commandments of the Church. Would you please identify the present Commandments of the Church and comment on the fact that these seem to have changed in recent years?

Answer:

The seven Commandments of the Church which I memorised as a primary school student were as follows:

1. To hear Mass on Sundays and Holy Days of Obligation.

2. To fast and abstain on the days commanded.

3. To confess our sins at least once a year.

4. To receive worthily the Blessed Eucharist at Easter or within the appointed time, that is, from Ash Wednesday to Trinity Sunday.

5. To contribute to the support of our pastors.

6. To send Catholic children to Catholic schools.

7. To observe the laws of the Church regarding the Sacrament of Marriage.

None of these laws has been revoked. They are not, of course, of equal gravity. Certainly not all of them 'bind under pain of mortal sin', as the moral theologians used to say.

Moreover in this post-Vatican II era, some of these regulations might need to be phrased differently. 'To hear Mass' is definitely the terminology of a past age, thankfully. It suggests a point of view which saw the offering of Mass as the function of the priest alone, with the laity as the audience.

Catholics in the 1980s would surely see their participation in the Eucharistic celebration as going somewhat beyond that of 'hearing' Mass.

Question 26:

Currently just what are the 'Commandments of the Church?' I think I recall learning six, but can bring to mind only two or three with any clarity, and I find I am not alone in this.

This enquiry arises from a discussion regarding Confession, so please deal with that in particular.

Answer:

There are in fact many more 'Commandments of the Church' than six. This description could justifiably be applied to all ecclesiastical laws which make up the Code of Canon Law, and run into several hundreds. For pastoral reasons, the Australian bishops chose to highlight and emphasise six of the Church's laws.

Traditionally they have been phrased as follows:

1. To hear Mass on Sundays and Holy Days of Obligation.

2. To fast and abstain on the days commanded.

3. To confess our sins at least once a year.

4. To receive worthily the Blessed Eucharist at Easter or within the appointed time, that is, between Ash Wednesday and Trinity Sunday.

5. To contribute to the support of our pastors.

6. To observe the laws of the Church regarding the Sacrament of Marriage.

Later a seventh commandment was added, 'to send Catholic children to Catholic schools'. But this was not enforced in all Australian dioceses.

You ask me to deal in particular with the commandment regarding Confession. I am not sure what aspect of this commandment you would like me to comment on. All I can say is that the precept which obliges Catholics to confess their serious sins at least once a year to a priest remains in force.

In fact, all six commandments remain in force. In some cases, the requirements may have changed, for example, 'the days commanded' for fasting and abstinence, and the laws of the Church regarding marriage. But none of the six precepts has been revoked.

Question 27:

When I was younger I was taught that there were six Commandments of the Church. And now you mention seven. I should be grateful if you would kindly tell me how the one about the schools arose.

I also do not understand how they are all not of equal gravity. For example, to deliberately eat meat on say, Good Friday, is surely the same as deliberately missing Mass on Sunday — or is it?

Answer:

You are quite right in saying that in earlier days, only six 'Commandments of the Church' were listed in the Australian catechism. I am not sure of the origin of these commandments. Probably they come from an Irish source, and were transplanted by the Irish-Australian Bishops to the Australian scene.

In actual fact, there are many more commandments of the Church than six. One could justifiably apply this description to all ecclesiastical laws, of which the old Code of Canon Law comprises 2414! For pastoral reasons, the Australian Bishops chose to highlight and emphasise six of the Church's laws.

Following on the Fourth Plenary Council of the Australian Bishops in 1937, a seventh commandment was added for the Australian Church: the obligation to send Catholic children to Catholic schools.

The lateness of this addition would explain why you were taught that there were only six.

As a matter of fact, the seventh commandment concerning attendance of Catholic children at Catholic schools was never enforced in all Australian dioceses.

As for the relative gravity of these commandments, let us take an example other than the one you presented. Surely the commandment about Sunday Mass is of greater importance than that of contributing to the support of pastors — or of sending Catholic children to Catholic schools. The commandments of the Church are not all of equal gravity.

Question 28:

I would like to comment on your reply on the question of the commandments of the Church. There must be many thousands of migrants (like myself) who memorised a slightly different list of precepts: there are six in the English catechism, with no precept requiring parents to send Catholic children to Catholic schools. Besides some of the others were slightly different in their emphasis and even in their requirements.

For example, one was expected to make one's 'Easter Duty' between Ash Wednesday and the octave of the feast of Sts Peter and Paul. If such commandments are still considered necessary, it would be helpful if a new set, relevant to today's Australian Catholics, were to be proclaimed by the Bishops.

Actually I grew up in South Africa, but we learnt from the English catechism. Speaking of South Africa, it took me some years to realise that Australian Catholics practise their own version of 'apartheid': discrimination against children and the families to which they belong who wear the 'wrong' school uniform. So I hope the Catholic education commandment is dropped.

Answer:

As my answer to a previous question indicates, there is a 'national' flavour to the formulation of these commandments. For example, the commandment 'to contribute to the support of pastors' would have no relevance in countries where the Catholic Church is the established religion and priests are paid a government salary.

As for your suggestion that the Australian Bishops might consider it timely to promulgate a new set of Church commandments, I would prefer to leave that to the Bishops themselves. However, I believe that our Bishops rightly operate on the principle that laws should not be multiplied unnecessarily, but that the Gospel ethic should be more powerfully proclaimed.

This, of course, encompasses the whole area of social justice, which is conspicuously absent from the traditional six or seven commandments of the Church. As for the commandment to send Catholic children to Catholic schools I would refer you again to my answer to a previous question.

Contraception and Conscience

Question 29:

Just a little background knowledge before I ask my questions. My fiancee and I are to be married shortly. We are both Catholics. We hope to raise a family, God willing, and bring our children up within the Church.

However, we are a little concerned about family planning and the Church's laws. We have a good working knowledge of the Billings Method, but are concerned that we won't be able to follow it and use it properly.

Some friends have used it and have found themselves with 'unplanned' children. They are now using contraceptive pills. This leads me to my question.

Can we use the pill or is it against the teaching of the Church? Please note here that as far as we both know we are completely healthy.

Also, if it is against Church law, is it a mortal or venial sin? And is the sin committed by both husband and wife or just the wife?

If by some chance we found out before marriage that we were unable to have children, could we still marry? Do the teachings of the Church forbid a marriage if prior to the marriage both parties know that children cannot be produced?

Perhaps you could advise us of some books and people to contact if we wanted to find out more about the Church's teachings on this matter.

Answer:

The Vatican Council's document, *The Church in the Modern World*, states that parents should exercise 'human and Christian responsibility' in the raising of their family.

Procreation involves not only having but also raising children. God does not demand that a couple have as many

62

children as is physically possible. How many children a couple should have is something that only they, in dialogue with God and one another, can determine.

Having said that the Church promotes and encourages family planning, it must also be said that the method of birth control approved by the Church is Natural Family Planning. It is called 'natural' since nothing mechanical or artifical is used; it depends on periodic abstinence and self-discipline.

A 'good working knowledge' of natural family planning is not really sufficient. You and your fiancee would be wise to attend one of the marriage preparation courses offered by the Catholic Family Welfare Bureau, and to attend at least one of the sessions of its Natural Family Planning Clinic.

In this area, simply to read a book and then expect to be competent to use the method reliably can be a trap.

You may well find that those friends of yours who found themselves with 'unplanned' children either had an in-adequate understanding of the method, or failed to exercise the required self-discipline on one or another occasion.

Use of the contraceptive pill is one of the artificial methods of birth control forbidden by the Church.

The Church's teaching is based on its understanding of the nature of the sexual act. It teaches that one of the major functions of the sex act is to bring new life into existence. To place a direct obstacle in its way is to prevent life in an act intended by God to give life.

Moreover, artificial birth control can frustrate the total physical self-surrender which is so essential to married love.

In July 1968, Pope Paul VI, in his encyclical, *Humanae Vitae*, reiterated the Church's traditional opposition to all forms of artificial contraception. He stated that 'each and every marriage act must remain open to the transmission of life.'

This was not an infallible pronouncement, but an official statement of the Church's moral teaching which Catholics must take seriously nevertheless.

In the aftermath of *Humanae Vitae*, several national conferences of bishops pointed out that, in certain circumstances and for serious reasons, Catholics might in conscience feel justified in exempting themselves from the Church's teaching.

There might be the situation in which a couple are trying

their best to live a truly Christian marriage and are not acting out of selfish motives. However they feel that their present situation is such that for grave physical, financial or psychological reasons they are unable to practise periodic abstinence.

They should not, however, presume to decide the morality of this solely by themselves, however well-intentioned they might be. While their conscience is always their ultimate guide, they must also consider the objective standards of morality proposed to them by the teaching Church.

They would be wise to consult an informed pastor before deciding to take such a step.

When a husband and wife consent to practise a form of birth control which in conscience they believe to be wrong, they are equally guilty of sin.

There may be certain circumstances, for example, in the case of a wife submitting to pressure from the husband for the sake of the peace of the marriage, which would diminish or even remove the responsibility of one of the partners.

The discovery by a couple before marriage that they are unable or unlikely to have children does not prevent them from marrying. It is the inability to perform the sexual act at all (physical impotence) which could render a marriage invalid, not the incapacity to have children.

Question 30:

Your reply to Q29 was very informative about the Church's explicit stance on contraception, as clearly defined by Popes Paul VI and John Paul II. Several parts of your answer referred to allowable present-day practices, and your elaboration on these points would be appreciated.

You state 'in the aftermath of Humanae Vitae *several national conferences of bishops pointed out that, in certain circumstances and for serious reasons, Catholics might in conscience feel justified in exempting themselves from the Church's teaching'.*

Does a national conference of bishops have the jurisdiction or authority to proclaim moral judgments binding in conscience on Catholics of their own or any other country?

In the instance quoted, they have gone over and above the teaching of the Church, and made their own moral judgment. The net result in practice is that the Pope's explicit teaching, in a case where it is 'binding on earth as it is in Heaven', has been drastically altered by adding exceptions, etc.

It surely causes chaos in the Church to have national conferences of bishops deciding for their flocks teachings on morals which are in opposition to one another.

This poses the question for Catholics, 'Does morality or Church teaching vary according to nationality or place of living?'

This question is not hard to answer, but the problem exists. The cause appears to be the unwillingness on the part of some members of the hierarchy of the Church and some clergy to obey the Pope's teachings as they are.

They change them to suit their own different interpretations or personal beliefs, which are generally the easy way out.

In your answer to the question whether a mortal or venial sin would be committed in breaking the Church's law on contraception, you appear to avoid the full anwer by saying 'when a husband and wife consent to practise a form of birth control which in conscience they believe to be wrong, they are equally guilty of sin.'

Do you consider that such a sin is so serious as to sever one's relationship with God, until proper reconciliation is made?

Answer:

Your letter poses a number of questions about the nature of the Church's teaching authority, the ways in which this teaching authority is exercised in the Church, and the kind of assent which Catholics are obliged to give to authoritative pronouncements.

Perhaps the best approach would be to leave aside the matter of *Humanae Vitae* and contraception for the moment, and consider the wider question involved.

Let us begin with the gift of infallibility. Infallibility is an effect of Christ's guidance of the Church through the Holy Spirit, so that the Church is preserved from error in handing on the Gospel message.

Infallibility is found in the consensus of belief of the whole Church in union with the Pope and bishops.

Vatican II's constitution on the Church teaches that 'the

entire body of the faithful, anointed as they are by the Holy Spirit . . . cannot err in matters of belief' (No.12).

Christ's infallible guidance of the Church resides in a special way in the leaders of the Church, the Pope and bishops.

The Church teaches that this gift of infallibility is enjoyed and expressed by the Pope when certain conditions are fulfilled: when he teaches as the visible head of the Church, to all Catholics, on matters of faith or morality, intending to use his full authority and to give an unchangeable decision.

In such a situation the Pope is the spokesman for the faith of the Church. He speaks on behalf of all the bishops and the believing people, and his teaching is binding on each and every individual Catholic.

The whole body or college of bishops can also teach with infallibility. In union with the Pope, they can pronounce infallibly on matters of faith and morals, in such a way as to require the acceptance of the entire Church.

This normally takes place when they gather together for a general council, but it may also be exercised by them separately, when they teach the same doctrine throughout the world.

Obviously, there is another kind of Church teaching which doesn't fall within the area of infallibility. This is called the 'ordinary' teaching of the Church and is often communicated by decrees or papal encyclicals (letters from the Pope to the whole Church on important matters).

It is also necessary to realise that some of the Church's teachings are more important than others.

'In Catholic doctrine there exists an order or "hierarchy" of truths since they vary in relation to the foundation of the Christian faith' (*Decree on Ecumenism*, No. 11).

It was in July 1968 that Pope Paul VI issued his encyclical letter *Humanae Vitae* which stated the Church's teaching on sexual morality in marriage.

In it, the Pope argued that 'each and every marriage act must remain open to the transmission of life', and thus restated the Church's traditional ban on any form of contraception.

The diverse reactions on the part of Catholics to this encyclical raised the important question: to what extent are Catholics bound to obey the ordinary, non-infallible teaching of the Church. *Humanae Vitae* was not an infallible papal statement.

Your choice of words in the first paragraph of your leter is therefore unfortunate when you refer to 'the Church's stance on contraception, as clearly *defined* by Popes Paul VI and John Paul II'.

The words 'define' and 'definition' are technical terms in theology to describe infallible Church pronouncements. In this sense nothing has been 'defined' by any Pope or Council on the matter of contraception.

However, although not an infallible statement, *Humanae Vitae* was an important statement on morality by the leader of the Church, and this demanded a serious response from the whole Church.

Various national conferences of bishops met to consider the pastoral implications of the teaching of the encyclical.

All affirmed the Pope's right to speak with authority on this matter. At the same time they recognised the difficulties which many couples would face in adhering strictly to the letter of the Pope's teaching.

What the bishops did was to issue for their people pastoral interpretations of the principles laid down by Paul VI in his encyclical letter.

Catholics are obliged to follow the guidance of the Pope and their bishops in religious matters, even when they are not teaching infallibly. But there is another important principle enunciated by the Second Vatican Council: 'In all his activity a man is bound to follow his conscience faithfully . . . according to truly Christian values and principles.'

What is the situation then when a Catholic sincerely finds himself or herself unable to accept in conscience an ordinary, non-infallible teaching of the Church?

This was the question which the bishops faced when drawing up their pastoral interpretations of the Pope's encyclical.

In most of their statements, the common factor was the primacy of conscience, but also the need for a well-informed conscience — a conscience which takes seriously the teaching of the Church before deciding on the morality of a course of action.

It is therefore possible that a Catholic in good conscience — after prayer, consultation and serious deliberation —

might assume the serious responsibility of humble dissent.

Dissent in clear conscience from an ordinary, non-infallible teaching of the Church is possible.

These pastoral interpretations of the papal teaching on birth control should not be seen in terms of national or local rules and regulations, or as suggesting that the morality binding on Catholics depends on their place of residence.

It is rather a case of the bishops, in union with the Pope, acting as pastors for their people, fully aware of their being part of the universal Church.

To say they have gone 'over and above the teaching of the Church' is really to confuse the issue.

There is one further comment in your letter which demands a response. You claim that in an earlier reply in *Question Box* I avoided the question 'whether a mortal or venial sin would be committed in breaking the law on contraception.'

In the light of what I have said above, it should be clear that this is a difficult question to answer even when confronted with the penitent in the reconciliation room. It would be rash indeed to attempt to give a generalising answer to such a question.

Your other question is easier to answer, concerning a couple who 'consent to practise a form of birth control which in conscience they believe to be wrong'.

If people act in bad conscience in any serious matter, they should certainly make use of the Sacrament of Reconciliation before presuming to receive the Eucharist.

Question 31:

I read with interest your reply on family planning (Q29). There are some points on which I would like you to comment further.

● *One criticism of Natural Family Planning which I find difficult to answer is that abstinence is not in fact, natural, as it interferes with the spontaneity of lovemaking which is a precious part of married life.*

● *Abstinence and the Pill (preventive type) are means to the same end, namely the prevention of conception. Why then does the Church come out so strongly against the Pill?*

One could argue that the failure rate of the Pill (2 per cent) fulfils the Pope's criteria regarding the transmission of life in each and every marriage act. The theoretical failure rate of the Billings Method is less than this, although I know that in practice it is greater.

Finally, from a booklet by the International Planned Parenthood Federation, I quote: 'St Augustine explicitly condemned periodic abstinence as an unacceptable practice for a Christian.'

The reference given is J. T. Noonan, Contraception: A history of its treatment by the Catholic Theologians and Canonists *(Harvard University Press, Cambridge, Massachusetts, 1965).*

What are your comments on this statement? And do you have any further comment on the International Planned Parenthood Federation?

Answer:

As I said in my reply, to which you refer, the method of family planning which involves periodic abstinence is considered 'natural' in the sense that nothing mechanical or artificial is employed to prevent nature taking its course.

The Church has consistently taught that one of the main purposes of the sex act is to bring new life into existence. To interfere with this act 'unnaturally' is to prevent life in an act intended by God to produce life.

It is also argued that artificial birth control frustrates the total physical self-surrender that is vital to married love.

It must be admitted, however, that there is much debate within the Church today about this question.

Some would argue that a consideration of what is 'natural' should involve not only the physical act, but the total context in which the act is performed (including the number of children a couple already have; their physical, mental, and material capabilities, etc.)

As with any action, it is claimed, the circumstances of the sexual act must be considered in determining its morality.

But to come to your specific question. You ask whether abstinence can be considered natural if it 'interferes with the spontaneity of lovemaking which is a precious part of married life.'

I believe that this objection is best answered by inviting people to reflect on the nature of Christian love in general.

If our love for one another is to be modelled on the love of

Christ, then sacrifice must be accepted as an integral part of this love. Jesus displayed this important aspect of love not only by his death, but throughout the whole of his public life.

As for married love in particular, St Paul in his letter to the Ephesians urged husbands and wives to love one another 'as Christ loved his Church' (Ephesians 5:25).

I believe that when Paul proposed Christ's love for his disciples as the model for the love between Christian spouses, he had uppermost in his mind two Christ-like qualities of love: fidelity and self-sacrifice.

Periodic abstinence for the good of one's partner, far from being seen as a negation of love, should therefore be regarded as a positive expression of the kind of love which is 'a precious part of married life'. Married love must surely involve more than just the sexual expression of that love — important though this is.

While abstinence and the use of the contraceptive pill are intended to produce the same result, the prevention of conception, the difference lies in the means employed.

Periodic abstinence follows and uses the laws of nature, the means that Christians should accept as designed by God, the author of nature, whereas artificial contraception is a human intervention which is aimed at frustrating the law of nature or of God.

Granted this distinction, then the success or failure rate of artificial means of contraception, vis-a-vis that of the Natural Family Planning method, is not really relevant to the moral issue involved.

Finally, you quote J. T. Noonan as saying that 'St Augustine explicitly condemned periodic abstinence as an unacceptable practice for a Christian.'

I have not verified this quotation from St Augustine, but I have no reason to doubt its authenticity. Great theologian though he was, many of Augustine's views on matters sexual must be considered dubious, and are not part of Catholic teaching today.

Those who regard theologians as a suspect group in the 20th century should not be surprised to learn that they could promulgate erroneous opinions in the 5th century as well.

Of course, it is true that even the practice of natural family planning can be sinful, if it is motivated by selfishness and the refusal to accept the responsibilities of parenthood.

As for the International Planned Parenthood Federation, this is an American based organisation with branches or affiliated groups in other countries. The positions it holds on contraception and abortion are far removed from the teaching of the Catholic Church. Though enjoying an aura of respectability and claiming not to promote abortion, it does in fact act as an abortion referral agency. It accepts abortion as a necessary back-up to contraception failure. In its own literature it states explicitly that abortion is 'a necessary and integral part of any complete or total family planning programme.'

To what extent some Australian family planning associations are affiliated with the IPPF or share its views I am not certain.

Question 32:
I find your answer on 'family planning' (Q29), most unsatisfactory and misleading. No Catholic couple with a fully informed conscience could conclude that their circumstances justify the use of the Pill.

You stress the 'primacy of personal conscience' but have failed to fully inform it.

The teaching of the Church is quite clear, as Pope Paul VI in 1968 expressed it. You have made it unclear, as indeed, I suspect, many parish priests do.

Answer:
The Second Vatican Council had already recognised the difficult situation of many married couples.

It said: 'The Council realises that certain conditions often keep couples from arranging their married lives harmoniously, and they find themselves in circumstances where at least temporarily the size of their families should not be increased.

'As a result, the faithful exercise of love and the full intimacy of their marriage is hard to maintain.

'But where the intimacy of married life is broken off, its faithfulness can sometimes be imperilled and its quality of fruitfulness ruined. For them the upbringing of children and the courage to accept new ones are both endangered.' (The Church in the Modern World, No. 51).

Following Pope Paul's encyclical letter (*Humanae Vitae*, 1968) many national conferences of bishops undertook to apply the principles enunciated in the encyclical to the various circumstances of these married couples.

All of these episcopal conferences affirmed the Pope's right to speak authoritatively on the subject. But a number of them recognised the difficulties for many couples to stick to the letter of the encyclical.

For example, the bishops of Belgium said: 'We cannot assume that those who do not see the convincing value of the Pope's reasons are acting out of selfish motives . . . We must recognise, according to the traditional teaching, that the ultimate practical norm of action is conscience which has been duly enlightened.'

The German bishops urged pastors in the administration of the Sacraments to respect 'the decisions of conscience made by believers in the awareness of their responsibilities.'

The bishops of Austria stated that if someone should go against the teaching of this encyclical, 'he must not feel cut off from God's love in every case, and may then receive Holy Communion without first going to Confession.'

The bishops of the United States, after affirming the objective evil of artificial contraception, urged those who had resorted to this 'never to lose heart but to continue to take full advantage of the strength which comes from the Sacrament of Penance and the grace, healing and peace in the Eucharist.'

The Canadian bishops recognised that in this matter, 'many Catholics face a grave problem of conscience'. They quoted Vatican II: 'In all his activity a man is bound to follow his conscience faithfully . . . according to truly Christian values and principles.'

They went on to state that confessors should show 'sympathetic understanding and reverence for the sincere good faith of those who fail in their effort to accept some point of the encyclical'.

The Canadian bishops acknowledged that there are some who, while accepting the teaching of the Pope, find that 'because of particular circumstances they are involved in what seems to them a clear conflict of duties.

'For example, the reconciling of conjugal love and responsible parenthood with the education of children already born or with the health of the mother.

'In accord with the accepted principles of moral theology, if these persons have tried sincerely but without success to pursue a line of conduct in keeping with the given directives, they may be safely assured that whoever honestly chooses that course which seems right to him does so in good conscience.'

These are not the opinions of radical or disloyal theologians. They are extracts from statements made by various national conferences of bishops from around the world, in full communion with the Bishop of Rome.

I submit that my reply to the question on family planning stated no more or less than these episcopal statements.

If my answer was 'most unsatisfactory, unclear and misleading', the same judgment must be passed on these pastoral applications of the Pope's teaching, by his brother bishops, to the many and varied circumstances of individual married couples.

Question 33:

Your reader's objection to your watering down of Humanae Vitae *is fully vindicated by the answer you gave him (Q32).*

Against the one sure guide Christ gave us in the charism of the infallibility of the Pope, you pose the chasm of fallibility shared by bishops, priests, scholars and the rest of us.

It will be an object lesson for centuries.

Indeed the same judgment is passed on them as on you, to quote your own words.

Thomas More, on trial for his life in 1534, was informed by the court that 'all the bishops of England' had signed away the papal supremacy in favour of the King's supremacy. 'Bishop for bishop!' he retorted, pointing out that the whole of Christendom had far more faithful bishops.

Compassion for the circumstances of the sinner cannot be elevated into approval of the sin in those circumstances. No one questions this about the widespread sin of drunkenness.

In this respect the advice given by the American bishops is in a class of its own and should never have been included in the fallible category you quoted.

In conclusion, I could wish that your column had more

*pastoral warmth in urging the fullness of the faith on strug-
gling believers.*

Answer:

I think your comments are misleading. Your contrast between the infallibility of the Pope and the fallibility of
others, including National Conferences of Bishops, is not
really relevant to the matter in question.

Infallibility is a charism, or gift of God, which is used by
Popes only in rare and exceptional circumstances. Certainly
it was *not* invoked by Pope Paul VI in his encyclical
Humanae Vitae.

Infallibility resides primarily in the Church as a whole. It
is expressed by the belief of the people of the Church who
are in union with the Pope and bishops. When there is a
consensus among the whole People of God about a doctrine
its truth is guaranteed by the Holy Spirit. 'The entire body of
the faithful, anointed as they are by the Holy One . . . cannot
err in matters of belief' (Constitution on the Church, No.
12).

In using the charism of infallibility the Pope acts as the
spokesman of the Church. He speaks on behalf of all the
bishops and the believing people.

In the matter of contraception, there was obviously no
consensus fidelium, or agreement among members of the
Church. There are some who regret that the Pope did not
make an infallible pronouncement on the matter. But the
question arises: Could Paul VI have done so, given the
circumstances, even had he so wished?

Certainly he did not do so, nor did he want to invoke this
privilege. Consequently there seems no justification for in-
voking this distinction (infallibility versus fallibility) in the
matter at hand.

Your comments infer a vision of Church in which the
pope is set over against the 'bishops, priests, scholars and the
rest of us'. This model conflicts with the Vatican Council's
presentation of the Church as the one People of God.

The aim of the National Bishops' Conferences whose
teaching I quoted was to provide a pastoral application (not
a 'watering down') of the papal teaching to the circumstances of married couples experiencing difficulties in this
area.

These were statements made by bishops in full communion with (and, I assume, with the approval of) the Bishop of Rome, the Vicar of Christ, the Pope.

Question 34:

Is the use of the condom as a form of male contraceptive morally acceptable in the eyes of the Church? Is it a mortal or venial sin to use it, and what punishment or penalty occurs?

If a woman's life is in danger should she fall pregnant, is this form of contraception (as well as the Pill etc) still wrong in the eyes of the Church?

Also, is there any literature I could read which states the Church's ruling on this subject of contraception?

Answer:

I presume that your letter envisages the case of sexual relations within marriage, between husband and wife. It was Pope Paul's encyclical *Humanae Vitae* (1968), which restated the Church's traditional opposition to *all* forms of artificial contraception. Much has been written on this controversial papal document, but there is no substitute for reading the encyclical itself.

After the publication of the encyclical, attention focused almost exclusively on its ban on contraception, but it also contains much positive teaching on marriage and sexuality.

This encyclical letter *Humanae Vitae — on the regulation of Birth* is published by St Paul Publications.

As far as the Church's opposition to artificial means of birth control is concerned there is no difference between the male condom and the contraceptive pill.

In a previous answer to a question on the matter of the authority of this teaching, I pointed out that several national conferences of bishops subsequently considered circumstances in which Catholics might experience difficulty in adhering strictly to the letter of the Church's teaching as formulated by Paul VI in *Humanae Vitae*.

In the same reply, I referred to the primacy of conscience as the ultimate factor in determining the morality of all human activity.

However, I also stated that a Catholic has the duty to cultivate a well-informed conscience — 'a conscience which takes seriously the teaching of the Church before deciding on the morality of a course of action.'

On the matter of birth control I suggest that the first necessary step towards a well-informed conscience would be careful, prayerful study of *Humanae Vitae* itself.

In an earlier issue of 'Question Box' I was asked whether a mortal or venial sin is committed by those who break the Church's law on contraception. I stated then, and I repeat now, that this is a very difficult question to answer.

The question of individual conscience is such that a generalising answer is just not possible.

However, those who practise a form of birth control which in conscience they believe to be wrong are guilty of serious sin.

You asked what punishment or penalty is incurred. There is no question of any penalty such as excommunication or interdict.

But, as in the case of any serious sin, the effect is the estrangement from God, which demands the Sacrament of Reconciliation to repair the spiritual damage that has been done.

Finally, there is your question about the danger to a woman's life from a pregnancy and whether in such a circumstance the use of some artificial means of contraception would be morally justified.

In some individual cases, perhaps so.

But it needs to be said that no method of birth control is 100 per cent effective. The method of family planning which is approved by the Church is Natural Family Planning.

Before concluding too readily that artificial means of birth control are morally justified in cases where a woman's health is in question, a Catholic couple have the duty to inform themselves of the workings of this natural method.

Refinements to the ovulation method in recent years have made it a relatively 'safe' means of birth control.

Question 35:
I would appreciate it if you would explain the teaching of the Church on birth control for young marrieds just starting out.

Question 36:

I believe any sort of contraception by artificial methods is a type of abortion. If the prescribed 'tablet' is for medical purposes, such as to regulate the "middle years symptoms" from which some people seem to suffer, the woman is evidently allowed to use them with a free conscience.

However, recently I have been in this situation and was prescribed a 10-day tablet to regulate heavy bleeding. Upon inquiring whether this was also a contraceptive I was informed it was not, but upon reflection I seem to think the doctor was a bit vague about the use of the the pill affecting a possible conception.

As my symptoms were irregular anyway, I wasn't sure if the three months I spent taking the tablet were normal or not. The fourth time round I realised the 'tablet' was not working to my expectations and was only making me have a 25-day cycle instead of actually regulating the bleeding.

It occurs to me that even specialists are not trained properly in this field and I wish I could find someone who knows.

Someone suggested a stronger tablet and I have no doubt that if I went back to the same doctor he would put me on the whole cycle pill which he had already considered (asking if I wanted more children at the time).

I am horrified when I hear of practising Catholic girls deciding that a 12-month course on the pill will give them a break from having their children too quickly, because it is affecting their early married life.

One of these girls is also cognisant with Dr Billings' findings on the Natural Method of Family Planning.

Answer:

The teaching of the Church on birth control 'for young marrieds just starting out' is no different from Catholic moral teaching on the subject in general.

The Church accepts the legitimacy of birth control, but teaches that a couple should exercise such control by using natural means — by restricting their intercourse to those days when the woman is biologically incapable of conceiving a child.

What the Church opposes is not birth control in this general sense, but contraception — the intentional use of a mechanical or artificial obstacle preventing the conception of a child.

Responsible parenthood is a perfectly acceptable principle. Parents have the right, indeed the duty, to plan their family responsibly. What is at issue is not this principle, but the means open to Catholics to regulate the birth of their children.

The Natural Family Planning Method, involving periodic abstinence, is the method of family planning approved by the Church. It is 'natural', since nothing mechanical or artificial is used.

Sometimes this can involve great self-sacrifice on the part of a couple, and they should therefore seek God's grace by frequent prayer and reception of the Eucharist.

Also desirable is the guidance of a competent doctor who believes in this method and is prepared to take the time to give advice.

Unfortunately, many doctors are unsympathetic to, and ignorant of, recent developments in research into Natural Family Planning.

Their prejudice is directed against the old 'rhythm' method of birth control, while they ignore those refinements of the Natural Family Planning Method such as have resulted from the work of Drs John and Evelyn Billings.

And, of course, it is much easier for an over-worked doctor to write a prescription for the pill than to explain the procedure of natural family planning.

Pope Paul VI restated the Church's traditional position in his encyclical *Humanae Vitae* (1968). He did not say a couple must have as many children as possible, but that 'each and every marriage act must remain open to the transmission of life.'

This letter of Pope Paul's provoked a strong reaction from those who insisted that for serious reasons Catholics may follow their conscience in this matter even though the Pope had spoken. And indeed, the primacy of the personal conscience was one of the basic principles laid down by Vatican II.

What needs to be remembered, however, is that in forming their conscience, Catholics must weigh seriously the ordinary teaching of the Church.

They would not be justified in taking this teaching lightly, and considering themselves exempt from it, without a serious effort to inform themselves about the ways and means of natural family planning, and without much thought and prayer.

It may happen that after going through this process, a couple might conclude that their circumstances are such as to justify their use of some form of contraception, such as the pill, to regulate their family, at least for a time. If their consciences are clear they should continue to receive the Sacraments without guilt or anxiety.

My strong recommendation, however, both for 'young marrieds just starting out' and for other Catholic couples not familiar with the Natural Family Planning Method, is for them to seek competent guidance.

In response to the second query, it must be said that not every form of contraception by artificial methods is 'a type of abortion'.

Abortion is the destruction of a human life already conceived (and modern genetic evidence indicates that the embryo and foetus are a full human person.)

Where artificial contraceptives are of a kind which prevent conception from taking place, there is no question of abortion.

It is true that some forms of the pill and intra-uterine contraceptive devices act by expelling the product of the union between male sperm and female ovum; that is, after conception.

In such cases the contraceptives do come into the category of producing an abortion, and take on a much more serious degree of immorality.

There is the question of the prescription of the contraceptive pill for medical reasons other than contraception. Although I am not qualified to comment on all the medical symptoms and treatments mentioned, the pill does have positive medical purposes which could be summed up under the heading of treatment of menstrual irregularities, especially the control of a woman's painful and heavy periods.

When such is the case, a Catholic woman or girl need have no feelings of guilt or anxiety about taking the prescribed pill. As in every moral act, the intention of the person is paramount.

And if the intent is not to prevent conception, the question of the morality of the use of the pill takes on a different dimension. (There is also the other question, of course, of the possible harmful side effects of the pill, which some doctors regard as very real.)

Moralists would invoke in such a case 'the principle of the double effect', which permits an act for the good effect intended — in this case, treatment of a medical condition, even though an 'unintended' negative effect will follow, in this case the prevention of conception.

Question 37:

In a recent reply you said, 'The Church teaches that contraceptive birth control as a means of prevention of the generation of children is morally wrong in normal circumstances.'

I would like to know what you mean by 'in normal circumstances', as I claim it should be in all circumstances — always.

Then in the next paragraph you said, 'One of the main purposes of the sexual act is to bring into existence new human beings'. Should this not be 'the main purpose of the sexual act'?

Answer:

I think the first part of your question has been covered by my lengthy reply (Q30) to a question about contraception.

As for your second question, there has been a change in the Church's presentation of the ends or purposes of marriage. The old Code of Canon Law, promulgated in 1917, stated that 'the primary purpose of marriage is the procreation and education of children; the secondary purposes are mutual help and the remedy (or lawful outlet) for human carnal concupiscence'.

However, the new Code, which was promulgated in 1983, avoids this terminology and states: 'The marriage pact, by which a man and woman constitute together a partnership of their whole life, and of its very nature directed to the welfare of the spouses and the procreation and education of children, has been raised by Christ to the status of a Sacrament for baptised partners'.

The new Code thus follows the teaching of the Vatican Council's document, *The Church in the Modern World*.

Some bishops at the Council wanted to retain the distinction between the primary and the secondary purposes of marriage, but their proposal was overwhelmingly rejected.

It is now the Church's position that marriage (and the sexual act within marriage) has two equally primary purposes: the welfare of the husband and wife and their mutual love for each other, and the procreation and education of children.

In his encyclical letter, *Humanae Vitae*, Pope Paul VI stressed that these two aspects were really inseparable. He spoke of 'the inseparable connection . . . between the unitive significance and the procreative significance inherent, both of them, in the marriage act.

'The reason is that the fundamental nature of the marriage act, while uniting husband and wife in the closest intimacy, also renders them capable of generating new life . . .

'And if each of these essential qualities, the unitive and the procreative, is preserved, the use of marriage fully retains its sense of true mutual love and its ordination to the supreme responsibility of parenthood.'

Creation

Question 38:

How do Catholics interpret the Biblical word 'creation', that is, what meaning do they attach to this word? Do they believe that all things that exist were made out of nothing, and thus no prior substance or essence was necessary?

Secondly, who was responsible for the idea or concept of 'transubstantiation'? I am led to the belief that this word means 'the change of one substance into another without the loss of the appearance of the first substance'. Is that a true definition?

Answer:

Creation: When we say that God created heaven and earth, we do indeed mean that he fashioned the universe and everything in it out of nothingness. In other words, God alone is eternal: matter is not.

The biblical account of creation is meant to teach us that God made everything that exists. It is not intended to be understood as a scientific description of the origins of the world and the human race.

It is possible, therefore, for a believer to accept science's theory of the evolution of the universe. In this case, God would be seen as bringing the world to realisation, not by continual interventions, but by directing the whole evolutionary process. But however we perceive the process as taking place, we must acknowledge that the raw materials of creation are God's handiwork.

So even if you hold for the necessity of a 'prior substance or essence' from which the universe evolved, the doctrine of creation demands that you acknowledge God as the Creator of that prior substance or essence.

Transubstantiation: Your definition of transubstantiation is basically correct. The concept of transubstantiation is tied to a particular philosophical understanding of being. According to this view every created thing consists of its 'substance' and 'accidents'. The substance is what constitutes the thing in its being: it is the very nature, the 'whatness' of the thing in question. The 'accidents' are the superficial characteristics which enable the thing to be identified: size, shape, colour, taste, feel, etc.

Transubstantiation is the name given to the attempt to explain in human terms a mystery of faith: that in the celebration of the Eucharist the body and blood of Christ become really present under the forms of bread and wine. The substance of the bread is changed into the substance of the body of Christ, and the substance of wine is changed into the substance of his blood. Only the 'accidents' of bread and wine remain — that is, the external characteristics mentioned above.

This understanding of substance and accidents is very much tied to scholastic philosophy, of which St Thomas Aquinas (1225-74) was a leading exponent. But the term goes back much earlier than Thomas. As far as we know, the first to use the term 'transubstantiation' was Stephen, Bishop of Autun in France (he died in 1139). Certainly, it was used in the Fourth Lateran Council in 1215.

The Council of Trent, which was convened after the Protestant Reformation in the 16th century, affirmed the real transformation of bread and wine into the body and blood of Christ, and stated that 'the Catholic Church most fittingly (*aptissime*) calls the change transubstantiation.' (Note that this terminology does not rule out the possibility of another explanation of the process.)

Modern theologians tend to avoid the term. This is partly because the word embraces ideas like substance and accidents, which do not have the meaning for 20th century man that they had in centuries past.

But it is more a recognition that we are dealing with a mystery of faith to which no human explanation can do justice. It is through the power of the Holy Spirit that the bread and wine are changed into the body and blood of Christ. It is the real presence of Christ in the Eucharist which is important, not so much the mechanics of how the change takes place.

(See also Q128, 129.)

The Crucifixion

Question 39:

While meditating upon the sorrowful mysteries of the Rosary, the thought struck me that all the crucifixes I have ever seen show Jesus Christ nailed to the Cross with the backs of his hands touching the Cross, and his palms facing outward.

Now to have the arm twisted and the palm of the hand touching the wood would be more painful and I think it likely the Roman executioners would have known this, mediaeval artists possibly not.

Are there any signs of such torture on the Shroud of Turin? If there are, it would tend to prove the authenticity of the Shroud.

Answer:

There is no evidence to indicate that the punishment of crucifixion was carried out in the way you suggest, with the palms of the hands against the wood. However, the Shroud of Turin does indeed display some interesting features which are relevant to your question.

What the Shroud image clearly reveals are distinct wrist wounds and corresponding flows of blood. Because Christian art had always depicted Christ hanging on the Cross with the nails penetrating the palms of his hands, the evidence of pierced wrists proved at first to be something of a stumbling block for those who were disposed to accept the authenticity of the Shroud.

A person who devoted much of his life to a scientific study of the Shroud was Pierre Barbet, chief surgeon at St Joseph's Hospital in Paris in the 1930s. As a result of his experiments with corpses and amputated limbs, Barbet discovered that a nail driven into the wrist does not strike a mass of bone as

84

one might think, but when diverted slightly upwards, passes cleanly through.

This aperture in the wrist was probably well known to the Roman executioners, who knew too that a body suspended from a cross by nails through the palms would soon tear loose.

Barbet also notes that when the nail pierced the wrist, it damaged the median nerve, causing the thumbs to jerk forward against the palms. Interestingly enough, there are no thumbs visible on the Shroud image.

Extensive blood flows are visible on both forearms, originating from the wrist wounds. Physicians who have studied the Shroud are in general agreement that the angle of the blood flow is consistent with a crucifixion position of the arms.

In 1968, an Israeli surgeon, Dr Haff, examined the remains of an ancient crucifixion victim, which had been accidentally uncovered by a bulldozer in construction work. On examining the skeleton he found distinct scratch marks near the wrist end of the victim's forearms.

It would appear that the nails were driven not through the palms of Jesus' hands, but through his wrists.

Devotion to the Saints

The question of devotion to the saints comes up very often. Already there have been a few queries in this column on the subject. One reader asks 'Can we not go directly to God?'.

In a word, the answer is 'Yes'. Prayer to the saints is not a part of the spirituality or religious practice of all Catholics.

Properly understood, however, devotion to the saints is a valid and praiseworthy practice. It is an expression of the beautiful doctrine of the Communion of Saints, which means the family bond that unites believers on earth with those who have gone before us and are now with God.

Our belonging to the one family of faith as sons and daughters of God, and brothers and sisters in Jesus Christ, is a bond which physical death does not sever.

Another reader asks what advantage is there in praying to saints. Taking the question in its literal sense, the answer is none. Strictly speaking, it is wrong to pray *to* saints. We ask the saints to pray *for* us and *with* us, to God.

In this life, Christians know the value of community prayer. We ask other people to pray with us and for us. In the case of the saints, we invoke the support of people whose lives have been so conspicuous for holiness that the Church has officially declared them to be in God's close friendship.

Question 40:
What is the origin of the St Jude prayers that appear in newspapers or are left in Churches to be recited nine times? St Jude himself in his epistle would appear to disapprove of such practices.

Answer:
I am sorry that I do not know the origin of the St Jude prayers to which you refer. Certainly they cannot claim any support from the letter of Jude in the New Testament.

Whatever the origin of the practice it does not bear the official approval of the Church. On the contary, the Church disapproves of the numerology associated with these and similar prayers, whose devotees claim for them infallible powers. The whole practice of 'chain' prayer and of prayers to be recited a set number of times to achieve results, smacks of superstition and is to be avoided. It goes against the whole spirit of true prayer, as set forth in the scriptures and in the teaching of Jesus himself.

Question 41:

With respect, I wish to comment on your reply regarding the 'St Jude prayers' to be recited nine times. Is this what we used to call a novena? I interpret the 'nine times' to mean nine days. I grew up in a Catholic Church that approved and encouraged this form of prayer.

We never called it 'chain prayer', an expression which brings to mind the current secular practice of good luck chain letters, which are pure superstition. I find I am caught between the old and new ways of the Church.

However, I take the view that no prayer goes unheard, and whether it is said for a set period of time seems immaterial. A novena can bring great solace and consolation, even if the favour requested is not granted directly — and sometimes it is. I speak from my own experience.

My questions:

1. Are novenas now outmoded?

2. In view of your comments about numerology in prayers, why has The Catholic Leader *until recently published the 'St Jude prayer' as well as the thanksgiving notices from people who had requests granted through the 'nine days prayer to St Jude'?*

Answer:

First of all I want to say that I agree entirely with your statement that 'no prayer goes unheard, and whether it is said for a set period of time seems immaterial.'

You ask: 'Are novenas now outmoded?' If you mean: are they less popular as a form of devotion now than they were in the past, then the answer has to be Yes. Priests receive far fewer requests for novenas of Masses than was once the case; once popular parish devotions like the novenas to Our

Lady of Perpetual Succour, and Our Lady of the Miraculous Medal have all but disappeared; nor does one hear much these days about 'making the nine first Fridays'.

But if your question means: has the Church taken positive steps to ban or even discourage novenas, the answer is No.

The danger about a preoccupation with numbers is that it can lead to superstition. People can come to believe that there is something almost magic about the number nine or whatever. Also the mistaken idea that a prayer was effective only if said on nine *consecutive* days, seemed in the past to be part of the mentality of some Catholics.

Another misconception which was sometimes a part of Catholic piety and devotion was that observance of the nine first Fridays, or perhaps the five first Saturdays practically guaranteed salvation.

It was as though the person gained salvation by his or her own efforts, and God had to keep his end of the bargain. This way of thinking clashes with a basic truth of Christianity, namely, that God's grace and final salvation are pure gifts which cannot be earned, but only gratefully received.

Provided such superstitions and misguided ideas are avoided, there is nothing wrong with the practice of novenas. When I am asked to celebrate a novena of Masses for some intention, I do not feel an obligation to do so on nine consecutive days. Indeed, I often inform the petitioner of this and explain why, to safeguard against the possibility of superstition.

I am not familiar with the content of the 'St Jude prayer'. But if it is orthodox, I would approve of it in the same way as of any other practice of devotion to saints — provided it is understood as a request that the saint might pray to God, with and for the petitioner, for the favour requested.

It is true that the 'St Jude prayers' were formerly published in *The Leader*. But a policy decision was taken about a year ago to cease the practice, and this policy has been brought to the attention of readers.

Question 42:

Why do many Catholics pray to saints? Surely, although we honour the saints, we can only pray, together with them, to God through Jesus Christ?

Answer:

You are absolutely correct. When Catholics speak of praying to saints, they are using a loose and inexact terminology. Perhaps they understand the true point of devotion to the saints, but it is certainly a manner of expression which is open to misunderstanding.

All prayer can end only with God. To believe otherwise is to be guilty of idolatry. We should speak of asking the saints to pray with us, or for us, to Christ and the Father. The Church's liturgy always asks the saints to pray for us, through Christ, to the Father.

The Devil

Question 43:

At a discussion which I attended recently, a person with theological training strongly denied the existence of the Devil, and said that evil came from within a person.

Would you please comment on the theological teaching about the Devil, and how adults should explain evil to children.

Answer:

In the light of the Scriptures, and especially the words of Jesus in the New Testament, it would appear difficult to deny the existence of the Devil.

On one occasion, when the Disciples returned from a missionary tour full of enthusiasm over their new spiritual powers, Jesus told them, 'I saw Satan fall like lightning from Heaven' (Luke 10:18).

However, when referring to evil, Jesus naturally used the language of his own culture and tradition. The question that arises is to what extent the New Testament employs the language and imagery of myth to personify evil.

The origins of such language can be traced in the Old Testament, but especially in Jewish religious literature just before the time of Christ.

Theology today is reconsidering the whole question of angels and devils. Some theologians would say that Scripture simply presupposes their existence as part of the biblical environment without directly affirming it as part of divine revelation.

They claim that the popular biblical language does not represent any dogmatic statement about the existence of personal forces of evil.

They also question whether the existence of personal angels and devils is part of the strictly dogmatic teaching of the Church.

Other theologians, while admitting that popular imagery indeed lies behind many of the details given about demons in the New Testament, are less inclined to dismiss the reality itself.

After all, the existence of personal evil spirits is based firmly in the long tradition and liturgy of the Church.

Besides, the more we penetrate the vastness of the universe, the more we realise how little we really know about God's creation. We realise that there could be other rational creatures in the universe — on other planets, perhaps in other galaxies.

God's power and love certainly are open to the possibility of many kinds of creation, including purely spiritual beings. And so the matter is by no means as clear cut as your 'person with theological training' would have you believe.

What is certain is that evil does exist in the world and takes root within the human person. Some would say that evil becomes personal, not because of the Devil, but because we make it part of our person and our environment.

Others would claim that evil is the work of a personal devil.

But, whatever the cause of evil in the world, we must still act against evil in the same way, by avoiding sinful situations and by prayer.

Belief or non-belief in a personal devil does not alter the need to be on guard against sin, and to seek God's help in avoiding evil.

Question 44:

You stated (Q43) that 'theology today is reconsidering the whole question of angels and devils'.

In the light of this, how would you suggest that teachers speak of angels and devils to the children they teach today?

Question 45:

Thanks so much for your words of wisdom on many aspects of our faith in The Catholic Leader. *However, I would like to comment on your wisdom in replying to questions on the Devil.*

I couldn't help but feel in all honesty that folk reading what you have to say on this topic would not go away with that clarity of knowledge — rooted in Scripture and tradition, and expounded by the Fathers and the magisterium — that the evil one, the Devil, Satan, is a real evil personality.

God's people need to know clearly that there is an enemy and his servants, 'the wicked spiritual powers of this dark age' (Ephesians 6:12).

I will close with the words of Paul VI. He described Satan as: 'A living spiritural being which is perverted and perverts. A terrible reality, mysterious and fearful. This hidden and disturbing being truly exists and, with unbelievable cunningness, still is at work. He is the hidden enemy who sows errors and disasters in human history.'

Personal experience also confirms his existence as far as I am concerned.

Answer:

I made it clear that there was disagreement among theologians and biblical scholars today about the existence of personal spirits of good and evil (angels and devils), or at least about how literally we must take the biblical account of their widespread activity.

At the same time Pope Paul VI obviously accepted the existence of a personal power of evil.

In the light of this 'ordinary' teaching of the Pope and the lack of consensus among theologians, I suggest that catechists continue to speak to children of angels and devils as personal spiritual beings, as they are described in the Scriptures themselves.

The contrary view which sees Satan as the personification of evil demands a theological sophistication which can hardly be expected of children. Perhaps in upper primary, but probably not until secondary school, such an alternative viewpoint may be introduced.

Might I make one further point. I believe that the best approach in religious catechesis is to speak of the Devil no more than is absolutely necessary.

Some might question this approach, and argue that to ignore him (or it) is to water down the content of Revelation. And I am well aware that a Gospel like Mark contains a high proportion of 'demonic' activity.

However, if we take the New Testament as a whole the overwhelming emphasis is on the positive aspect of Christ's teaching and Christian living. If we stress the virtues of love and forgiveness and tolerance and patience, then we can safely play down Satan and all his works.

In his case I believe there is no such thing as bad publicity. Concentration on his activity and influence only serve to increase his power.

As a child who played the part of Adam in his school's dramatisation of the Creation complained, 'the Devil has all the good lines.'

This is just one of my concerns about a fundamentalist approach to Scripture. Some fundamentalist preachers seem to devote more attention to the power of Satan and the forces of evil, than they do to the power and love and mercy of God.

The result is often a distorted and unbalanced understanding of the Gospel of Jesus Christ.

His Gospel or 'Good News' is that the power of evil has been defeated, at least in principle, by his life, ministry, death and Resurrection.

Over those who believe in him and strive to put into practice his teaching about love of God, of neighbour, and of self, Satan or evil has no power.

Question 46:

If theologians are uncertain about the existence of good and evil spirits, to whom would the Old Testament be referring in Job 1:6 when it refers to Satan?

And to whom is the New Testament referring when it says God sent the Angel Gabriel to tell Mary that she was about to become pregnant with the child Jesus (Luke 1:26-38)?

And to whom is the New Testament referring in the temptations of Jesus? The Devil tells Jesus (Luke 4:5-7) that God has given him (the Devil) all power and wealth, and that he will give it to Jesus if he worships him.

My other question is this: In Luke 2:34-35 some Bibles put the sentence 'and so reveal their secret thoughts', after Simeon has finished speaking about the child Jesus, and other Bibles put the sentence after Simeon says to Mary 'and sorrow, like a sharp sword, will break your own heart'.

I am hoping you can tell me where this sentence belongs. And how come we have this difference?

Answer:

(a) In the Book of Job 1:6-12, we have a picture of a heavenly scene. God is represented as a king seated on his throne, receiving the reports of his servants and issuing commands.

Among these ministers or servants, the agents through whom God governs, is the Adversary — which is the meaning of the Aramaic word *Satana*.

In the Book of Job, Satan should not be interpreted as a personal name. The Satan is rather the prosecutor who spies on men's wrong-doing, and reports back to God, his master.

It is incorrect to identify him with 'the devil' of later Jewish and Christian theology. To do so would distort the meaning of the story of Job.

However, as the story unfolds, he does emerge as a cynical and unpleasant character whose pessimism about human possibilities for good contrasts with God's optimistic attitude.

The Satan is sceptical about Job's apparent virtue and interprets it instead as self-interest. Does Job, he asks, serve God purely out of love, or does he have his own welfare at heart?

The Satan, or Adversary, obtains God's permission to put Job to the test and thus reveal where his loyalties really lie. The withdrawal of God's gifts from Job will demonstrate whether his affections are focused on the gifts themselves or on the giver.

(b) The essential truth contained in Luke 1:26-38 is that God revealed to Mary that she had been chosen to be the mother of the Messiah, his own Son.

The 'how' of the revelation is not of the essence of the saving truth which we are invited to discover in this passage.

In the Old Testament, 'the angel' (or messenger of the Lord), was a literary device used by the authors to describe one of God's channels of communication with human beings.

This originally grew out of the idea that the infinite distance between God and his creatures required intermediaries to make the divine will known to man.

This understanding of the role of angels or divine messengers was carried over into the New Testament. In the late Old Testament and the New Testament period, angels gradually came to be personified — described as personal beings and given personal names, like Raphael, Gabriel and Michael.

As far as the Annunciation is concerned, faith demands that we accept that God revealed his will to Mary. We are not required to believe that she carried on a conversation with a visible, personal being.

(c) The story of the Temptation of Jesus at the beginning of his ministry is also a matter of separating the literary form used from the truth which God intends to communicate.

In the Gospels of Matthew and Luke, the account of the testing of Jesus in the wilderness teaches us that he was tempted to renounce the way of service, self-sacrifice and suffering which the Father had mapped out for him. He was tempted instead to choose the way of power and prestige and comfort.

Because this alternative conflicted with his Father's will, it was rightly seen as an attempt by the power of evil to dissuade him from his messianic mission. This conflict is dramatically presented in terms of personal struggle between Jesus and the Devil, the personification of the power of evil.

In both the Temptation and Annunciation accounts, it is better to understand the action as taking place entirely within the minds of Jesus and Mary respectively.

(d) Your final question concerns Luke 2:34-35, the report of the prophecy of Simeon on the occasion of the Presentation of Jesus in the Temple. The correct translation of the original Greek reads thus:

'This child is set for the fall and rising of many in Israel,
And for a sign that is spoken against,
(and a sword will pierce through your own soul also),
That thoughts out of many hearts may be revealed.'

The brackets above do not appear in the original text. They are included to show that those words are like an 'aside' addressed to Mary, interrupting the continuity of the thought.

Simeon's prediction was that the child would be a sign of contradiction for people. They would be forced to make a decision for or against him. His person and his message would challenge people to search the depths of their own hearts, and decide where they really stood in relation to him.

Simeon included Mary the mother of Jesus in this prophecy. There is no mention of sorrow in the original Greek text, and translations which include this are not really faithful to the original.

It has been assumed that Simeon's words referred to the sorrow Mary would experience at the Cross, but this is restricting the meaning of the words attributed to the old prophet.

The best guide for understanding the words of Simeon is a passage from the Epistle to the Hebrews (4:12): 'For the Word of God is living and active, sharper than a two-edged sword, piercing on the division of soul and spirit, of joints and marrow, and discerning the thoughts and intentions of the heart.'

The similarity between Hebrews 4:12 and Luke 2:34-35 is obvious. The sword to which Simeon referred was not primarily a sword of sorrow, but the Word of God which penetrates to the depths of every person's being and forces each one to make a decision for or against Christ. Even Mary, Jesus' mother, he inferred, would not be spared this test of faith.

You ask why the order of words is different in different versions of the Bible.

Every translation of the Bible is a compromise between fidelity to the original sequence of words and readability.

Some translators may err in one direction, some in the other. The most literal translation may not always be the most intelligible.

For this particular passage (Luke 2:34-35) the translation given above, taken from the Revised Standard Version, represents the best compromise between accuracy and intelligibility.

Question 47:

The 'serpent' of Genesis is mentioned in Revelation 12:9 as the huge dragon, the ancient serpent known as the Devil or Satan, the seducer of the whole world.'

Other relevant readings are Wisdom 2:24, John 8:44, as well as the recapitulation of Genesis 3:1-19.

'Less certain' exegetes than your good self need to identify the serpent of Genesis quite positively as the Devil, the author of evil, lest God be charged with dualism — the

creation of both good and evil, or with creating an imperfect universe.

Similarly, their implied reflection on Genesis as primaeval history damages the concept of the Fall by our first parents as the cause of original sin. This destroys the rationale for the Incarnation and the Redemption, and all our salvific theology.

Hence you would readily appreciate, I am sure, why your readers might be concerned about any apparent relegation of the 'serpent' of Genesis to a purely symbolic role as a feeble tribal folk-myth.

Answer:

I fear that a basic difference between our respective methods of interpreting the Scriptures is illustrated by your final phrase, 'a purely symbolic role as a feeble tribal folk-myth'.

Your choice of words indicates your view that all myth is of the 'feeble' variety, and that 'symbolic' is an unworthy appellation to apply to the contents of Sacred Scripture. This is a view which I cannot accept.

The ancient civilisations of Mesopotamia and Egypt had a very extensive mythology. Certainly there are differences between the mythological thinking of other ancient people and the thinking of the biblical writers, but this is not to say there is not myth or mythology in the Scriptures, especially in the Old Testament.

The reason why many people deny the existence of myth in the Old Testament is because of the presumption that myth is essentially false.

But this is not necessarily so at all. It is true that many ancient myths presuppose the existence of many gods, and give a distorted view of the universe. However, the goal of mythological thinking is truth, not falsehood.

Myth is expressed in story or narrative form, but the narrative is not historical and it is not intended to be taken as history. It aims to present the reality of the universe in story form. It does not pretend that the symbolism *is* the reality, but it uses symbol to give an insight into reality beyond human understanding.

For example, the ancient Mesopotamians had a creation myth.

The first chapter of Genesis exhibits the same superficial

and unscientific view of the structure of the universe as the Mesopotamian myth.

Certainly there are striking differences. The biblical account has nothing about any cosmic conflict between different gods as a vital part of the process of creation. Instead we have a description of a tranquil act of creation by word, which demonstrates the effortless superiority of God the creator over all other cosmic forces.

The Genesis account is openly critical of the other ancient myths of creation, which it corrects. But it does not replace these myths with history or science but with another myth. The difference lies in Israel's concept of God.

In his encyclical, *Divino Afflante Spiritu* (1943), Pius XII taught that the human authors of Scripture, under divine inspiration, were able to make use of any of the literary forms that were common in their time and culture, provided these were constant with God's sanctity and truth. Myth is one such literary form.

In other words, God inspired the human authors to employ this literary form of myth, among others, to teach truth — not scientific truth or historical truth — but religious truth, God's truth.

The story of the flood is an even clearer example of the correction or revision of a foreign myth. There are striking similarities between the Genesis account of the deluge and other earlier ancient stories of a great primitive flood.

The Mesopotamian myth of the flood was an attempt to explain the problem of natural disasters, accompanied by random destruction.

This myth described the arbitrary and irrational anger of the gods. In the face of this capricious wrath, man could do nothing but submit helplessly to their superior power.

The Israelites, with their more elevated belief in one God, could not accept this. They did not, however, reject the story entirely but rewrote it, under divine inspiration, in such a way as to show that Yahweh's anger was not arbitrary or irrational but was a response to human wickedness.

They saw in natural disasters the righteous judgement of God on sin, and they expressed this insight by re-telling and re-casting an ancient story.

Again it is a case of the inspired use of the literary form of myth to teach truth.

There is no known ancient myth that parallels the account of the origin and fall of man in Genesis chapters two and three. But many features of ancient mythology have been woven into this story, which is one of the most profound and creative pieces of literature in the entire Bible.

Here the concept of God is balanced by a concept of man which differs remarkably from what we find elsewhere in ancient literature.

In narrative form, the story describes the human condition: man's dignity and fall from Grace, his relations with God and the material world, his moral responsibility, the origin and meaning of sex.

To present these profound insights, the human author, inspired by God, uses the symbols of mythology: the garden, the tree of life, the tree of knowledge of good and evil, the serpent, the man's rib.

It may be myth, but who can deny the truth which it expresses?

Pius XII, in a later encyclical, *Humani Generis* (1950), repeated a warning which earlier biblical scholars had issued, not to reduce the beliefs of the Old Testament to the level of the mythology of other peoples.

The method of interpretation proposed above does not run foul of this admonition, precisely because Israel's mythology enshrines a completely different concept of God, man, and the relationship that exists between them.

What elevates the biblical accounts on to an altogether different level is the concept of God which underlies them — the belief in the personal character of Yahweh, the one true God.

The people of Israel attributed this understanding of God's nature and character to divine revelation, to a personal encounter with the God who revealed himself to them as their saviour and their judge.

Frequently they express their insights in the only forms of thought and speech which were avilable to them — literary forms which they shared with other peoples in the ancient east, especially myth.

I submit that such an interpretation of these biblical passages accepted and taught by all Catholic biblical scholars in no way destroys 'the rationale for the Incarnation and the Redemption, and all our salvific theology.'

Myth in the Old Testament is anything but feeble. It is a most powerful vehicle of human thought and expression, used by God to convey the most profound truth. It expresses most effectively the need of the human race for redemption.

Question 48:

Being a high school student, I am more than ever aware of the Devil in my life. No matter which way I turn, the Devil is there, ever ready to tempt me.

We should be made aware of the Devil and his works. If you teach people about the Devil and his works and how evil he is, then maybe their lives won't centre around evil as much.

People have to be taught how evil he is and how he tricks them into his ways. There is no way we can 'stress the virtues of love and forgiveness and tolerance and patience and then safely play down Satan and all his works.'

How can we ignore the fact that Satan is always and constantly trying to win people over, and he is winning them over, even without them knowing it? If we think that when we teach love and patience, etc, we can safely play the Devil down, well I think he'll be laughing all the way to Hell.

Answer:

My intention is to draw attention to the problems which can arise in our relationship with God from an over preoccupation with the influence and power of the Devil.

For example, you say: 'No matter which way I turn, the Devil is there, ever ready to tempt me.' I should much prefer to hear you say: 'Which ever way I turn, Christ is there, ever ready to help and support me.' This would reflect a more positive and peaceful and less anxious outlook on life.

To say that our relationship with God should be free from anxiety is not to say that we may ignore the reality of sin, or the possibility of sinning.

However, the danger of making fear of sin (or of the Devil) the basis of our relationship with God is that fear and anxiety will come to dominate that relationship. It can lead to a distorted concept of God as a stern judge rather than as the loving, forgiving Father that he is.

I believe that St John in his first letter strikes the right balance. He has plenty to say on the subject of sin. For example, in 1:8 he states bluntly: 'If we say we have no sin, we deceive ourselves, and the truth is not in us.'

Yet he also says: 'No one born of God commits sin; for God's nature is in him, and he *cannot* sin because he is born of God' (3:9).

John explains what it means to be 'born of God'. In 4:7, he says: 'Let us love one another; for love is of God, and he who loves is born of God and knows God.'

In other words, John says that the one who loves God and his neighbour *cannot* sin. This might seem a surprising statement, because we all know from experience how easy it is to fall. What John means, however, is that sin cannot co-exist at the same time with genuine love of God and neighbour.

Some might say: we love God, if we avoid sin. I should think it is much more true to the Gospel message to say: if we love God, we will avoid sin.

Difficult Scripture Texts

Question 49:

What do you understand by 'God created man in his own image' (Genesis 1:27) and 'God created man, he made him in the likeness of God' (Genesis 5:1)? What does it mean for us?

Answer:

The message of Genesis 1:26-28 is that man (that is, mankind) is the crowning achievement of God's creation. This is brought out by the placing of his creation at the end, in the position of climax and emphasis. It is described as a personal act of God who makes humanity in his own image and likeness.

The two words, *image* and *likeness*, are not precisely the same in English or in the original Hebrew. *Image* is an exact reproduction, whereas *likeness* denotes only a resemblance. Man is said to have been created as one who is a *copy* of God; but then the author immediately modifies this statement, since no one can be an exact image of the transcendent God.

In what, in the author's mind, did man's likeness to God consist? According to our psychology, we have no difficulty in understanding this likeness to lie in man's spiritual nature, his intellect and will. These separate him from the rest of animal creation and make him similar to God.

Our psychology, however, was not that of the biblical author, who did not have the same concept as we do of a rational soul with its spiritual faculties.

The second part of Genesis 1:26 gives us the clue to the author's intention. It is man's God-given dominion over creation that makes him like God, who has dominion over all.

Man is given a share in God's Lordship. So in reply to

your question 'what does it mean to us?' — I believe that these texts first of all impress on us the dignity of man, and his dominion — under God — over all other living beings. At the same time, we must take care that our Lordship over creation, having been delegated to us by God, does not clash with his own benevolent rule.

In man's history, especially his recent history, life has all too often been seen in terms of a struggle of man *against* nature rather than as a joint venture between the two.

We have a responsibility to future generations for the way we exercise the Lordship over God's creation which he has entrusted to us.

And although it was not the original author's primary intention, the text does pave the way for the higher revelation which appears later in Scripture: man's share in the divine nature by virtue of grace.

Question 50:
Could you comment on symbolic language in the Bible, in particular, Noah's Ark? This came up in a discussion and I did not feel confident enough to reply. I do not believe there was an 'ark' and I am not clear on the symbolic language of the Bible.

Answer:
As far as history is concerned the first 11 chapters of Genesis must be considered as being in a separate category. Some commentators refer to their contents as pre-history, others as primordial history. They do not satisfy the criteria of history, in the sense that a modern scientific historian would understand the term.

These early chapters of Genesis speak in popular style of the origin of the world and the human race. They are written in a simple, pictorial style, suited to the mentality of primitive, unsophisticated people.

Yet they declare the fundamental truths on which God's plan of salvation rests. These truths are: creation by God at the beginning of time, God's special intervention in the creation of man and woman, the unity of the human race, the origin and nature of sin, mankind's fall from God's favour, and the punishment which the human race suffered as a consequence of sin.

All of these truths are guaranteed by the authority of Scripture. While not satisfying the strict criteria of historical truth, this section of the Bible is certainly *true* in the sense that Vatican II defined biblical truth: 'The truth which God wanted put into the Scriptures for the sake of our salvation.'

The story of the flood and of Noah and his ark is one of the stories contained in these first chapters of Genesis.

There are several earlier Babylonian stories of a great flood, which are in some respects remarkably similar to the biblical narrative. All draw on the same source, the memory of one or more disastrous floods in the valley of the Tigris and Euphrates rivers.

Tradition had enlarged this to the dimensions of a world-wide catastrophe, but there is a fundamental difference in the biblical account.

The author has used the tradition as a vehicle for teaching eternal truths: that God is just and merciful, that man is innately perverse, and that God saves those who are faithful to him.

The vessel in which Noah and his family escaped the deluge is called an 'ark', which is the common English translation of a Hebrew word which means a box or chest. According to the measurements given in Genesis 6:14ff., the vessel would have been about 138 metres long, 23 metres broad and 14 metres high.

It must be said that these measurements designate a house of palatial dimensions rather than a ship. Such a fantastic vessel would hardly have been suitable even for a house-boat.

Interestingly, the same Hebrew word 'tebah' (box or chest) occurs elsewhere in the Bible only in Exodus 2:3-5, where it is used of the basket in which Moses was saved from death as an infant.

The connection is no doubt intentional: the instrument of salvation for Israel on the one hand (Moses), and of salvation for all mankind on the other (Noah and his family).

In later biblical writings, the flood, and salvation from the flood, were often used as symbols of subsequent disasters in which God's mercy and justice were both revealed; for example, the Exile and Restoration of Israel (Isaiah 54:6-10), and the Last Judgment (Matthew 24:36-39).

The New Testament also sees the ark as a symbol of

Christian Baptism, which saves from eternal destruction and makes possible the new life in Christ (1 Peter 3:20-22).

The literary form of Genesis 1-11 and the multiple symbolism associated with the story of the flood must be taken into account if we are to understand correctly the author's intention and the truth which God intends to reveal.

Question 51:

What happened to David's wife Michal? And why does 2 Samuel 1:14-16 relate that someone was killed for killing Saul, when I Samuel 31:4-5 tells how Saul committed suicide?

Answer:

Michal, the younger daughter of King Saul, was David's first wife. David had been promised the elder daughter Merab, but Saul failed to honour his promise. However, Saul gave Michal to him as a reward for his victory over the Philistines in a battle which the jealous Saul had hoped would result in David's death.

Michal loved David (1 Samuel 18:20), and proved her loyalty to her husband when Saul attempted to murder him. She revealed the plot to David and deceived Saul's men by placing a dummy in David's bed, while he escaped. But after David's flight, her father gave her to another man as his wife.

When David later, after Saul's death, made a treaty with Abner, one of the conditions which he imposed was the return of Michal to satisfy his wounded honour. Abner agreed to this, and David and Michal were reunited.

David's introduction of the Ark of the Covenant into Jerusalem was the occasion of the final estrangement between him and Michal. David threw restraint to the winds with his frenzied dancing before the Ark. Michal's pride and sense of dignity were offended.

She considered his conduct unbecoming and undignified for a King and reproached him with biting remarks for making as ass of himself. David reacted furiously to her criticism and excluded her from his bed for the rest of her life.

The mention of Michal's sterility in 2 Samuel 6:23 would appear to be the result of his casting her aside. As a result, the line of Saul was not continued through David. The whole sorry episode reflects little credit on him.

As you say, 1 Samuel 31:4-5 reports that Saul committed suicide, while 2 Samuel 1:14-16 describes how David had an Amalekite killed for having confessed to killing Saul. Though the two versions differ in detail, both agree that Saul's death was suicidal, one account making it self-inflicted and the other making it the request of Saul to a passerby.

Perhaps we have a case here of two variant traditions which have been inadequately reconciled. On the other hand, the clear implication is that the Amalekite who told the story of his part in Saul's death was lying. He probably hoped to obtain a remuneration from David for his action. If so, he miscalculated badly, and paid for it with his life. David had him put to death for having raised his hand against 'the anointed of the Lord'.

Perhaps there was a mixture of policy and impulse in David's act of vengeance. Although he reaped the advantages of Saul's death, he had to make it very clear to the nation that he had in no way connived at it.

Question 52:

In Genesis, chapter 18, Abraham not only talks to three heavenly visitors but actually feeds them; and again in chapter 19 Lot, in the city of Sodom, plays host to two messengers from the Lord who are so real that the perverted men of Sodom wanted to have sex with them.

If they were 'literary devices' as you have suggested, why did the writer/s go to so much trouble to make them real?

I would also like your opinion on a statement made by our parish priest in a recent sermon. Father told us that many Scripture scholars now believe the story of Jonah and Nineveh is a satirical story made up to teach the Hebrews a lesson.

Yet Christ says that the people of Nineveh will stand up at the Last Judgment as an example of the way the Jews should have received his word and did not.

The sense of Christ's words seems to indicate to me that the story of Jonah and Nineveh was a true story.

Perhaps you can set me straight on these two issues.

Answer:

I hope that the first part of your question has been sufficiently covered by my lengthy treatment on the subject of angels (see Q1-4). I do not think there is anything further that I can add to that.

As for the story of Jonah and the whale, your parish priest is correct.

Although biblical scholars differ as to the precise term that should be used to describe this literary form, they would agree that the book is not to be classified as history. Some refer to it as a parable, but it seems best to use the broader term, didactic fiction.

It should therefore be seen as a fictional narrative, with clear elements of satire, but having a profound theological purpose.

Writing at a time when the Israelites were tempted to hope more for the destruction of their enemies than for their salvation, the author's aim was to convey an important message in story form about the extent of the Lord's mercy.

This was his main theological intention: to teach that the Lord's mercy is universal, extending far beyond the boundaries of Israel.

The fact that Jesus referred to the story by saying 'just as Jonah was in the belly of the whale for three days and three nights', (as if it were a factual account), is no proof that the story is historically true.

To illustrate this point, I would invite you to consider the following: most would regard the parable of the Prodigal Son as a fictional narrative created by Jesus to teach that God is always ready to forgive a sinner.

A preacher might say: 'Just as the father welcomed back his prodigal son, so God will always welcome back the sinner who repents'.

In speaking this way the preacher's intention is not to assert his belief that the parable is historically true. He is rather drawing attention to the religious truth which the parable contains.

In the same way, the truth to be looked for in the book of Jonah is not historical truth but God's saving truth.

Question 53:

Does the Church still believe in the book of Wisdom, where it says in 3:16 that 'the children of adulterers will remain without issue, and the progeny of an unlawful bed will disappear' and 4:6, 'children born of lawless unions give evidence of the wickedness of their parents when they are examined'. (New American Bible translation). This worries me as I could be one of them.

Answer:
There are some traditional Jewish views of moral issues expressed in the Old Testament which never carried over into Christianity. For example, the Jews believed that sterility or childlessness was a curse. This was tied up with their understanding of immortality.

It was only in the last couple of centuries before Christ that some sections of Judaism came to a belief in the resurrection of the dead and a meaningful after life.

In earlier days they saw God's favour and blessings confined to this life, and so their hopes for immortality dwelt above all in the memory of their children. To see one's children's children to the third and fourth generations was the surest sign of God's favour.

Conversely, the children of the wicked, it was believed, would either live to a dishonourable old age, or die young with no hope of immortality. This is the view expressed in Wisdom 3:16-19.

Jesus on one occasion explicitly rejected this notion that the sins of the parents are visited on their children, or that a person's misfortunes are the result of parental sin.

In John 9:2 his disciples, on seeing a blind man, ask Jesus: 'Was it his sin or that of his parents that caused him to be born blind?'. He replied that no sin, either of the man himself or his parents, was responsible for the man's condition.

Nor is there any sign of this Jewish belief anywhere in the moral teaching of Jesus. Throughout the Gospel his message is one of personal responsibility for the good or evil that one does.

Question 54:
In one of the Gospels Jesus is quoted as saying that John the Baptist is the greatest man born of a woman. How is it that

Jesus can show precedence to John over both himself and St Joseph?

Answer:

The passage you refer to is Matthew 11:11, in which Jesus states that 'among those born of women there has risen no one greater than John the Baptist.' (*Revised Standard Version*).

First of all, I think we can safely dispense with the possibility that Jesus would have been thinking about himself when he was singing the praises of John the Baptist.

As for St Joseph, I think he can be eliminated on the grounds that Jesus was thinking of the role of the prophet in Israel, when making this evaluation of John and his part in God's plan of salvation.

The spirit of prophecy was thought to have grown silent in Israel after the last canonical prophet, Malachi, but now in the voice of John it was speaking again.

But John was more than a prophet. He was a prophet allowed to see the time of the fulfilment of all prophecy. He was part of the age he prophesied.

The remainder of the verse is a statement not of John's greatness, but of his limitations. The disciples of Jesus (and his later disciples in the Church) enjoy a higher status: 'yet he who is least in the kingdom of Heaven is greater than he.'

John's greatness lay in the fact that he stood on the threshold of the new age. But even the least of those who stand beyond the threshold is greater than he. This statement implies that Jesus, who brought in the new age, has a greatness and dignity far surpassing that of the Baptist.

Clearly, from the overall context, Jesus' words are not to be understood in the sense of John's personal sanctity or virtue, but as a reference to his role and function in God's plan as the last and greatest of the prophets, the one privileged to introduce Jesus to the world and so to prepare immediately for the coming of the age of salvation.

Question 55:

My question concerns trying to prove points by scriptural argument. The Scriptures are too often vague, incomplete, and downright ambiguous — if not contradictory. I often

*think of the 'render to Caesar . . .' statement (Matthew
22:21). In answer to the question: 'Is it lawful to give tribute
to Caesar?' I would have answered (a) yes; (b) no; (c)
sometimes it is not! Of the three options I would choose (c),
as it is the only truthful answer.*

*But Jesus never did get around to answering the question.
He threw in a red herring, that at the time seemed like a
satisfactory answer, but probably confused his questioners.
And since he never really answered the question, he has left
us all confused ever since. Just what are 'the things that are
Caesar's', and just what are 'the things that are God's?' No
one can answer that!*

Answer:

I appreciate the freshness of your interpretation of that
Gospel incident, which describes the barbed question of the
Pharisees to Jesus about the lawfulness of paying tax to the
Roman government (Matthew 22:15-22). And I agree with
your comment, at least up to a point.

I too believe that Jesus never did get around to answering
the question. This is not the only occasion in the Gospels
where he declined to answer the question that was put to
him. The reason for his refusal to do so was that he judged
that the question should never have been asked, at least in
the way it was framed.

A classic case is the question: 'who is my neighbour?'
(Luke 10:29). This question was asked by a well-meaning
scribe in response to Jesus' teaching about the importance of
love of neighbour.

He answered the question by telling the story of the Good
Samaritan, which does not exactly answer the question
asked (Luke 10:30-35). In fact, this is confirmed by the
question which Jesus himself then turns back on his
questioner 'which of these . . . acted as a neighbour?' — a
somewhat different question from the one originally posed,
but one that is intended to bring out the real point of his
teaching.

The answer to the question about paying taxes to Caesar
is in effect Jesus' way of avoiding the trap set for him by the
Pharisees — the danger of falling between the two stools of
disloyalty to Rome and loss of credibility with the people.

But as for your statement, 'just what are the things that

are Caesar's, and just what are the things that are God's? No one can answer that!' — I beg to differ. I believe that what Jesus was saying was that everything belongs to God, including what belongs to Caesar.

He might have been saying, 'work it out for yourself', but he was also saying that whatever decision one reaches must be subordinate to God's over-ruling claim on our allegiance.

This is very similar to his directive in the Sermon on the Mount: 'Seek first his kingdom and his righteousness, and all these things shall be yours as well' (Matthew 6:33).

I do not agree with you, therefore, in holding that 'he has left us all confused'. It is true that Jesus's teaching on one's debts to God and to Caesar has been misinterpreted by many people down the centuries, because they have thought he meant to divide secular and religious obligations into distinct compartments.

In fact, he intended no such thing. His intention was rather to establish the priority of God's claims over all others.

However, I appreciate your drawing attention to this biblical passage because it illustrates something that too many people are still not prepared to do: to take responsibility for their own decisions and the consequences of those decisions.

Vatican II's teaching on the primacy of conscience confirms this. It is certainly wise to consult one's pastor when one is confronted with a moral dilemma, but he cannot take upon himself the conscientious decision which the person alone must make.

In the instance which you bring forward Jesus' own response reveals the prototype of this truth.

Question 56:

(a) What did Jesus mean by the 'new wine' in his Father's Kingdom (Matthew 26:29)?

(b) 'No one can confess "Jesus is Lord" unless he is guided by the Holy Spirit' (1 Corinthians 12:3). Is it not possible to say 'Jesus is Lord' and not really understand what it means?

Answer:

(a) According to Matthew's account of the Last Supper,

Jesus, after pronouncing over the cup the words 'This is my blood of the covenant . . .' added: 'I tell you, I shall not drink again of this fruit of the vine, until that day when I drink it anew in my Father's Kingdom'.

The picture of a banquet or feast as an image of the Kingdom of God is one that occurred quite often in Jewish religious thought and literature. It is found in both the prophetic writings and the psalms of the Old Testament.

That Jesus took over this image can be seen in his earlier reference to the 'many who will come from east and west and sit at table with Abraham, Isaac and Jacob in the Kingdom of Heaven' (Matthew 8:11).

In the same context, wine was used as an image of the gifts and blessings that would be bestowed on those belonging to the Kingdom. At the Messianic banquet, God's Messiah would preside as host and dispense the Messianic wine (the gifts of salvation) to those who had entered the Kingdom.

The first Christians understood the Eucharistic meal celebrated in the Church as an anticipation of the Messianic banquet.

In our proclamation of this mystery of faith after the consecration of the bread and wine at each Mass, we express this connection between the Eucharist and the coming Kingdom: 'Christ will come again; Lord Jesus, come in glory; We proclaim your death, Lord Jesus, until you come in glory'.

The first Christians were also convinced that there was a real sense in which the Kingdom of God was already present.

They believed that with the Resurrection and glorification of Jesus, God's reign had entered a new and decisive phase. This way of thinking seems to underlie John's account of the marriage feast at Cana (John 2:1-12).

When Jesus at first rejected his mother's approach about the scarcity of wine, he gave as the reason, 'My hour has not yet come'. By this, he meant that the time of his glorification had not yet arrived, so it would be premature to be thinking about the dispensation of the Messianic wine.

Ultimately he did perform a miracle, as a sign of the good things that would be provided when the Messianic age had dawned.

Perhaps, then, underlying Jesus' words in Matthew

26:29, there is also the idea that each time the Eucharist is celebrated, those who participate are taking part in a banquet at which Jesus is present.

(b) It is true that one can *say* Jesus is Lord without understanding the meaning of the phrase, or even without meaning it at all.

But Paul speaks of *confessing* that Jesus is Lord. It is a confession of faith which he is referring to, and such a confession, he says, is not possible unless the Holy Spirit has enlightened the mind and moved the heart of the believer.

The formula, *Jesus is Lord*, seems to have been the earliest and the most basic statement of the Christian faith.

The word 'Lord' (in Greek, *Kyrios*) was the title or name reserved in the Old Testament for Yahweh, or God alone. To confess Jesus as Lord was therefore to acknowledge his full divinity.

An early witness to this belief occurs in the ancient hymn incorporated by Paul in his letter to the Philippians (Philippians 2:6-11). There it is said that God has 'exalted' Jesus and given him 'the name which is above every other name, so that at the name of Jesus every knee should bow . . . and every tongue confess that Jesus Christ is Lord'.

Such faith cannot be attained by human initiative: it is the gift of the Holy spirit.

Question 57:

If there was no 'virgin birth' was Our Lady 'ever virgin' as we were taught? Or is it possible that Jesus did have brothers, as interpreted by some Protestant theologians?

Answer:

In previous answers to questions on this topic, I expressed the view that the Church's dogmatic definition of Mary's virginity, 'before, during and after birth', should be understood as a comprehensive affirmation of her perpetual virginity.

It is traditional Christian teaching that Mary remained a virgin all her life, but this does not mean that a Catholic need accept that the actual '*birth*' of Jesus was miraculous in the sense that it did not happen in the normal way. Mary's virginity should be seen as more than physical inviolability.

As for the brothers and sisters of Jesus mentioned in the

Gospel, I repeat that the word 'brother' was commonly used among the Jews for any blood relation. The references in the Gospels (for example, Mark 6:3) *need* not therefore be taken to mean that Joseph and Mary had other sons and daughters.

At the same time, let us not be too hard on the 'Protestant theologians'. As Catholics, our belief in the permanent virginity of Mary is based on the subsequent teaching of the Church, and not on the biblical evidence itself.

It is not surprising that those who did not feel bound by some later Church pronouncements should interpret references to Jesus' brothers and sisters as meaning other sons and daughters of Mary and Joseph.

Your question does, perhaps, betray too physical or clinical an understanding of Mary's virginity. I should like to counterbalance this with a quote from a modern Protestant theologian. Max Thurian, form his work: *Mary, Mother of all Christians.*

'Her unique relation with the Spirit sets her in such close proximity to God that she must remain alone in order to point out to our eyes this unique choice of her Lord . . .

'Her viginity appears at one and the same time as a sign of consecretion and a sign of solitary powerlessness which gives glory to the fullness and power of God . . .

'A sign of poverty, humility and of waiting upon God . . . a sign of emptiness and total trust in God, who makes rich such poor creatures as we are.'

(See also Q16-18.)

Question 58:

I would be grateful if you could explain what Christ meant when he said: 'So in the same way, none of you can be my disciple unless he gives up all his possessions' (Luke 14:33).

Answer:

If we were to speak of the Gospel of Luke in modern terms, we might describe it as the 'social' Gospel.

Luke has many warnings about the danger of riches, and is more emphatic on this score than the other evangelists. It is not so much the possession of wealth as such that is condemned, but rather the selfishness of the rich which is severely censured.

Not surprisingly, therefore, Luke's Jesus is the one who insists most on renunciation. Confidence is not to be placed in riches (12:31-21) but in God who will provide (12:22-32). 'Sell your possessions and give alms' (12:33).

The follower of Christ must renounce all: 'Whoever of you does not renounce all that he has cannot be my disciple' (14:33).

So too, a ruler who comes to him is told: 'Sell all that you have and give to the poor . . . and come, follow me' (18:22).

I presume that the point of your question revolves around how literally we must take Christ's command to give up *all* possessions.

The normal understanding of this text, as of so many others in Luke, is that it proposes not a law of discipleship, but the ideal of total renunciation which must be the spirit of every true disciple of Christ.

It is a binding ideal in the sense that it demands of us the spirit of complete detachment from material possessions.

It is not ownership of goods as such which is forbidden, but the Christian must hold the things of this world with a light grasp.

To become a slave of material possessions, or to be pre-occupied with acquiring and retaining them, is in direct conflict with the way of discipleship demanded by Jesus.

The Christian must always be prepared to share his goods and use them in the service of others.

Of course, there have been many saints in the history of Christianity who have taken Christ's words in their full literal sense, and actually divested themselves of every material support.

By choosing such lives of total poverty, they have provided us with a powerful and necessary living witness to this particular Gospel ideal.

Question 59:

The Apostles' Creed describes how, after he died, Jesus 'descended into Hell', and only after 'the third day' did he ascend into Heaven. The Scriptures also report that Jesus on the Cross turned to the 'good thief' exclaiming: 'this day you shall be with me in Paradise' (Luke 23:43). If Paradise is to be equated with Heaven, and if Hell is something entirely different from the two, then where did Jesus go immediately after his death? Did he go 'up' as described by Luke, or did he go 'down' as stated in the Creed?

Answer:

It is not necessary to hold that Jesus went 'up' or 'down'. The classical description of the Ascension of Jesus is found in Acts 1:9-12, where Luke says he was taken up before the eyes of his disciples until a cloud received him out of their sight.

But is Luke intending to give any more than a symbolic account of Jesus' return to the Father, which marked the end of his post-Resurrection appearances to the disciples?

In ancient times, man's view of the world was of a three-tiered universe — the heavens above, which were the dwelling place of God; the earth; and Hades, or *Sheol*, below, the abode of the dead.

Ascension was the natural way of depicting Christ's return to the Father. The symbolic intent of the author is further suggested by his mention of the cloud, a common biblical image for the presence of God, as when the pillar of cloud guided and protected the Israelites during the Exodus (Exodus 13:21ff. and elsewhere).

The descent of Jesus into Hell poses a more difficult problem. This phrase 'descended into Hell' appears in early Christian creeds, and is based on the language of the Old Testament. 'Hell' here does not represent the place of the damned, but is the equivalent of the Hebrew '*Sheol*', the abode of the dead.

In the Old Testament, the concept of *Sheol* implies neither reward nor punishment, nor any distinction between the good and the wicked. To 'descend into *Sheol*' was simply 'to die'.

Is the credal formula 'Jesus descended into Hell' therefore intended to emphasise anything more than the *reality* of Jesus' death, prior to his Resurrection?

Luke 24:43 presupposes a different concept where Jesus tells the penitent thief, 'today you will be with me in Paradise'. Perhaps it would be unwise to force the strict chronological sense of the word 'today', but Jesus seems to be saying that the 'good thief' because of his act of faith in acknowledging Jesus, will share his glory without having to be detained in *Sheol*.

A problem text is 1 Peter 3:19ff., where it is stated that Jesus went to those who were kept in prison and there 'announced' or 'declared' to them. The original Greek does not say what he announced or declared. It would seem that the declaration in question was an announcement of his triumph over sin and death.

Some commentators have found in this text justification for the theory that Jesus descended into the limbo of the fathers and informed them of their deliverance, but Fr Bill Dalton, an Australian Jesuit, wrote a brilliant doctoral thesis some 15 to 20 years ago, which I believe effectively demolished this interpretation. Space does not allow me to expand on Fr Dalton's thesis here.

But to get back to your question: many passages in the New Testament about the death, Resurrection and Ascension of Jesus employ the language of Judaism, which conceived the Heavens (the sky) as the abode of God and *Sheol* (Hell), beneath the surface of the Earth, as the abode of the dead. This childlike view of the structure of the universe is not part of the Christian faith in Jesus' death, Resurrection and Ascension.

His 'descent into hell' affirms the reality of his death; his 'Ascension into heaven' affirms his triumph over death and his return to the Father.

The belief in a liberating visit of Jesus to the limbo of the fathers, and their accompanying him in his Resurrection does not, I am afraid, have any foundation in the New Testament.

Question 60:

In John's Gospel, Jesus is quoted as saying, 'Before Abraham was, I am', I would like you to discuss this statement from two points of view, the experiential knowledge and the faith knowledge of Jesus himself.

Answer:

Actually, I should prefer to approach this statement of Jesus, 'Before Abraham was, I am' (John 8:58) first of all from another direction, and that is from the theological perspective of John the Evangelist himself.

It is the Gospel of John, the last to be written, which emphasises most the divinity of Jesus and his own awareness of his divinity. The phrase, 'I am', is an important feature of John's Gospel.

First, there are a number statements attributed by John to Jesus which begin with the phrase, 'I am', and go on to describe some important aspect of himself and his mission: I am the bread of life (6:35), I am the light of the world (8:12), I am the Good Shepherd (10:11), I am the Resurrection and the life (11:25), I am the way, the truth and the life (14:6), I am the true vine (15:1), etc.

If we were to look for a common element in all these statements we would have to isolate the notion of life. These 'I am' expressions all focus directly or indirectly on the idea of life — that life which comes from accepting in faith the word of God revealed and embodied in Jesus. This is the essence of John's theology.

But there are a few instances in the Gospel where John describes Jesus using this formula in an absolute sense, that is, without any complement or predicate. Space does not permit me to survey the Old Testament background and evidence, but there are more than enough indications there to suggest that 'I am' was a recognised form of the divine name. The use of this expression by Jesus in this absolute sense is understood by John as an explicit claim to divinity, to equality with Yahweh himself.

And so the desire of the Jews to stone Jesus for blasphemy (8:59) was not just because he claimed to have existed before Abraham, but because he attributed to himself the divine name, 'I AM'.

Although it doesn't always come through with the same clarity in English translations of the Gospel, John makes the same point in many other texts, for example, 8:24; 8:28; 13:19; 19:6. In all of these instances John intends the words 'I am' to be understood as a statement of Jesus' divinity.

But when you ask whether Jesus knew this from experiential knowledge or faith knowledge you are posing a very tough question.

That Jesus did have at least an intuitive awareness of his divine Sonship in a special sense, no orthodox Christian could doubt.

But the problem is in determining to what extent the portrait of Jesus in John's Gospel is the result of many years of theological reflection on his person and work and of the evangelist's own faith interpretation, and to what extent it reflects the self-awareness of the historical Jesus. The Jesus portrayed in the earlier Gospels does not assert his divinity with anything like the same clarity that we find in John.

John would certainly say that Jesus' knowledge of his divinity was of the 'experiential' variety. On the other hand the 'faith knowledge' of Jesus is not apparent to the same extent in John as in the earlier Gospels which present a more human figure. The Jesus who speaks in John's Gospel is really the risen Christ. He is one who transcends time and space; he is a Jesus already in the company of the Father.

Although his words are placed in the context of human situations, he is really speaking from Heaven.

Question 61:

Please, this is a serious question. I have asked it of several well-instructed people, and their answers have ranged from laughter, through 'nobody but you would think of such a thing', to 'this is scrupulosity run riot'.

I have been told that the rulings of a General Council require the same obedience as the infallible pronouncements of a Pope. This gives rise to the following question: I abstain from fornication, we behead our chooks and I believe few abattoirs now strangle oxen, calves or sheep. But I do eat black pudding. Just how serious is this sin? Why this ruling was made does not matter. That it was, surely must. Please believe me, I am not being facetious. If nobody else would think of it, still I do. And I do not think I am particularly scrupulous. I ask because I want to know.

Answer:

You certainly have an imaginative way of phrasing a question. For the benefit of readers, I will try to explain what I think you are getting at.

Chapter 15 of the book of the Acts of the Apostles describes the proceedings of a special assembly of the Apostles and elders of the Jerusalem Church. It was called to debate the big issue — at that time — of whether pagans could be received into the Church without having been circumcised or to observe the Jewish Law in its entirety.

This assembly took place about the year 50 AD, just 20 years after the Church began. It has commonly been referred to — perhaps loosely — as the first 'General Council' of the Church. The decision reached was that gentile Christians or converts from paganism were to be baptised and admitted into the Church without the obligation of circumcision or observance of the Law of Moses.

However, in deference to Jewish Christian sensitivities these converts from paganism were asked to abstain from four things which Jews found particularly abhorrent. These are spelt out in Acts 15:19-20 and again in 15:29. Gentile-Christians were asked to 'abstain from what has been sacrificed to idols and from blood and from what has been strangled and from unchastity' (fornication).

In other words, Gentile Christians were requested not to eat meats which they knew were 'left overs' from animal sacrifices to the pagan gods and not to eat any food with blood in it. The Jews had (and still have) their religious reasons for abstaining from eating any meat from which the blood had not been fully drained. Carcasses of animals that had been strangled would not have met their requirements.

As for the word translated in many versions of the Bible as fornication or unchastity, it appears to mean marriages contracted within degrees of blood relationships which were acceptable in pagan Greek and Roman law but prohibited by Jewish law. The Jews regarded such union as concubinage. Again, out of respect for Jewish-Christian feelings, converts from paganism were asked to respect Jewish marriage laws.

You say in your letter that 'why this ruling was made does not matter'. On the contrary, I would suggest this is the only thing that matters. It was a ruling drawn up to regulate relationships between Jewish and Gentile Christians in the early Church. It reflects a situation which is no longer relevant, and therefore its provisions no longer bind.

This disciplinary decision contained in Acts 15: 28-29 can in no way be equated with an infallible pronouncement of a Pope or with a dogmatic definition of a General Council of the Church.

Question 62:

I would be grateful if you could explain what St Paul meant when he wrote: 'My conscience is clear, but that does not prove that I am really innocent. The Lord is the one who passes judgment on me' (1 Corinthians 4:4). St Paul seems to me to be asserting that a person could unknowingly be committing sins, but this is contrary to what I have been taught.

Answer:
Regarding the quotation from 1 Corinthians, I would not draw from it the conclusion that it is possible to commit sin unknowingly and involuntarily.

As with all quotations from Scripture, it is important to look at the context in which the statements appear. In the whole section of 1 Corinthians from 3:5 to 4:21, Paul is giving an exposition of the apostolic ministry, his own and that of his fellow workers. He has been critical of the way the Corinthians have split into factions or party groups each group claiming allegiance to different 'apostles': Paul himself, Peter or Apollos.

Paul has argued that they are all merely the instruments through whom God has called the Corinthians to the faith. Each of them has a distinct mission assigned to him by Christ. But any success they have achieved in their ministries is due to God alone.

In the course of his exposition, Paul reflects on different categories of ministers of the Gospel: the unworthy whom God will punish; those who have been lacking in zeal, though not to the extent that their work has been useless; and finally the good and faithful servants (1 Corinthians 3:12-15).

Paul would like to think that he is among the latter, but he is aware of what he has told the Corinthians in 1:31 — that they have no reason to boast except 'in the Lord'. so now he is reluctant to deliver a favourable judgment on his own ministry.

Certainly, the Corinthians themselves have no right to pass judgment on his word, or that of the other Apostles. Not even he himself, but only the Lord can judge the faithfulness of Paul's ministry. It is in this context that Paul says: 'My conscience (about how I have discharged my ministry) is clear, but that does not prove that I am really innocent (that is, that I have been as zealous and faithful as I might have been). The Lord is the one who passes judgment on me.'

I think that Paul's comment in 1Corinthian 4:4 has to be seen in the light of his own situation. It would be dangerous to extend it to cover the whole general question of sin, conscience, and personal responsibility.

Question 63:

In these days when the people of God are liable to be misled by moralists proclaiming that sex relations between engaged couples are not necessarily immoral, that is, in every possible situation, it is good to have your assurance that you do not suggest any possible discontinuity between Catholic teaching on this point and that of St Paul.

However, you have not answered, or even attempted to answer, my contention that 1 Corinthians 7:9 puts it beyond doubt that, when in the preceding chapter Paul condemns sexual licence, alleging cogent motives for this from Christian revelation, he was thinking not only of prostitution, although this receives greatest stress, but of all forms of extra-marital or pre-marital sex.

St Paul's advice to those who are unable to remain continent is to marry rather than be tortured — 'burned' — by sensual inclinations.

This is not properly a principle, but a prudential rule of sound casuistry, presupposing the principle that all sex activity outside marriage is immoral.

This implication cannot be dismissed by saying 'it is not one of his (St Paul's) better principles' — the Apostle is simply saying that a strong sexual appetite can, in marriage with a suitable partner, be elevated into the expression of unitive and procreative love.

I do not see why you speak of the Apostle's expectation of a speedy second coming as his basis for comparing marriage and virginity, when the basis is the Coming itself, whether next week or in millions of years, as can clearly be seen in the teachings of Vatican II, Paul VI and John Paul II.

St Paul's expectation of a speedy Coming merely adds urgency and insistence to his teaching.

In conclusion, I don't want to be further side-tracked. When you produce arguments I shall consider them.

Answer:

I suggest you might consult a good reputable commentary

on St Paul's first letter to the Corinthians, such as the *Jerome Biblical Commentary*.

The first six chapters of 1 Corinthians deal with serious abuses which had come to Paul's notice concerning the Church at Corinth.

From chapter seven on, Paul deals with questions that were submitted to him by the Corinthians themselves, such as whether it is better to marry or to remain celibate in view of the expected imminent coming of Christ (Ch.7).

This matter, dealt with in chapter seven, is quite distinct from the issue of chapter six which concerns the reversion of some Chistians to a pagan way of life including intercourse with 'sacred' prostitutes, a feature of pagan Corinthian worship.

Paul's teaching on marriage and celibacy in chapter seven occurs in a completely different context. It is important to read the whole chapter.

His advice to the Corinthians is clearly based on his expectation of the imminent return of Christ: 'The time is short, so do not change your present state of life; however, if you are unmarried and cannot cope with celibacy or virginity, if you are "tortured", then marry.'

When I say that it is not one of Paul's better principles, I mean simply that it presents a less than ideal motivation for marriage. This is because his advice to the Corinthians is conditioned by his expectation of a speedy second coming of Christ.

A much more positive approach to marriage can be found in Ephesians 5:21-33 written at a time when Paul had come to terms with an indefinite postponement of the return of Christ.

You state: 'The Apostle is simply saying that strong sexual appetite can in marriage with a suitable partner be elevated into the expression of unitive and procreative love'. In fact, the Apostle is 'simply saying' nothing of the sort.

I do not dispute the truth and beauty of the sentiments which you express and I agree with them whole-heartedly. But it is you who are expressing them, not the Apostle Paul. There is no ihdication whatever of any such line of thought in 1 Corinthians 7.

You say that you don't want to be 'further side-tracked'.

I, too, should prefer not to be further side-tracked by a

fundamentalist approach to scriptural texts which takes into account neither the problems of the Corinthian Christians who wrote to Paul seeking advice, nor his own expectation of an imminent return of Christ when he replied to their questions.

(See also Q101-6.)

Question 64:

Would you please comment in depth on the change from the word 'Charity' to the word 'Love' in modern versions of the Scriptures.

Answer:

Your difficulty, I suspect (if you have one), confirms the changing meaning of words which can cause real problems in communication.

Both love and charity are rich and beautiful words, but both are ambiguous and subject to misunderstanding.

Unfortunately, charity has come more and more to be identified with the area of social welfare — the dispensing of charity to those in need.

At the same time, it has taken on a pejorative sense in such expressions as 'I don't want your charity', or 'As cold as charity'.

For these reasons, while we may regret the depreciation of the word, the result is that the term no longer does justice to what the Word of God intends by the concept.

The term love is for that reason superior.

However, it is important to realise that love, too, is one of the most abused and ambivalent words in the English language.

Perhaps the best way to approach your question is to explain the various Greek words, widely different in meaning, which can all be rendered by the English word, Love.

The reason I refer to the Greek language is because the New Testament was written in Greek and so this should serve best to illustrate what Jesus and the biblical writers meant when speaking of love or charity.

The Greek language uses the words *eros, philia* and *agape* to designate love.

Eros signifies the passion of sexual desire. Although this word does not appear in the New Testament, it is this meaning that is most frequently attached to the word love in our modern world.

Philia denotes primarily the love of friendship. It does occur in the New Testament, especially in the writings of John.

But the principle word for love in the Scriptures is *agape* — a word that is found less frequently in secular Greek language.

Probably it was for that reason that it was chosen to designate the unique and original Christian idea of love in the New Testament. It is this word, *agape*, which is used in the passage in which Jesus identifies love of God and love of neighbour as the greatest commandment of the law (Matthew 22:34-40; Mark 12:28-34; Luke 10:25-28).

The two commandments are put on an equal plane, and it is precisely in this that we have the Christian revolution in the concept of love.

In his Gospel, St Luke goes on to answer the question 'Who is a neighbour?' by telling the story of the Good Samaritan (10:29-37). Jesus chose a Samaritan as the hero of the story because there was a deep and long-standing hostility between Jews and Samaritans.

The significant point of the parable is that neighbour is identified with a person or a group that was most alien to the people who heard Jesus preach.

This parable is a beautifully vivid illustration of Jesus' teaching about love of one's enemies (Matthew 5:43-48; Luke 6:27-28, 32-36).

Jesus here presents God's attitude towards people (sinners) as the model of the Christian attitude towards those who are alienated from them.

This is how Christian love must show itself as special and distinctive.

No one would question the duty to love one's friends but Jesus demands more than that.

There is much more that could be said about love (*agape*) in the Christian sense of the word.

The writings of John and the letters of Paul add further dimension to the notion of Christian love. The famous 13th chapter of Paul's first letter to the Corinthians gives a detailed description of the qualities of Christian love.

But the two qualities that stand out when we say that the love of Christians must be modelled on Christ's love, or God's love, are the qualities of fidelity and self-sacrifice.

Fidelity is exemplified in Jesus' final words to his disciples in Matthew 28:20 'I will be with you always even to the end of time.'

Self-sacrifice is expressed in Jesus' farewell words to his disciples in John 15:13 'Greater love than this no man has, than to lay down his life for his friends.'

Perhaps the best way to describe Christian love (*agape*), modelled on the love of Christ, is to say that it is a love which is unselfish and disinterested; is prepared to risk — not counting the cost; is faithful — no matter what might be the behaviour of the other person; is prepared to go on giving, even though the gift might be not appreciated, or even rejected.

This is what is distinctive about *agape* (Christian love) as opposed to *philia* (the love between friends) and *eros* (sexual passionate love).

Question 65:

I have been reading Spirituality and the Gentle Life *by Van Kaam. In Chapter 10 on 'Gentleness and Aggression' he says: 'The wages of repressed anger include not only a distorted spiritual life, but also in the long run, poor psychological and bodily health, damage to my togetherness with others, and diminishment of my apostolic effectiveness.*

'As I try more and more to live for God I see I should not be concerned about health and effectiveness for their own sake of his Kingdom.

'The Lord may take away my physical and psychological health; he may choose for a life of suffering, letting me share in the lowliness of the kenotic Christ who emptied himself to glory.'

Could you explain what 'kenotic' Christ means?

Answer:

'Kenotic' comes from the Greek word *Kenosis* which literally means an emptying. When applied to Christ the term is derived from a very ancient Christian hymn which was included by St Paul in his letter to the Philippians. This hymn in praise of Christ occupies Chapter 2, verses 6-11 of this letter.

In this passage it is said Christ Jesus did not consider his equality with God something to be clung to, or jealously hoarded, but instead that he 'emptied himself', took the form of a servant (human nature) and became like all other men in appearance.

He went further still and humbled himself, becoming obedient unto death, even death by crucifixion.

The hymn goes on to say God rewarded this humble obedience of Jesus by exalting him in his humanity and giving him the name which is above all names, the name (and function) of Lord.

The 'kenotic' Christ is therefore a reference to the Son of God who emptied himself of glory, and chose rather to immerse himself in the suffering human condition, and ultimately to accept a sacrificial death.

Question 66:

I find difficulty in understanding the passage in the Book of Apocalypse, chapter 12 verses 1-6: 'I saw a woman clothed with the sun, and with the moon beneath her feet'. Please explain.

Answer:

Space does not permit me to give a verse by verse explanation of this difficult passage. The whole of Apocalypse chapter 12 is a symbolic description of the power of evil, represented by a monster (the Great Red Dragon) which is radically opposed to the Messiah and his people. Filled with hatred, the devil goes to any length to destroy Christ and his Church. Most modern commentators see the heavenly 'woman clothed with the sun' as a symbol of the Church. The persecution of the woman is intelligible only if she represents the Church, which throughout the book is oppressed by the forces of evil.

The Messiah sprang from the people of the 12 tribes (Israel); this same people, directed by the 12 apostles, is the mother of those who believe in Christ (see also v.17). The Apocalypse makes no clear distinction between the old and the new Israel, that is, between Israel and the Church.

The crown of 12 stars seems to symbolise the 12 tribes and the 12 apostles; the male child is, of course, Christ; the woman's birth pangs are a common biblical symbol for the inauguration of a new age.

The heavenly woman is adorned in splendour with the sun covering her like a cloak. It is well to note that the Church which is envisaged here is not the earthly Church with its faults and failings but the ideal, heavenly Church. This celestial Church or heavenly Jerusalem was believed to exist in God's presence as a model for the growth of the Christian community here on earth.

This interpretation of the woman of the Apocalypse is not new. In fact, most ancient commentators identified her with the Church. In the Middle Ages she was believed to represent Mary, the Mother of Jesus; but several of the details in Apocalypse 12:1-6 make it difficult to sustain that this was the primary meaning intended by the author of the book.

However, it is possible that a secondary reference to Mary is intended. The author may well have written with a twofold viewpoint in mind, individual as well as collective.

He may have intended to suggest at the same time both the people of God, the Church, and Mary, the member of Israel who gave birth to the Messiah.

Freemasonry

Question 67:

Can a Catholic join the Freemasons? If so, can he still receive Holy Communion and also does he lose his right to a Catholic burial?

Answer:

The old Code of Canon Law explicitly forbade Catholics joining a Masonic lodge or affiliated organisation under penalty of excommunication reserved to the Holy See (Canon 2335).

This prohibition followed numerous papal condemnations of Freemasonry during the 18th and 19th centuries.

Such a penalty deprived a person of reception of the Sacraments, Christian burial, and such rights as acting as a godfather in Baptism. At the same time, a Mason who wished to enter the Catholic Church was obliged to sever all ties with the lodge.

Basically, the reason for the Church's stance against Freemasonry has been the strong anti-Catholic ideology of the society, especially on the continent of Europe.

Many European lodges tended to atheism and/or anticlericalism from the beginning, although not all branches of Freemasonary were so explicit in their direct opposition to the Church.

The new Code of Canon Law, which came into force on the first Sunday of Advent 1983, does not contain any condemnation of Freemasonry by name.

What the new Code does say (Canon 1374) is that 'anyone who joins a society which works against the Church is subject to a just penalty; whoever promotes or presides over such an association incurs the penalty of Interdict'. (The penalty of Interdict includes exclusion from the Sacraments and loss of the right of Christian burial).

In the light of the new law, it would appear that it will become the responsibility of national bishops' conferences to decide whether the local brand of Freemansonry comes into the category of a 'society which works against the Church'.

The bishops' decision will, naturally, be made more difficult, in proportion to the degree of secrecy practised by the Masons themselves.

Indulgences

Question 68:

What is the Church's teaching about indulgences these days?

Answer:

An 'indulgence' was the name given to a practice that began quite early in the Church's history. The first instance of the practice seems to have been in the case where a bishop would reduce a sinner's public penance because a martyr had offered his sufferings to atone for the penitent's sin.

Gradually, the Church came to declare that certain prayers or good works could gain an 'indulgence'. This was usually stated as the equivalent of a certain period of penance, for example, seven years or 300 days, etc. These times attached to indulgences did *not* refer to equivalent periods which would otherwise be spent in Purgatory after death, but to the remission of penances imposed on sinners.

The practice of indulgences grew up alongside, and partly because of, the long and severe penances which were imposed in earlier centuries of the Church.

In fairness, indulgences were never considered 'automatic' ways of atoning for sin. Their effectiveness depended ultimately on God's love and mercy, and on the faith and repentance of the sinner. But it cannot be denied that the practice was open to abuse, and often was abused. The sale of indulgences by some mediaeval preachers brought forth Martin Luther's justifiable protest.

Today, indulgences are considered as of minor importance in Catholicism. Indeed, their relevance to Christian living is highly questionable. The proposal was put before the second Vatican Council to present the practice of indulgences in a more acceptable way, but the Council did not pronounce on the subject.

More recently, the whole practice was simplified by new regulations. But it seems best, if we have to think in terms of indulgences at all, to consider them simply as the Church's recommendation and approval of a particular prayer or good work.

Question 69:

With reference to your answer to Q68, I would strongly urge you and all Catholics to read the booklet entitled Indulgences, Their Meaning and Value *by Rev O. Corr.*

After reading this booklet no true Catholic would dare to say in print or otherwise 'Today, indulgences are considered as of minor importance in Catholicism.' Your casual approach to the subject leaves one with a feeling of irrelevance towards God's generous gifts from his love and mercy.

By your attitude and remarks, you undermine and minimise the very love and mercy of God, when you reduce indulgences to 'minor importance'. These indulgences are gifts from his love and mercy, of which we are free to partake. Pope Paul VI, Revision of Sacred Indulgences, 1967, *reaffirms the value of indulgences, their importance and assistance towards sanctity and renewal.*

Answer:

You suggest on several occasions that my statement, 'Today, indulgences are considered as of minor importance in Catholicism,' somehow amounts to a minimising or undermining of the love and mercy of God. I find such a suggestion puzzling, to say the least.

The love and mercy of God are a basic datum of the Christian life. We are the beneficiaries of that love and mercy every moment of our lives, and they are connected to us in many different ways.

The idea that God's gifts of love and mercy are somehow tied to the practice of indulgences does not make a lot of sense to me. I am aware that recently the whole practice has been simplified by new regulations, in an attempt to make indulgences more relevant.

Despite this, they remain peripheral to the faith, and rightly so. To say they are of 'minor importance' is simply a statement of fact.

It is true that in times past, their importance came to be exaggerated. It is also true that they were one of the contributing factors to the tragedy of the Protestant Reformation. His attack on the abuse of the practice of indulgences was one area, at least, in which Martin Luther was right.

Question 70:

If the practice of Indulgences is of minor importance to the faith, why did the Second Vatican Council again recommend this practice and still condemn those who say that Indulgences are useless, or that the Church does not have the power to grant them?

Answer:

The Second Vatican Council dealt with *all* questions pertaining to the faith of Catholics, some of greater importance, some of lesser importance. It is not a matter of denying the authority of the Church to grant Indulgences; nor of saying they are 'useless'. Nevertheless, the matter of Indulgences is of secondary importance, when one considers the full richness of the Catholic tradition of Christianity.

In more than 20 years of priesthood, I don't think I have ever preached on Indulgences. Certainly, I have never attacked the practice. But neither can I recall any discussion on spirituality with a lay person who thought or spoke in terms of Indulgences. In the light of this, how can one say otherwise than that Indulgences are of minor importance to the faith and practice of Catholics?

Intercommunion

Question 71:

Could you please explain to me something I cannot understand? I married into a very good Anglican family. We were married in the Catholic Church. Our children attended Catholic schools. In fact, their father worked more for the Catholic Church than many Catholics did. Another member of his family also married a Catholic, but in the Anglican Church.

This happened many years ago when mixed marriages were forbidden, although neither changed religion. The other member is allowed to go to Holy Communion, but my husband has been forbidden to go. He was told it is not allowed unless he becomes a Catholic.

I would like to know why the difference, as we have never had a word over religion since the day we met. Everything went the Catholic way. Now he comes with me and I feel so sad when he is forbidden to receive Communion when other Anglicans can go because the priest says so.

I would appreciate your opinion.

Answer:

There are some statements in your letter which I find a little confusing. If my reply shows that I have misunderstood you on any point you might wish to clarify the issues in a follow-up letter.

You say that a member of your husband's (Anglican) family married a Catholic in the Anglican Church at a time when mixed marriages were forbidden by the Catholic Church. I would question the latter part of this statement.

Mixed marriages were strongly disapproved of, and some bishops and priests no doubt held stronger views on the subject than others. But mixed marriages were not forbidden by the Church. It was always possible for a mixed marriage to be celebrated in the Catholic Church with a dispensation from the bishop. Church law still requires such a dispensation.

You go on to say that this other family member (an Anglican) is allowed to receive Holy Communion, presumably in the Catholic Church, while your husband is forbidden to do so. I presume you mean that some priest has given approval to your Anglican relative to receive Communion in the Catholic Church, whereas another priest has informed your husband that this is not permissible in his case.

If this is the situation, then the priest who has approved of your relative receiving Communion is not acting strictly in accordance with the Church's law. His action may appear more pastoral and compassionate, but he is really taking the law into his own hands.

The whole question of inter-communion is a difficult and delicate one, but a commission of leading Catholic and Anglican theologians has been looking into this matter, and we may see in our lifetime a change in the Church's position. But I do not think that the cause of ecumenism is advanced by individual priests anticipating such a change.

On the other hand, you may be misinterpreting the situation. I have myself given the Eucharist to people whom I have known to be non-Catholics. I did not believe that I would be justified in refusing them in the context of community worship. This would be a serious offence against charity.

Were they to ask my advice or permission beforehand, I would be obliged then to point out to them the law of the Church and the reasons behind it. Should they, in spite of this continue to come forward to receive the Eucharist I would presume that they were acting in good faith, and that their conscience was right in the sight of God.

The reason for the Catholic Church's apparent 'hard line' on this matter is that we see the Eucharist as both a source and a sign of unity. Those who advocate a more liberal approach to inter-communion stress the first aspect: that the Eucharist is a Sacrament which promotes and achieves unity.

But the second aspect, the 'sign of unity', must not be ignored. Communion, that is common participation in the body and blood of Christ, is a public expression of a complete unity of faith on the part of the participants.

If that unity of belief and practice is not complete, then the reception of the Sacrament is an expression of something which does not exist.

Sadly, this unity is not yet a fact. Communion in the body and blood of Christ must wait until such unity is a reality.

Liturgical Issues

Question 72:

Has the Church changed its attitude about Benediction of the Blessed Sacrament?

Answer:

I am not aware of any change in the Church's attitude towards the practice of Benediction of the Blessed Sacrament. It continues to be regarded as a valid form of Eucharistic devotion.

The practice of Benediction has declined in frequency for two reasons. The first is a practical one. The introduction of evening Masses naturally led to the suspension of parish Sunday evening devotions, including Benediction, which were a regular feature of Catholic piety 20 years ago.

The second reason is a more theological one. With the increasing emphasis on the celebration of the Eucharist, there has been a corresponding de-emphasis on the reservation and adoration of the Eucharist. However, these two aspects of Eucharistic worship, though they should be kept separate, need not be mutually exclusive.

It would be a pity if parishes were to dispense completely with the practice of Benediction. Surely the opportunities are still present for this form of devotion to be made available to people in a meaningful way. In some parishes on special Sundays, the Sacrament is left exposed on the altar after the final morning Mass, to be venerated by the people. This time of adoration then concludes with Benediction, perhaps at mid-day.

Feasts like Corpus Christi and Christ the King are obvious occasions when such a practice is appropriate. Other parishes may choose to encourage this form of devotion when urging people to pray for some particular cause, for example, on Vocations Sunday, or Right to Life Sunday.

It is not necessary to adhere exactly to the traditional structure. The actual Benediction or blessing may be surrounded by a variety of songs and prayers of praise, and appropriate readings from scripture or other devotional books. Imaginative members of parish liturgy committees should have no problem in devising a form of Benediction which would be most appealing and conducive to prayer.

Question 73:

Do you think that, in the future, parishioners might be able to select the topics for the Sunday sermon?

Answer:

There are a few problems associated with this proposal as I see it. The Sunday homily is meant to be constructed on the biblical readings chosen by the Church for that Sunday, to give the whole Eucharistic celebration a unified theme.

Many parishes have liturgy committees which, in conjunction with the priests, prepare the Sunday liturgy and decide what theme should be followed on a particular day.

Possibly you are suggesting that this procedure means that there are important theological moral and social issues which are not covered. The priest does, of course, depart on occasions from the regular practice and devote his homily to such questions as Aboriginals, immigration, abortion, and the like.

I do not believe, however, that the Sunday homily is the right forum for many of the issues people would like to hear discussed. The homily is not meant to be the place for faith education in the sense I understand it. Ten or twelve minutes is hardly adequate anyway for the kind of treatment of the topic that would be required.

I think that people who feel this lack should make their views known to their Parish Council representatives and push for courses in adult faith education in the parish.

At the same time, the people could then be invited to submit topics which could be part of such adult education courses.

Question 74:

Could you please enlighten me why, in some of our churches, the Blessed Sacrament has been removed from the

*place of honour in the centre of the church? I do not know
how far-reaching this practice is; I do know that it is very
confusing to enter a church and not know where to
genuflect.*

*Belief in the Real Presence being central to the teaching of
the Catholic Church, and speaking on behalf of many fellow
Catholics, it is difficult to see the justification for removing
the Blessed Sacrament from the main altar.*

Answer:

There are two ways of looking at the Eucharist. First, we can
consider the Eucharist as an *action*, a celebration that is
done in Christ's memory and in obedience to his command.
It is this action which is performed every time the Mass is
celebrated, and the bread and wine become the body and
blood of Christ — to be offered to the Father, and received
in communion by those who participate.

The other way of looking at the Eucharist is as something,
or rather Someone, to be preserved and adored — what we
call the Blessed Sacrament. It is interesting to see how this
devotion grew up in the Church.

In Rome, back in the third century, Christians used to
keep the Eucharist in their homes under both forms, bread
and wine, so that they could give themselves Communion
every day.

Gradually, the practice grew of reserving the Eucharist in
churches mainly for the purpose of taking Communion to
the sick. This led later still to the adoration of Our Lord
present in the reserved Sacrament. The tabernacle came to
be placed in a central position in the church. This custom
became universal Church practice only in the 16th century.

But the principal form of eucharistic devotion remains the
celebration of Mass, and the receiving of Holy Communion
at Mass. The other forms of eucharistic devotion — including exposition and adoration of the Blessed Sacrament,
Benediction, processions, etc. — are indeed an important
part of Catholic piety. However, in relation to the celebration of Mass and the reception of Holy Communion, they
remain secondary.

In a number of newer churches, the Blessed Sacrament is
reserved in a separate chapel. This is in keeping with strong
recent recommendations from Rome.

The document promulgated by Pope Paul VI in 1975 on *Holy Communion and Worship of the Eucharist* states explicitly that the Eucharist chapel should ideally be separate from the main body of the church. The major space of the church is designed for the eucharistic *action*, that is, for the Mass.

The purpose of this separation is to avoid confusion between the celebration and reservation of the Eucharist. There is something less than ideal in the arrangement which has the Eucharist already present in the central place in the Church, where the action is to be performed which makes the Eucharist present.

Having the Eucharist reserved in a place apart is not meant to play down its importance. Rather, a chapel carefully designed and appointed should give proper attention to the Blessed Sacrament.

The Roman document I have referred to stresses that the Eucharist chapel should be prominent, properly set up for individual prayer and adoration, and that the presence of the Blessed Sacrament be clearly indicated by a light or lamp.

It is urged that there should be easy access from the body of the church, as well as from the church surrounds. It should be left open daily for people who wish to pray there. It should be free of statues and pictures which would distract people from its primary purpose of adoration of Christ in the Sacrament.

Question 75:

You may have noticed recently an increasing number of advertisements for gentlemen's hairpieces — 'wigs' to those who like plain speaking. Now my question is this: In the 18th century it was the custom for men to shave their heads with, I think, the purpose of denying a home to vermin.

They wore wigs over their shaven heads, but did they wear those wigs in Church? Would you be classified as bareheaded if you did wear a wig?

And while we are on the subject, could you give a ruling on whether a lady is under any obligation to wear a hat in church?

As far as I know it was something said by St Paul that caused them to wear hats in church. But was it ever a

Church ruling that caused all the girls to wear hats, even if it
was only a handkerchief, until the Second Vatican Council?
If it was a rule I have never heard of it being repealed.

Answer:

I am not really familiar with the customs of the 18th century, as far as the wearing of wigs or hairpieces is concerned.
I presume there was no problem raised about men with wigs
attending church.

Regarding this question, and that of women having their
heads covered, it is true St Paul commands the women of
Corinth not to pray or prophesy with their heads unveiled.
He backs up his command with some argumentation of
dubious enduring value (see 1 Corinthians 11:3ff.).

In this passage he rebukes the behaviour of women attending the assemblies without wearing a veil as unbecoming, because, he says, God has established a hierarchy, in
both the natural and religious areas, in which the female is
subordinate to the male sex.

This hierarchical subordination of the woman should be
recognised in her behaviour and dress. The veil covering the
head is a symbol of this subordination.

And so Paul rebukes both men who pray with their heads
covered and women who pray with their heads unveiled.

This might seem strange reasoning by our standards. But
we must remember Paul was influenced (as we would
expect) by the male dominated culture and social conditions
of his day.

A good rule for interpreting Paul is that when he is teaching doctrinal truths, or general principles, then his teaching
must be taken as basic Christian dogma of permanent
validity.

But when he gets down to particular rules and regulations
of a practical nature then his remarks don't necessarily
contain timeless theological truth.

Although the Bible is the word of God, even the word of
God has sometimes to be seen as time conditioned, and
some of Paul's practical directives certainly reflect the social
and cultural circumstances of his time, and are tied to them.

I publish the following letter without comment:
A reader asked about the obligation for women to cover

their heads in church. These are Our Lady's words to Veronica Leuken, of New York: 'My heart is torn, my children, at the manner in which you do honour to my Son in his house.

'The angels demand proper deportment during the Holy Sacrifice of my Son. A woman must have her head covered. It is the command of the angels who are present at the Holy Sacrifice.

'All flesh and nakedness shall burn with the Ball of Redemption. Cover your bodies. They are temples of the Holy Ghost.'

I hope this will clear up the matter.

Marriage Concerns

Question 76:

I am puzzled as to the meaning of Matthew 5:31-32: 'It has also been said, "anyone who divorces his wife must give her a writ of dismissal" but I say this to you: everyone who divorces his wife, except in the case of fornication, makes her an adulterer; and anyone who marries a divorced woman commits adultery.'

As it stands it makes no sense to me. Surely if A divorces B, that does not make B an adulterer (or adulteress).

I realise my translation is very literal, but I would appreciate your help.

Answer:

Matthew 5:31-32, from the Sermon on the Mount, differs from Matthew 19:9. In the later passage, the author quotes Jesus as saying: 'Whoever divorces his wife . . . and marries another, commits adultery'. Whereas, as you point out, in 5:32 the words are changed to read: 'Everyone who divorces his wife . . . makes her an adulteress'.

I think the phrase has to be understood in the sense that the man who divorces his wife exposes her to the danger of becoming an adulteress.

Having been divorced by her husband, the woman is left exposed to the possibility of marrying again and so being guilty of adultery. For this her former husband, who divorced her, must bear a major share of the responsibility.

It also needs to be remembered that at that time in history, a woman was very much regarded as a man's possession. She did not have the independence or the opportunity for a career and a different lifestyle that so many women enjoy today.

This made the divorced woman so much more vulnerable.

I suggest therefore that we should understand Matthew

5:32 to mean 'everyone who divorces his wife . . . makes her
an adulteress' (if she marries again).

Question 77:
*The short statement by Jesus regarding the indissolubility of
marriage poses a problem.*

*I do not believe in divorce for very practical reasons, but
the phrase 'whatsoever God has joined together, let no man
put asunder' (Matthew 19:6; Mark 10:9) is a very broad
form of command that seems dubious in its argumentation.*

The term whatsoever *is so general that we might forbid
doctors from separating Siamese twins or physicists from
splitting the atom.*

*When two people marry, we argue that the man and the
woman confer the Sacrament upon each other and that the
priest (the representative of Christ) is only a witness.*

*Perhaps when two people elect simply to live with one
another the Sacrament may still be conferred in the eyes of
God — if not in the eyes of some people. The marriage bond
is principally a secular and legal contract.*

Answer:
Your comments on the teaching of Jesus and the practice of
the Church regarding marriage betray a scepticism which is
unwarranted.

To extend the meaning of the words of Jesus: 'What God
has joined together man must not divide,' beyond their
immediate context, is not a justifiable procedure. Clearly
from the context, he has marriage alone in mind.

The primary rule for the interpretation of any Scriptural
text is to take account of the surrounding context.

Jesus' words were spoken in the context of a debate with
the Pharisees about the permanence of marriage, and it is in
this area alone that we are justified in applying them.

You say, rightly, that in the Sacrament of marriage it is the
bride and bridegroom who are the ministers of the Sacrament to each other. In this, marriage differs from the other
Sacraments where the minister is the priest or bishop. In the
case of marriage, the priest is the Church's official witness.

But in saying '*only* a witness,' I think you are losing sight
of the fact that the Sacraments are Sacraments of *the Church*

and have no status apart from the Church. They are means by which the risen Christ acts through the community of the Church to confer on people his special gifts.

It might be an over-simplification to say the earthly Jesus instituted seven Sacraments; there is no biblical evidence for this. But the Church has determined that there are seven Sacraments and it has so decided by virtue of the authority vested in it by Christ.

If we take the Church itself seriously as *the* Sacrament of Christ, or the sign of his continuing presence in the world, then we must accept in faith the Church's teaching on the individual Sacraments.

And for those with a Catholic vision which sees Jesus Christ as the Sacrament of God, and the Church as the Sacrament of Christ, there is no possibility of the Sacrament being conferred 'in the eyes of God', in the case of those who 'elect to live with one another'.

Finally, I must reject your statement that 'the marriage bond is principally a secular and legal contract.'

When Jesus was challenged by the Pharisees to declare his position on divorce, he appealed to the book of Genesis and to the story of creation which states that 'a man must leave his father and his mother and be joined to his wife and the two become one' (Genesis 2:24).

The Church's teaching on the Sacrament of marriage is a thing of beauty and power. It teaches that all Sacraments are actions of the risen Christ.

In the case of marriage, Christ gives two people who already belong to him as individuals by their Baptism now to belong in a special way to each other. Christ acts through them as they exchange the gifts of themselves.

The priest is the Church's witness, but not 'only a witness'. Without his presence, as the official representative of the Church community, there can be no Sacrament of marriage.

When two people elect simply to live with each other there can be no question of a Sacrament.

Jesus' quotation of the word of God was intended to demonstrate that marriage is not a man-made institution for economic or biological reasons, but an intergral part of God's original plan for the human race which he created.

The State may subsequently have seen fit to legislate for

the marriage institution; but this in no way reduces marriage 'to a secular and legal contract'.

Question 78:

I would like to know the position the Church adopts in relation to the obligations of the Catholic partner in a mixed marriage. I refer specifically to a marriage between a Catholic and a Muslim. I am aware that in the past, the non-Catholic partner had to undertake to commit himself to bringing up all children in the Catholic faith.

Does this still hold, and does the Catholic Church allow the marriage to be conducted according to both Muslim and Catholic rites?

A last point — is it sufficient for the Catholic partner to hope sincerely, at the outset of the marriage, without explicitly demanding if of the other partner, that the children will be brought up Catholics?

Answer:

The Church law which required the non-Catholic partner to sign a guarantee that all children of the marriage would be baptised and brought up as Catholics has been discarded for many years. According to current Church practice, what is required is that the *Catholic* partner sign a statement about the baptism and upbringing of the children.

The exact wording of the statement is as follows: 'I re-affirm my faith in Jesus Christ, and with God's help, I intend to continue living that faith in the Catholic Church. I promise to do all in my power to share the faith I have received with our children, by having them baptised and brought up as Catholics. My future partner has been informed of this declaration and promise I have made.'

So the non-Catholic is not asked to make any promise at all before the priest, but is to be informed of the promise made by the Catholic.

Where there are serious difficulties, a bishop may dispense the Catholic from the requirement to be married in a Catholic ceremony. The bishops of Australia have adopted two general criteria which they use for granting such a dispensation:

1. When the person who is not a Catholic is a close

relative by blood or marriage to a minister of another Church; or:

2. When the bishop judges that the refusal of the dispensation could cause a grave danger to the faith of the Catholic person, or to the peace and harmony of the couple.

(No. 1 above may be extended to cover a close personal relationship between the couple and a Minister of another Church — apart from blood or marriage relationship.)

The dispensation mentioned above may be granted for serious pastoral reasons, whether the marriage is between a Catholic and a person from another tradition of Christianity (Anglican, Lutheran, etc.) or with an unbaptised person. The Church does not, however, permit the Catholic to go through two marriage ceremonies, for example, according to both Catholic and Muslim rites.

In the case of an inter-faith marriage between a Christian and a Muslim, the Christian would need to consider carefully the Muslim belief that it is lawful to have more than one wife. Though Australian marriage law does not permit this, a serious difficulty could arise if the couple were to move to another country such as Malaysia, where the practice is permitted by law.

For more precise information about the exact procedure to be followed, and how to go about obtaining any dispensation that might be required, the Catholic partner would need to consult his or her parish priest.

Question 79:

Is not re-marriage after divorce a state of permanent adultery? Is not adultery expressly forbidden by one of the Ten Commandments? Have the Ten Commandments been relegated to the wastepaper bin along with the Tridentine Mass and the sacred statues of saints?

Answer:

When Jesus was asked by the Pharisees whether it was lawful for a man to divorce his wife, he replied by pointing out that marriage was an institution created by God. It is therefore not within the power or authority of any human agency to sever a union which is valid in the sight of God.

He went on to say that the person who divorces his wife

and marries another commits adultery (Mark 10:1-12; Matthew 19:1-12).

In this absolute prohibition of divorce and re-marriage, and defence of the permanence and indissolubility of the marriage bond, Jesus therefore does say that re-marriage after divorce amounts to adultery. So the answer to your first question is 'Yes'.

The answer to your second question is also 'Yes'. Adultery is expressly forbidden by the Sixth Commandment.

The answer to the first part of your final query is 'No'. The Ten Commandments have not been 'relegated to the wastepaper bin'.

I am not sure of the point you are trying to make by your comment about the Tridentine Mass and the statues of saints. It does not seem to me particularly helpful or relevant.

(See also Q136.)

Question 80:

Recently I have come in contact with a Catholic divorced mother of two children who divorced her husband. She is taking courses in marriage counselling, so that she can have something to do in her spare time.

Does the Catholic Church allow a Catholic divorced mother to do marriage counselling? Or any divorced person? I have asked a few people and their reply was: 'You must be joking.'

Answer:

Although it may seem an anomaly to you that any divorced person should set himself or herself up as a marriage counsellor, there is no prohibition on the part of the Church on this matter.

I cannot comment on the specific case you mention because I do not have all the facts.

For example, does the person in question intend to work as a marriage counsellor in a Church agency, or elsewhere? And why did she divorce her husband? Was she the 'guilty' party or was it he whose conduct was mainly responsible for the breakdown of the marriage?

You could even argue that her experience of a 'failed'

marriage might make her more qualified to advise others of the pitfalls to be avoided.

Certainly there is a place for the divorced in the Church's ministries. In many parishes, divorced people fill leading lay ministerial positions — in liturgy, catechetics, care and concern, etc.

This might seem less appropriate in such an area as marriage counselling, but it should not be too readily assumed that a broken marriage renders one unfit for this work either.

Question 81:

I read your letter from a lady whose daughter married a divorced man, who was a convert to Catholicism. Since the daughter was not married in the Catholic Church, when her marriage failed and she obtained a divorce, she was free to marry again in the Church. I, on the other hand, did what I felt was right and married a convert in the Catholic Church in 1942. After 30 years, my husband deserted me for another woman, divorced me and then married this woman in another Church. We had four children. I worked hard at being a good wife and mother, loved my husband, and worked hard to help him in every way. I have had a struggle for the last 10 years to preserve my health. I was so upset about it all that my nerves were shattered. The loneliness has almost been unbearable, not to mention all the tears I have shed.

I still cry for the husband I loved. Sometimes I feel I need a man around the home to help me, someone to talk to, someone to love, and someone who would care for me. But I must go on, on my own. There is no choice for me because I love my God, I believe in my Church and I feel I must struggle on no matter how I feel about all this. I just hope the good Lord will continue to give me the courage to go on. I am 64 with my family in all parts of Queensland, I think the older I get the more lonely I get. Is there any answer for me please?

Answer:

I consider your letter to be one of the saddest I have so far received in 'Question Box'. To say all the things I would like to say would require an hour's conversation; it is very hard to do justice to your case in a few paragraphs in a news-paper.

Every pastor is conscious of the pain involved in cases such as yours. It is true that the Church's teaching on marriage and divorce sometimes has the side effect of great suffering for the innocent partner. Not that this in itself justifies a change in the Church's law, but it does mean that some people are called to carry a very heavy cross as an act of witness.

Have you explored the possibility of an annulment of your marriage which would give you the freedom to re-marry in the Church? Thirty years of marriage and four children do not necessarily rule out that possibility. If you have not, a phone call and a request for an appointment with the Catholic Marriage Tribunal would not do any harm. Before you do this, some advice from your own parish priest might be advisable.

In the meantime, you might consider becoming involved with a group like the Paulian Solo Parents Association. I don't know whether there is a branch of this organisation in your parish or district. It provides the opportunity for mutual faith sharing and support among people like your-self. Again, your parish priest could direct you towards making contact with this association.

It is a fact of Christian history that God asks those he loves most to shoulder the heaviest crosses. This is in keep-ing with Jesus' own words that true disciples must be pre-pared to take up their cross and follow him. His own mother and his disciples — many of whom died for the faith — are proof of this, as is the story of the saints down through the centuries. The suffering one is called on to endure can evoke different reactions. It can cause bitterness or resentment, which defeats God's purposes; or it can call forth the kind of response which led St Paul to say that he rejoiced in his suffering because he consciously united them to the suffer-ings of Christ and so recognised their redemptive value.

Do try, with God's help, to accept your suffering 'for the sake of the Kingdom.'

Question 82:
How can you advise your reader (Q81) to seek a marriage annulment? On what grounds? If you take your vows to

*each other before Christ in the Catholic Church, then either
you are married, or you are not.*
*My own case is exactly the same as hers. I have feeling for
her. My wife ran off, got a divorce, got the children, house,
etc., and on the surface seems very happy (after 25 years),
while I am leading a lonely life because I follow the Church's
law.*
*Moreover, I know in my heart that I pledged myself to
that woman, and I am still married to her.*
*I suppose you would advise me to try for an annulment,
too.*

Answer:
I have no idea whether the inquirer whom you mentioned
has grounds for an annulment. She may or may not have. A
priest who has specialised in Church Marriage Court procedure would be in the best position to advise her.

The presumption is that two people who exchange their
vows before Christ in the Catholic Church are validly married in the sight of God and the Church.

In many cases, however, a Church Court has subsequently decided that some obstacle existed at the time of the
marriage which made the marriage invalid.

Your case would not be 'exactly the same' as the other
inquirer. No two cases are exactly the same.

If you have any reason to suspect you may have grounds
for an annulment of your marriage, and wish to obtain one,
you are perfectly free to approach your parish priest, who
may then refer you to someone in the Catholic Marriage
Tribunal in your area, or you may go directly to the
Tribunal.

Of course, not everyone who seeks an annulment of his
marriage is successful in his petition.

On the other hand, because the Church's decision is based
on the mind and the circumstances of the parties at the time
of the marriage, it does not follow that many years of
marriage or a number of children necessarily rule out the
possibility of an annulment being granted.

Each case is decided on its merits.

Question 83:
I am writing to you with reference to your response given to

*the question on 'divorce and adultery', Q79. You said, 'It is
therefore not within the power or authority of any human
agency to sever a union which is valid in the sight of God.'
My question is this: Is it true that some marriages, even
though they take place in a Catholic Church, are invalid in
the sight of God?*

Answer:

I admit that my reply to the question about divorce and
adultery left many things unsaid. My statement that 'It is not
within the power or authority of any human agency to sever
a union which is valid in the sight of God', is, of course, just
a re-statement of the words of Jesus: 'What God has joined
together man must not divide.'

So, the issuing of a 'decree absolute' on the part of the
State may dissolve the marriage bond from the legal point of
view, but it has no bearing on the status of the marriage in
the sight of God, or in the eyes of the Church.

Your question, however, concerns the validity of marriages celebrated in the Catholic Church. Is it possible that
some marriages entered into with the blessing of the Church
might also be invalid?

First, it needs to be said that the presumption is in favour
of their validity. It is possible, however, for marriages that
have been celebrated in the Catholic Church to be declared
null. This is not the same thing as divorce. It is rather a
declaration by the Church that no true marriage bond existed in the first place.

There are several possible grounds for annulment. These
grounds, of course, have to be established. The Church has
its own system of marriage tribunals or courts, staffed by
trained priests and lay people, whose duty it is to investigate
and judge each case.

When a marriage is declared null, this means that some
serious impediment existed at the time of the marriage,
sufficient to affect its validity. This can be true of marriages
undertaken within the Catholic Church or anywhere else.
This is not necessarily any reflection on the priest who
instructed or prepared the couple and who officiated at the
wedding ceremony.

He can only act on the evidence presented to him and on
the assurances of the couple concerned — regarding such

things as freedom, their belief in marriage as a permanent union, etc.

In answer, therefore, to the question proposed, some marriages celebrated in the Catholic Church may indeed be invalid. A Church declaration of their nullity is a statement to this effect.

Question 84:

There have been reports in the press recently of a couple in the United States being refused permission to marry in the Catholic Church because the man is a quadraplegic unable to consummate the union. Previously there was a report of a similar case where, after an initial refusal, the couple appealed and won approval for a Catholic wedding. These instances have caused misunderstanding and some bitterness. What is the current Church teaching on the matter?

Answer:

The issue is whether an impotent person can contract a valid marriage in the Catholic Church. Impotence means the inability to perform the act of sexual intercourse. Sterility means the inability to conceive children. The two must not be confused, as sometimes happens.

Every person of whatever age or physical condition has a right to marry. The desire to exercise this right must always be based on natural and worthy reasons, though the reasons may vary. No one is to be presumed completely impotent. Any person, priest or otherwise, who is engaged in preparing a couple for marriage, is not required to investigate the physical or sexual capacity of the couple, nor obviously would it be prudent to do so. People are presumed to be normal, and have the right to this presumption.

It is true that according to current Church law, a person who is permanently and totally impotent cannot contract a valid marriage. This law was made and evolved at a time when much greater emphasis was placed on what were called the primary and secondary 'ends' of marriage. The primary end was designated as the procreation of children, and consequently there was strong emphasis on the person's sexual capacity.

Today, the Church's theology of marriage and consequently the Church's marriage law acknowledge many serious and desirable reasons for marriage, or ends of marriage: mutual love, community of life, sexual compatibility, psychological capacity for marriage, and a general ability to recognise marriage as a wonderful, life-long, joyous sacramental union.

To sum up, every person has the basic right to marry. A condition like impotence is never presumed. In the very rare case of a man with no physical genital equipment at all, that case alone should be referred to the local bishop.

Although it is difficult to make an assessment from this distance of the American case publicised in the press, it might appear that the Church authorities adhered too scrupulously to the letter of the law. It is difficult not to sympathise with the man involved who is reported as saying: 'I thought marriage was a unity of two people in love, respect and understanding.'

Question 85:

A recent letter to 'Question Box' expressed concern about my comment that the physical inability to have sexual intercourse could make a marriage invalid.

The questioner, a middle-aged married man with four children, is anxious about his situation because of the present state of his marital relationship with his wife.

Answer:

I think that the questions which you raise are best not treated in this column but should be discussed on a personal level with your parish priest or any priest in whom you have confidence as a counsellor.

I want to say, however, that the situation which you describe would not make your marriage invalid. Impotence can be a ground for annulment when this is the situation as it exists at the time of the marriage.

Since you have a number of children to the marriage this is not your situation.

At the same time the other questions which you raise are matters that should be discussed with a competent counsellor and for that reason I strongly urge you to consult someone about your obligations towards your partner.

Question 86:

My cousin, who is a Catholic, is getting married outside the Church to a non-Catholic girl. He has told the family that there will be a Catholic priest present, even though, as far as we know, a non-Catholic minister will be performing the ceremony.

In my opinion, the couple will not have a valid marriage in the eyes of the Church even though the priest is there. Am I correct, Father?

Also, is it at all possible for a Catholic priest to marry a couple in a non-Catholic Church? There has been some family discussion on this, although I have never heard of the practice.

Father, if I am correct and the marriage is not valid, is it not wrong for a priest to witness it, just for the sake of keeping people satisfied.

Answer:

The validity of the proposed marriage in the eyes of the Church depends on whether the permission of the Bishop has been obtained. The rules of the Church regulating mixed marriages allow for a Bishop in a case of 'serious difficulties' to dispense a Catholic from the requirement to be married in a Catholic ceremony.

In allowing the Bishops to dispense a Catholic from the obligation to marry before a priest, Pope Paul VI asked the Bishops of each country to agree to certain criteria for granting such a dispensation. The Australian Bishops adopted two general criteria:

1. When the non-Catholic is a close relative, by blood or marriage, of a minister of another church; or

2. When, in the judgment of the Bishop, refusal of a dispensation could cause a serious danger to the faith of the Catholic person, or to the peace and harmony of the couple.

This second criterion could be verified in the following examples:

● Avoidance of strained relations between the two families, so that both may offer better support to the couple;

● Active participation of the non-Catholic party or his family in the life of his own Church, for example, Sunday School teacher, Elder, Warden, etc.

● To keep the person who is not a Catholic from breaking with his or her own church;

● A close personal relationship of the couple with a
minister of another church, who, because of this relationship, would be in a good position to assist them in any
difficulties that could arise in their marriage.

This is not meant to be a complete or exhaustive list of
circumstances which might warrant a dispensation. Each
case is dealt with pastorally and personally. In general, the
Bishop will be looking for some positive spiritual advantage
to the couple as the ground for granting the dispensation.

If a Catholic marries before anyone other than a Catholic
priest *without* a dispensation from the Bishop, then the
Church does not recognise the marriage as valid. But if a
dispensation has been granted, then a Catholic priest may be
present and assist at the ceremony in a non-Catholic church.

In such cases it is not the Catholic priest who is the
celebrant of the marriage nor is the presence of a priest
necessary for validity. He may attend and play a supporting
role.

If a dispensation by the Bishop has not been given, a priest
may not take any part in the ceremony.

Question 87:

*It must be admitted that annulments by the Catholic Church
of the marriage vows are many (though the numbers are
fewer than during the reign of Pope Paul VI), as also are
dispensations from religious vows.*

*Is it possible for a Church-approved annulment or dis-
pensation to be unsatisfactory, and therefore displeasing
and illegal in the eyes of God?*

*I base my query on the fact that false evidence may be
given to the Church's judges with the intention of obtaining
a wrongful decision. This results in the judges being misguided, and in their wrongfully granting an annulment or
dispensation.*

*It would not be hard to establish that, on many occasions,
guilty persons charged with criminal offences have been
exonerated because of fabricated evidence, technicalities, as
well as many other reasons, including conspiracy.*

*In the eyes of the civil law such persons are therefore free
of any guilt. However, in the eyes of God, the judge who*

*cannot be deceived, these people are full of guilt, for which
they will have to answer to him.*

Answer:

It is true that the number of laicisations of priests has fallen
dramatically in recent years. The present Pope has been
adopting a much stricter line in this matter than did Paul VI.

But as regards marriage annulments, there has been no
change of Church policy or practice. I would challenge
therefore your statement that 'the numbers (of annulments)
are fewer than during the reign of Pope Paul VI'.

As for your main query — of course it is possible for the
Church's judges to err in the decisions which they make
regarding annulments.

They are human and must therefore act in a human way.
They can only go on the evidence which is placed before
them.

The same is true of priests who celebrate marriages in the
first place. They ask the couple the pertinent questions
about their intention to marry: whether their decision has
been taken freely and willingly; whether they believe in
marriage as a permanent, lifelong union; whether they intend to have children and bring them up according to God's
law, etc.

Sometimes, there is also the difficult decision about the
sufficient maturity of those intending to marry.

So, in both cases, there is the possibility of human error. If
the parties concerned deliberately present false evidence,
then, as you say, this is a matter between God and their
conscience.

Question 88:
*Please explain the teaching of the Church today on parents
or relatives attending the marriage of children who marry
outside the Church. Is it permissible to attend, or is this still
not allowed?*

Answer:

It is permitted, and even encouraged that Catholic parents
(and relatives) should attend the marriage of their children
who marry outside the Catholic Church.

Your presence does not imply that you condone their

decision. There are other ways of expressing your disappointment and disapproval than by boycotting such an important occasion in their lives.

Of course, it depends on the individual's ability to cope. If a parent or relative were psychologically unable to handle the situation, and should find it altogether too painful an experience, then he should lovingly and calmly explain his inability to attend, and ask the young people to be understanding.

But, except in this extreme case, much more is to be gained by attendance than by non-attendance. For the average young person getting married, the absence of his or her parents would be a saddening and perhaps embittering experience. It could lead to an estrangement and a lifelong resentment and nothing is to be gained from that.

I believe the chance that young people who marry outside the Church might ultimately return to their true spiritual home is increased by their parents and relatives displaying real Christian charity in this regard.

On the other hand, I think that generally the boycotting of their marriage by parents and family would only lessen the prospect of their reconciliation with the Church.

Question 89:

In Q88, you were asked to explain the teaching of the Church today on parents attending the marriage of their children who decide to marry outside the Church. 'Is is permissible to attend, or is this still not allowed?' You answered: 'It is permitted and even encouraged that Catholic parents and relatives should attend such marriages, as their presence does not imply that they condone the decision.' I believe this is completely against Catholic teaching. It is hard to imagine what presence does, if it does not condone or recognise the decision. I would believe such attendance is still forbidden; certainly not encouraged. The reason which you give is that the attendance of parents and relatives increases the chances of a subsequent return to the Church by the people involved.

The parents, you say, display real Christian charity in this regard. I am afraid we have completely lost the meaning of words when we call this Christian charity. Perhaps the same

could be said of parents who drive the car for their child
when he robs a bank! Christian charity? Hardly!
   Secondly, you seem to be astray on the question of Sunday
work. I do not remember reading of any change in the law
on this matter. It hardly seems that the only thing required
to fulfil the Sunday obligation is to set aside an hour to
worship God by attending Mass, then have no worries
about any work that needs to be done.

Answer:

Even in my limited pastoral experience, I have come across
tragic cases of permanent estangement between parents and
children, and later grandchildren, because of the refusal of
Catholic parents for the best of motives to attend the weddings of children who marry outside the Church.

   In the same cases, animosity towards the Church itself has
been the result and prospects of any ultimate reconciliation
with the Church, or of having the children baptised and
brought up as Catholics, have been rendered very remote.

   You say it is hard to imagine what the presence of parents
could signify, if not to condone the decision of their son or
daughter to marry outside the Church. I would have
thought that their presence expresses nothing more or less
than the natural bond of love which exists between parents
and children. I must say that I consider your comparison
between marriage in another Christian Church and bank
robbery rather far-fetched.

   As for the question of Sunday observance, there is wide
variation of opinion among Christians about what constitutes violation of the Lord's day. If anything, the Catholic
Church has always tended to take a more human
and realistic view than most other Churches.

   There are those Churches which disapprove of the
playing of sport on Sunday, or of attendance at sporting
fixtures played on that day; there are others which condemn
the patronising of hotels on a Sunday, in those places where
Sunday trading is permitted by law; there are still others
which do not permit any work at all to be done. Probably it
is the Seventh Day Adventists, who observe Saturday as the
Lord's day, whose practice is most in keeping with biblical
teaching about observance of 'the sabbath'.

I agree with you that there has been no official change in the Catholic Church's position: the prohibition of 'unnecessary servile work' remains in force. But then, who but some incurable 'workaholic' would want to perform *unnecessary* servile work on Sunday — or any other day, for that matter?

Wisely the teaching Church has chosen to be non-directive in this matter and to leave it to the conscience and indeed the common sense of Catholics. I repeat that the most important aspect of keeping the Lord's day holy is to come together with the believing and worshipping community to join in honouring, praising and thanking God in the celebration of the Eucharist. A Catholic who has that awareness of the special character of the Lord's day is not likely to offend against its observance in the matter of work.

Question 90:

I was not sure if I should continue with The Leader *as some of your answers, I feel, have left a lot to be desired, especially regarding Sunday Mass and marriage outside the Church.*

How can Catholic parents go along and be happy at a marriage of their children outside the Church, when their hearts are breaking because their son or daughter have turned their backs on the greatest treasure we have, the Blessed Sacrament?

Answer:

Whether parents who attend the marriage of a son or daughter who marries outside the Church are 'happy' about doing so, is not the question. Committed Catholic parents would hardly be happy about such a situation. Nor has it ever been said that there is any obligation on them to attend.

All that has been said is that there is no universal law of the Church forbidding them to do so. Parents, out of natural parental love, may attend the weddings of their children outside the Church in spite of their disappointment and unhappiness.

Question 91:

I agree with your reader (Q90) in every way.

No way would I attend my children's weddings outside the Catholic Church. Why should you run after them or help them in any way?

Answer:
I would just like to make two brief comments. I do not accept your assumption that Catholics who marry outside the Church intend to turn their backs on their parents.

Secondly, I am afraid the attitude expressed in your letter comes across as far less caring and compassionate than those with whom you disagree.

I submit, without comment, the following letters from parents:

With regard to the letter in Q90 I would like to make the point that a great many of us Catholic parents do not have the 'luxury' of even marriages of our children outside the Church. Our young people live together without marrying.

A 'good' Catholic lady upbraided me for continuing to visit my son and his girlfriend in this situation. She said I was scandalising my younger children and condoning what I knew to be sinful.

Sacramental marriage is preached by the life my husband and I live, and our acceptance of all that this life involves. Our acceptance of alternative situations does not take away from our complete faith in Christian marriage which we try to demonstrate by our way of life.

Moreover, after six years, my son is beginning his return journey to the Church, and I would think the most necessary and attractive experience for him will be that he is forgiven.

Mary Magdalene, Zaccheus, the woman at the well and many others found joy not from Jesus' sermons but from his forgiveness.

Finally, having to face disappointment and embarrassment at our children's transgressions has made it easier for us to accept our own weaknesses, and to forgive ourselves and others — so this situation need not bring bitterness but much peace.

I cannot agree with your reader (Q91). It really stunned me to read her letter stating that 'no way' would she attend the marriage of her children outside the Church.

Jesus came to heal sinners. He does not condone their sins, but neither does he turn away from them.

I have a son who was married out of the Church last May. I did not attend the wedding because circumstances prevented my travelling hundreds of miles to do so. His action hurt me, but I still would have been there if it had been at all possible because he is my son and I love him and his wife very dearly.

Had I turned against him then, I could have driven him further from the Church, and anyway, it was not my place to judge or condemn.

My son and his Anglican wife were remarried in the Catholic Church just six months later — their own decision. They are now about to have a baby who will be baptised in the Catholic Church.

So prayer, love and understanding can and do achieve, but condemnation can often destroy.

This letter is written with my children's full approval. They are grateful for my support and I say keep supporting your children, and give them the love that God asked of you when he placed them in your care.

I feel that the attitude of your reader is what God might have envisaged when he spoke through the prophet Isaiah: 'Even if a mother forgets her children I will not abandon you.'

Question 92:

The question regarding attendance of parents at marriages of their children outside the Church is one that has far-reaching pastoral implications. A Catholic who does not observe the necessary form for the validity of marriage according to the laws of the Church (marriage outside the Church) rejects the authority of the Church in this matter, and enters, at least objectively, a continuous state of sin. It is a matter, therefore, of the moral principles regarding co-operation in the sin of another.

Marriage is a public act, and mere physical attendance is a public witness to that act, irrespective of intentions or mental reservations. Hence the effect on all other guests and all who become aware of that witness must be an important consideration.

It concerns me that, as a great authority would naturally be attributed to a feature such as 'Question Box' in a leading Catholic paper, replies must be theologically sound, otherwise priests and others involved in pastoral counselling could be placed in a difficult position.

Hence as the original question asked for an explanation of the teaching of the Church on this particular matter, I ask what justification is there from the magisterium of the Church, and/or in Holy Scripture, for your statement that 'it is permitted and even encouraged that Catholic parents (and relatives) should attend the marriages of their children who marry outside the Catholic Church'.

Answer:

If I did not directly answer the question: 'What is the teaching of the Church about parents attending the marriages of their children who marry outside the Church?' — it is because there is no general Church legislation on the subject.

Some individual dioceses may have particular legislation on the matter, but I am not aware of it. Certainly there is none in my diocese. It is left to the consciences of the people concerned.

In forming their consciences, it is true that one of the factors which Catholics must take into consideration is that of co-operation in another's sin, and the scandal that their attendance might cause to other people (guests, etc.).

In the case at issue such scandal, in normal circumstances, would appear to fall into the category of 'pharisaic scandal'. There may sometimes be particular circumstances which would lead to a different conclusion.

My reply was given from a pastoral point of view, and I stand by it. In saying 'it is permitted that parents . . .' I mean that there is no Church legislation explicitly forbidding the parents' attendance, and the degree of their co-operation would not seem sufficient to prohibit such attendance.

As I said, there are other ways for parents to express their disappointment and disapproval than by boycotting their son's or daughter's wedding. I doubt very much whether people of goodwill would see in the attendance of parents at such an occasion anything more than an expression of their natural love for their children.

Question 93:

I have another question about 'marriage outside the Church'. I am a Catholic and next year intend marrying a girl who is a Protestant. We rejoice in our common Chris-

tian faith and happily respect our differences. Her home is a farm in Victoria and we would like to ask a priest friend of mine to marry us in Katherine's home.

Failing that, we would like to be married in her home town Methodist Church by my friend. I have an idea that there are regulations preventing this. Could you please tell me what our position is regarding the wedding?

Answer:

As to the question of your marrying your fiancee in her home town Methodist Church — if you should apply for, and obtain, a dispensation to marry in the Methodist (or Uniting) Church, your priest friend could assist at the marriage in a secondary capacity only, but he would not be the celebrant of the marriage.

In their *Pastoral Statement on Mixed Marriages* (1977) the Australian Bishops adopted two general criteria for dispensing a Catholic from marrying in a Catholic ceremony.

1. When the non-Catholic is a close relative, by blood or marriage, of a minister of another church; or

2. When, in the judgment of the Bishop, refusal of a dispensation could cause a serious danger to the faith of the Catholic person, or to the peace and harmony of the couple.

This second criterion could be verified in the following examples:

● Avoidance of strained relations between the two families, so that both may offer better support to the couple;

● Active participation of the non-Catholic party or his family in the life of his own Church, for example, Sunday School teacher, Elder, Warden, etc.

● To keep the person who is not a Catholic from breaking with his or her own church:

● A close personal relationship of the couple with a minister of another Church, who, because of this relationship, would be in a good position to assist them in any difficulties that could arise in their marriage.

This is not meant to be a complete or exhaustive list of circumstances. Each case is dealt with pastorally and personally.

If you think that any of these criteria apply to your own

case, then your first step should be to get in touch with your parish priest, and discuss the matter.

If he judges that there are grounds for seeking a dispensation for you to be married in a non-Catholic church, he will apply to the Bishop on your behalf for the dispensation. In these cases, it is the Bishop of the Catholic party who must grant the dispensation, not the Bishop of the area where the marriage takes place.

With regard to your first choice — marriage by a priest in your fiancee's home — the Bishops' pastoral statement has this to say:

'There is a growing custom of couples wanting to be married in places other than a church, whether this be before a priest or, with permission, before another minister.

'We appreciate that there could occasionally be good reason for this, for example, the desire to have present at the ceremony a sick parent who could not possibly come to the church.

'But if the request to have a marriage in a place other than the church springs from a desire to water down the religious and sacred content of the ceremony, obviously it cannot be granted . . . a couple ought not to ask a priest to take part in what is to them no more than a civil ceremony with a few religious trappings. We express our strong disapproval of this as a growing social custom.'

I realise from your letter that this last paragraph does not apply to your situation. Permissions have been granted by Bishops for priests to perform marriages in places other than a church, if they consider there are 'good reasons'.

Once again, I would advise you to talk it over with your own Bishop.

Original Sin

Question 94:

A non-Catholic recently asked me for my thoughts on Original Sin. From my limited knowledge of Scripture this was my reply:

The story of Adam in Genesis is the story of the beginning of the history of salvation. The Adam story is saying that man has arrived at a point in history where he acquires human intelligence and freedom, what we call 'free will'.

Man can choose good, God's way, or evil, the opposite of God's way.

By choosing God's way of living man is agreeing with God's plan. And even though he may not realise it as such, man is seeking a covenant with God, that is, an agreement with God to do his will, and God in return agrees to give man the power (ability) to be part of God, this ability that we call 'Grace'.

Since acquiring free will man must want to do God's will to be able to become part of God. Man has to make a commitment for God, a covenant with God.

When a man is said to be in the 'state of sin', he is simply in a state of non-covenant with God. If a man has never made a decision (even subconsciously) for God, he is in his original state of non-covenant (Original Sin).

Baptism is the religious ritual (Sacrament) in which man formally makes his covenant with God. Subsequent sin is a total or partial breach of this covenant.

I think the idea that 'Baptism washes away Original Sin' allows the misconception that sins are black marks. The idea of God's side of the covenant is followed through into the Eucharist where the 'ultimate' is given to those who have Grace — physical and spiritual union with God.

I would like you to comment on this line of thought.

Answer:

I should like to make just a couple of comments on your interesting presentation of the concept of Original Sin.

Your treatment of 'covenant' might appear to reverse the correct order of things, in that you seem to suggest that the covenant between God and man arises from human initiative. Such, of course, is not the case.

I would not say therefore 'man is seeking a covenant with God . . . and an agreement with God to do his will, and God *in return* agrees to give man the power (ability) . . . that we call Grace'.

It is a datum of all biblical revelation that 'God loved us first'. It is he who freely initiated a covenant with the people he chose to be his own.

The covenant which he made with Israel, with Moses as the mediator, finds its fulfilment in the covenant which he has made with 'the new Israel', the Church, with Jesus Christ as the perfect mediator.

In each case it is God who has taken the initiative, contracting to love and protect his people. At the same time, he asks them to respond by loving and serving him and he offers them the Grace to be able so to respond.

I should prefer therefore a phrasing such as: 'By choosing God's way, even though he may not realise it as such, man is responding (saying 'yes') to God's invitation to enter into a covenant relationship with him. In agreeing to do God's will, man is in fact accepting God's free offer of Grace.'

The other point in your presentation that I would query is your definition of 'Original Sin' as a person's original state of non-covenant, or never having made a decision for God.

The term 'Original Sin' is not a biblical term but as it came to be used in Church tradition, the word 'original' referred not to the original state of each person, but to the fact that this condition results from sin which goes back to the origins of the human race.

Similarly, the term 'sin', as it is applied to this condition of every human being born into the world, is used in an analogous or derived sense.

Normally, the word sin refers to a conscious, deliberate act on the part of a person who is capable of wilfully disobeying God's law. Obviously, this cannot be the state or condition of a new-born baby.

For this reason we should understand both the words 'original' and 'sin' in the phrase 'Original Sin' as referring to the power of sin which was let loose in the world as the result of sin committed at the very origin of humanity.

This power of sin has been increased and multiplied by the countless personal sins committed by all human beings since the beginning of human history.

The result is that every human being is born into a sinful environment — the result of Original Sin followed by man's personal sins which have progressively increased the sinful climate of the world.

The New Testament message of hope is that Christ has broken this power of sin in principle, especially by his death and Resurrection, and provided a means for us to escape from this sinful atmosphere of 'the world, the flesh and the Devil'.

For each individual Christian, this means is faith accompanied by Baptism: faith in the saving power of the death and Resurrection of Christ; and Baptism, which is the participation in that saving death and Resurrection (see Romans 6:3-8). Through faith and Baptism, God draws each person into a covenant relationship with himself and into the life of grace.

I agree with your reservations about the phrase 'Baptism washes away Original Sin'. Rather than say: 'Baptism removes Original Sin', it would perhaps be more meaningful to say that Baptism removes the person from the power of sin which had its origins when man first received the gifts of intelligence and freedom, and chose to abuse them by disobeying God's will.

The symbolism of water in the Sacrament of Baptism is best seen as one of life, symbolising the new birth into a new way of life, life in the spirit (John 3:5). The symbolism of cleansing is secondary.

The dogma of Original Sin was defined by the Council of Trent and Catholics are thereby bound in faith to accept its existence.

How it is 'transmitted' is not clearly defined and we are allowed a certain freedom to speculate not about its existence but about its exact nature and precisely how it affects each individual.

I believe the explanation proposed above is in accordance

with the Church's teaching, and is at the same time more easily understandable and acceptable.

Finally, we must always remember that the dogma of Original Sin is merely the negative expression of the positive and more important truth that every human being born into this world needs to be redeemed by Christ to enter into eternal life.

Question 95:

What is the Church's current understanding of Original Sin? Comment on 'Baptism takes away Original Sin', in the old catechism.

Answer:

One of the main effects of the Sacrament of Baptism is the forgiveness of sin. In the case of adult Baptism, the Sacrament removes the personal sins which a candidate for Baptism has committed.

Original Sin is not an expression which is found anywhere in Scripture. The term arose only in the early centuries after Christ.

The Book of Genesis tells us that at the beginning of time, the human race became estranged from God by the deliberate sin of our earliest ancestors. Out of this biblical evidence, as well as a passage like Romans 5:12-21, grew the Church's belief that we are all born in that condition, which came to be called 'Original Sin'.

So in the case of adults the Sacrament of Baptism was seen to remove also this state of Original Sin. In the case of infants not capable of personal sins, one of the effects of Baptism remains the removal of Original Sin.

It is true that this aspect of the Sacrament is played down in the new baptismal rite for children, because the baptismal liturgy concentrates on the more positive side — rebirth and new life.

But in the Prayer of Exorcism and Anointing before Baptism, the celebrant says: 'We pray for this child: set him (her) free from Original Sin, make him a temple of your glory, and send your Holy Spirit to dwell with him.'

This is the only mention of Original Sin in the new rite, but it still remains a doctrine of the Church. The fact of Original Sin is a dogma of faith, but its exact nature and the question of how it is transmitted continue to be the subject of theological debate.

The religious truth behind the story of Adam and Eve is that human beings are responsible for sin in the world. God, the creator, is in no way the author of sin, which rather resulted from man's abuse of God's gift of free will. The following stories in the Book of Genesis reveal how the power of sin gradually gained a grip on the world.

The story of Adam and Eve is followed by the account of Cain's murder of his brother Abel. Human sinfulness subsequently increased, until in a world filled with sin only Noah and his family were judged by God to be worthy of salvation.

After the purification of the flood, soon sin raises its ugly head again in the affairs of man. The story of the tower of Babel is yet another example of human pride, and of man's futile attempts to achieve equality with God.

This build-up of sin in the world has never ceased, down to the present day. One could nominate many attitudes and situations in today's world which contribute to this increase of a sinful climate and environment.

To sum up — as a sequel to the first human sin, man's refusal to serve God, sin multiplied so that the whole human environment became corrupt and contaminated. The world became estranged from God as a result of sin.

Every human being born into this sinful world is thus affected by the climate which sin has created. The New Testament message is that the power of Christ's redemptive work far outweighs the power of sin. Christ's death and Resurrection have conquered sin, at least in principle.

Baptism is the Sacrament which enables us to share in the death and Resurrection of Jesus. And so Baptism lifts us out of the sinful condition. As St Paul says, it is through Baptism that we die with Christ to the old self and rise with him to life with God.

Question 96:

On the topic of Original Sin you said: 'The religious truth behind the story of Original Sin is that human beings are responsible for sin in the world' (Q95). Does this mean that Adam was not an individual historical person?

Answer:

What I actually said was: 'The religious truth behind the story of Adam and Eve is that human beings are responsible for sin in the world'. These words of themselves do not imply that Adam was not an individual historical person. But certainly his story and his sin are related in such a way that he must be seen as more than an individual.

His experience is to be seen as typical of human sinfulness, its origin, its nature and its consequences, rather than just the personal experience of one man.

The Hebrew word *adam* means simply 'man', or 'mankind'. The usual translation of the word as a proper name, Adam, has to be recognised as an error. He is called 'the man' up to Genesis 4:25 where the proper name first appears.

The man was made of dust from the soil, for which the Hebrew word is *adamah*. There is obviously a play on words here. Just as man came from the earth, so does his name, *adam*, come from the name of the clay from which he is formed, *adamah*.

It is important to recognise that the Genesis account is not a scientific explanation of the origin of man, nor a history of the beginning of the human race in the proper sense of the word.

Does the biblical account, therefore, demand that we hold that all human beings are descendants ultimately of one man and one couple (monogenism)?

Or is it possible to hold that the human race descended from a multiplicity of men who emerged, under God's creative power, in different places and at different times (polygenism)?

In other words, can what the Bible has traditionally been understood as saying about an individual, Adam, be perhaps understood rather as referring to a plurality of persons?

In 1950, Pope Pius XII issued an important encyclical letter, *Humani Generis*, part of which deals with biblical matters. The encyclical allowed scholars freedom to discuss the evolution of the human body, but allowed no such freedom on the question of polygenism.

Pius XII said: 'It is in no way apparent how such an opinion can be reconciled' with the traditional teaching on

Original Sin, viz that it proceeds from sin actually committed by an individual Adam.

For those, however, who are familiar with the careful
wording of papal statements it appears that the door was
not firmly closed. The Pope did not absolutely condemn the
theory of polygenism, that is, that 'Adam' represents a
number of first parents.

Pius XII's statement that 'it is in no way apparent how
such an opinion can be reconciled' with the Church's
traditional teaching on Original Sin, was not intended to
exclude the possibility of subsequent development in
Catholic theology.

Pius XII did not say that such a reconciliation was impossible. In the view of many theologians it is not only possible
already, but even necessary.

One might well argue that the intention of the author of
Genesis was not to teach the strict unity of origin of the
human race, but rather the universality of sin. The biblical
account is making a theological statement, not a scientific
one — viz, that all people have sinned and all need
redemption.

Other Religions

Question 97:

A regular contributor to The Leader *over the years writes that the Mormons are a religious group of some significance. He mentions that two Mormon women are most active in a local Right to Life group. He goes on, however, to express the view that real dialogue between Catholics and Mormons is still a long way off!*

Answer:

I am afraid I would have to agree. I suppose we should take satisfaction that Mormons are prominent in their opposition to a serious moral and social evil such as abortion, but I would not place too much ecumenical significance on that.

The Mormon opposition to abortion is in fact a consequence of their peculiar beliefs on the nature of God and of his relationship with human beings, or perhaps we should say, 'the nature of their gods and of their relationship with human beings'.

I am not sure to what extent today's 'Latter Day Saints' have modified the teachings of their prophet and founder, Joseph Smith. They are often evasive when it comes to teachings which are so obviously at variance with biblical views.

Certainly, Smith believed in the existence of many gods, who fathered a large number of spirit children. These are restless spirits until they are clothed with bodies. Bodies are provided for these spirit children of the gods by human procreation. Man's principal obligation is to glorify the gods by having babies and so procreation becomes man's primary duty.

Logically, therefore, the more children a person has the more virtuous he is. Hence the strong opposition of the Mormons to abortion.

It was this line of 'reasoning' which led to the practice of polygamy by the Mormons in their early days. It was only when the United States government imposed its will on their adopted State of Utah, and threatened to confiscate the property of the whole Mormon Church if they did not obey the laws of the land, that Mormonism officially forbade polygamy.

The Mormons are not a Christian Church. They have retained only a minimal amount of the biblical faith. On the whole, it must be said that their beliefs are a gross distortion and a parody of orthodox Christianity. For this reason, I see little mileage to be gained from ecumenical dialogue with them.

Question 98:

Is there any essential difference — theologically speaking — between the origin and nature of the Islamic and Mormon religions?

Answer:

This question leaves me somewhat confused. I will have to ask for further clarification before I attempt to answer it. I am not an expert in the field of comparative religion, so I may be missing something that should be obvious. In what specific areas do you see links between Islam and Mormonism?

As a layman in the field, I would see their main point of contact in that they are both non-Christian religions. Both Islam and the Mormon faith appeal to prophets who claimed to receive new and special revelation from God — Mohammed and Joseph Smith, respectively. Polygamy is perhaps another contact point. Off-hand, I cannot see any close parallels between the two faiths.

Pre-Marital Sex

Question 99:

During a discussion with the older children of our family, the question of virginity came up. We were told that a nun had told a group of girls, in general discussion, that 'it was quite all right for an engaged couple, promised to marry, to engage in premarital sex, but it was not right to "sleep around for sex".'

My question is, what is the Church's teaching on 'virginity'?

Answer:

More and more these days, priests preparing young people for marriage, when they come to fill out the pre-marriage documents, discover that the couple are living at the same address.

The young people mostly display no embarrassment about admitting this fact. The social mores of our permissive society thus present us with an ever-increasing pastoral problem.

Premarital chastity remains the Christian teaching, because sexual intercourse is meant to be the symbol and expression of a permanent union, of a lifelong commitment to one's partner.

Those who indulge in promiscuous behaviour are running away from the permanent commitment to another that true love involves.

They go from one affair to another, trying to convince themselves that they are involved in loving, whereas they are really avoiding any deep or mature human relationship.

There are, however, those who are capable of loving maturely, who intend to enter a permanent union, and who want to express their commitment to each other fully by sexual intercourse.

But even for those in this situation premarital chastity is the ideal. The public, life-long commitment of the marriage ceremony has not yet been made.

Young Catholics should be made aware of the nature of the Sacrament of Marriage, and of the beauty of the Church's teaching on marriage as a Sacrament.

All seven of the Church's Sacraments are actions of Christ. The risen Christ acts through the Church, and through his ministers (normally a priest or bishop) to give his graces and gifts to those who receive the Sacraments.

Marriage differs from the other Sacraments in that the officiating priest is not the minister, but the Church's official witness.

The ministers of the Sacrament are the bride and groom. Christ acts through them. He gives two people who already belong to him individually by Baptism, now to belong in a special way to each other.

They minister the Sacrament of Marriage to each other.

The act of sexual intercourse is the fullest possible expression of this total self-giving. The Church's teaching is that it should take place only when there has been the public, total and final commitment of one to the other in the Sacrament of Marriage.

The partners thus save for one another, as their wedding gift to each other, the fullest expression of their love. To act otherwise is to anticipate the sacramental activity of Christ who unites them in marriage, which carries with it the privilege of full sexual union.

Many couples have found it worth waiting until marriage before engaging in sexual intercourse because it makes the marriage so much more special.

However, there are others who feel they already have a deep, mature and permanent commitment to each other before the marriage ceremony, and choose to consummate that commitment in the sexual union.

In their view they are doing no wrong. Whatever the state of their conscience in the sight of God, priests, parents and Catholic teachers still have the obligation of presenting the Church's teaching on marriage and sexuality without compromise as a beautiful and attainable ideal.

Certainly a statement like 'it is quite all right for an engaged couple, promised to marry, to engage in premarital sex, but it is not right to sleep around for sex' is a gross over-simplification of the difficult and delicate problem of human sexual relationships.

Question 100:
Many things have happened in the Church in the past dozen years or so that have shocked me and many others, but never was I so shocked as when reading 'Church and virginity' (Q99) about what that nun told a group of girls: that it was 'quite all right for an engaged couple promised to marry to engage in premarital sex.'

I still think that the girls might have understood wrongly. Otherwise God help our youth. If it is true, that nun should be pleased that she is doing the evil one's work very well.

As for your answer you leave much to be desired. Is it a grievous sin or not to have sex before you are married? Please answer Yes or No, not with columns full of 'ifs' and 'buts' etc.

Answer:
First of all, with regard to your comment about the anonymous Sister who allegedly gave the advice you quote to a group of girls, you may very well be right in saying that the girls might have misunderstood.

Anyone who has been a teacher, on any subject, knows well how students can carry away garbled versions of what was actually said.

Personally, I have serious doubts that any Religious would have given the kind of advice which was reported.

Concerning your second comment about the inadequacy of my answer to the question posed, there are a few points I should like to make.

A number of correspondents have recently referred to 'frills' and to 'ifs' and 'buts' which I include in my replies and instead demand straight answers: Yes or No!

First it needs to be recognised that life itself is often a matter of 'ifs' and 'buts' and many questions cannot be answered with a simple Yes or No.

Some might regret that moral behaviour cannot always be categorised in black and white terms, but that is a fact of life. There are many moral and social issues which do not lend themselves to such facile and simplistic solutions.

The development of the modern behavioural sciences of sociology and psychology have inevitably had their effect on moral theology. We are no longer as confident or dogmatic about assigning moral behaviour into neat categories of mortal and venial sins as we once were.

The second point that needs to be made is that 'Question Box' was never intended to be just an intellectual exercise or a quiz session. It would certainly save me a lot of time and energy if I were simply to answer Yes or No to questions that are presented to me.

But this approach to the column would, I believe, be a disservice to those people for whom the questions raised are not merely academic or theoretical matters, but practical issues in which they are very much involved.

Some months ago a controversy raged in these columns about whether it was right for Catholic parents to attend the weddings of their children who marry outside the Church. (see Q88-92).

What I found significant was that those who advocated a 'hard line' approach were all people for whom the matter was a theoretical one.

Those who appreciated the more 'compassionate' approach were parents for whom the question was much closer to home. One's attitudes tend to change when one finds himself (or herself) in the hot seat.

The same polarisation would appear to be developing in discussion on the matter of premarital sex. In the same mail which contained letters from 'Shocked' and 'Disgusted' readers, I received also the following letter which restored my sense of balance:

'A special thank you for your reply on the Church and virginity, which has helped us to clarify our thinking in this area and present some positive teaching to our children.

'We have had the experience of seeing our daughter choose to live with her boyfriend without the benefit of the Sacrament of Marriage.

'While not wanting to condone the situation, and concerned for the younger children, we have tried to keep the door open and continued to show our love and respect for our daughter and her fiance.

'They are soon to be married, and although we have mixed feelings, we look forward to the event with hope and joy. We would appreciate a prayer for us, and especially for the young couple.'

I doubt whether my reply would have been of much use to the lady who wrote that letter had I omitted the 'ifs' and 'buts' and simply classified the conduct of her daughter as mortally sinful.

I am sorry to have kept you in suspense for so long, but I will now answer the question which you posed. At the same time, I ask you to keep in mind what I have said above.

Here is the answer you have been waiting for: when an unmarried man and an unmarried woman have sexual intercourse outside of marriage they commit the serious sin of fornication.

Question 101:

While I agree with most of what you say, I am very surprised that in your answer to Q99, you, as a Catholic priest, made no mention of Our Lady. In my opinion you had a duty to do this when speaking on the issue of virginity in a Catholic paper.

It seems to me that you wrote what you did with an eye to non-Catholics, making concessions to them, while avoiding the specifically Catholic viewpoint.

You have an obligation to point out the wrongdoing in cohabiting and in all sexual relationships outside of Christian marriage.

It appears that you are going along with, and not confronting, the permissive society, which by its very nature opposes the Church's God-given authority and true Catholic teaching.

Catholics, as you must know, have a special regard for the virginal state for one reason only. It has everything to do with the historical fact that, when God's Son became man, he was born not of a married woman already a mother, nor someone 'with a past' like Mary Magdalene, but a pure virgin girl.

Today Catholic girls along with the rest are being coerced into having sexual relationships outside of marriage. And it doesn't help to have a Catholic priest saying that what is wrong is sometimes OK.

When I was at convent school we used to be told the story of St Maria Goretti, with the inference that in the same circumstances we should act as she did (preserve our virginity even unto death). That was rather rugged I agree; but at least the rightness of her attitude was upheld.

Today girls are being told that they are 'freaky' and 'inhibited' if they are not sexually involved. They are coerced into living with a man — or boy — to prove their love. When he decides he prefers his freedom, a new car, or maybe a boat, the girl is discarded.

Although I think the scar remains also with him, she is permanently harmed — spiritually and emotionally. I myself lived through the trauma of mistreatment at the hands of a supposedly 'good Catholic' boy — in reality a spoilt, over-indulged son.

You say couples coming to you to be married are not ashamed of having lived together previously. I hope you set them right on that! But have you thought of those who are presently living together and will never come to you or to anyone else to be married?

To my mind this is a contemporary tragedy of enormous proportions. The last thing Catholics should be is complacent about it. As a mother and formerly a teacher, I believe I see these matters clearly.

You have my prayers at all times in the difficult work you are doing — no easy role, I am sure. May God and Our Lady bless you.

Question 102:

What has become of sin? Lots of young people reading your reply could almost be excused for believing that living together, and having a sexual relationship, if the couple is promised to marry, although not the ideal, is not a sin.

Why use such words as 'ideal' when in truth to say 'seriously sinful' would be more to the point.

The nun who taught that it was 'quite all right for engaged couples promised to marry to engage in premarital sex' was not only guilty of 'gross oversimplification' but was downright wrong, and she is doing more harm than good.

If a girl remains a virgin before marriage, as she should, she can then instruct her own children to be as she was. If young people are not instructed rightly, they cannot be expected to know right from wrong.

Question 103:

As a mother of eight such teachings in our Catholic schools worry the heart out of me. Our young people should be made very aware of what sin is all about and how it offends Our Saviour who died because of it.

This would give them a greater appreciation of what is good and right, and would, I believe, result in fewer young people dropping out from attendance at Mass and the Sacraments, particularly the awful neglect of the Sacrament of Reconciliation.

Answer:

In my reply to Q99 I expressed my serious doubts as to whether any nun would have given the advice as quoted. Certainly there is no justification for the fear that this represents the standard teaching given on the subject in our Catholic schools.

In the same issue of *The Leader*, in reply to the direct question whether premarital sex is sinful, I said: 'When an unmarried man and an unmarried woman have sexual intercourse outside of marriage they commit the serious sin of fornication.'

I cannot accept that young people reading my original reply 'could almost be excused for believing . . . having a sexual relationship, if they have promised to marry, . . . is not a sin,' or could interpret my words to imply that premarital sex is 'sometimes OK.'

To come to such a conclusion would need a very selective reading of what I said.

In my original reply, I did not approach the question from the angle of law and sin, partly because I do not believe that this approach is the most effective line to take with young people in that situation.

When composing my answer I certainly did not have 'an eye to non-Catholics, . . . making concessions to them, while avoiding the specifically Catholic viewpoint.'

The viewpoint I proposed was indeed 'Catholic'. If I had an eye to anyone in particular, it was to the parents of those young people who are in such a situation, to parents of those who are approaching that age when they will be confronted with difficult moral choices, and the young people themselves.

My own pastoral experience indicates that most young Catholics living together outside of marriage are quite aware that their conduct is in conflict with the Church's presentation of God's law, and that they are in a sinful situation.

This knowledge has not been sufficient to deter them from their way of life.

In the face of the many negative pressures of modern society I believe it is necessary to confront young people with the ideal of Christian discipleship, and to provide positive motivation for living the Christian life.

Some readers obviously react against the word 'ideal' apparently seeing it as a way of watering down the Gospel of Christ.

But surely it is perfectly correct to say, for example, that the Church puts before married people the beautiful *ideal* of faithful, self-sacrificing love or that Christ presents his disciples with the *ideal* of taking up their cross and following him.

This is in no way to water down the teaching of Christ or the Church.

I am not saying that these are *merely* ideals in the sense of vague general principles of morality. They are ideals which every follower of Christ is bound in conscience to strive to attain. Failure to do so results in sin.

In the case of casual sex or promiscuous conduct, the sin committed is against Christ's command to love one's neighbour as oneself.

Sex without love involves using (or abusing) another person as an object of pleasure.

The nature of the sexual act as the expression of a full loving relationship and of total commitment needs to be impressed upon young people.

In the case of those promised to marry, the immorality of full sexual sharing arises out of the nature of marriage itself, especially its sacramental character.

When two baptised Christians marry, it is Christ who gives them to belong fully to each other, and only then do they receive the right to that full expression of sexual intimacy which is an integral part of married life and love.

Those who do not accept this sacramental vision of marriage, and who therefore choose to continue 'living together' and having sex before marriage, are not likely to be dissuaded by being told that what 'they are doing is seriously sinful.'

I did not mention Our Lady in reply to the original question, because I do not agree with the statement that 'Catholics have a special regard for the virginal state for one reason only.'

Certainly Mary can and should be presented to young people as the highest model of chastity, but this is not the same thing as saying that the Church's teaching on the restriction of sexual intercourse to the marital state is based on Mary's virginal conception of Jesus. It is not.

The Church's position is based on the nature of Christian marriage itself.

Question 104:

My opinion is that youngsters today who decide on sexual intercourse before marriage are perhaps not so much sinful as ignorant of the commitment the total sexual act represents.

And, if ignorance is a sin, then I would suggest that we are all mightily guilty in many areas of life. I would suggest further that, although many of us did not indulge in sexual intercourse before marriage, often the reasons for our abstinence could have been fear — fear of becoming pregnant, fear of parents, or fear of going to Hell!

Were we more virtuous than our kids today? I think not. I think that kids today are more honest about their sexuality than we of the previous generation.

Let us educate ourselves so that we may adequately educate our children about their sexuality as children of the Father instead of dishing out a load of 'dos and dont's' that they just don't respond to.

Unlike many of us, our kids are being taught to think for themselves about important issues and make their own decisions. As parents we had better have some honest and direct answers for our honest and direct children.

Question 105:

Thank you for your words of wisdom, as I have a precious daughter who has chosen to live with her fiance before they marry. Who on this earth is in a position to judge them?

*I try to look on them with the eyes of Jesus, who said
about the woman who had committed adultery: 'Whoever
is without sin, let him throw the first stone,' and I pray and
suffer with Christ for them.*

Question 106:

*I don't expect you to answer this letter. Indeed I'll be lucky if
the people who open your mail let it reach you.*

I refer to your anwer to Q 100.

*You say you doubt if a Yes or No answer would have been
of much help to the woman who was upset because her
daughter was living with her boyfriend.*

*St Paul had no such qualms. In 1 Corinthians 6:9 he tells
me that fornicators, adulterers, homosexuals, etc. will not
inherit God's Kingdom, and I would rather believe St Paul
than any Fr O'Shea or Pope.*

*Why can't your 'Yea' be 'Yea', and your 'Nay' be 'Nay' in
your answers?*

Answer:

On the *objective* level, sexual intercourse before or outside
of marriage constitutes serious sin in the teaching of the
Church, which has a valid mandate to interpret the will of
God.

Having said that, I would advise caution about interpreting St Paul's words in 1 Corinthians chapter 6, as a condemnation of premarital sex in general.

There is certainly room for doubt about whether he intended his condemnation to cover engaged couples, or
couples promised to marry.

The Greek word which Paul uses in this passage is
porneia.

Porneia is a general term in the Greek language for
immorality, and can describe various kinds of illicit sexual
activity.

Often only the context can determine exactly the kind of
immorality which is under consideration. For example, earlier in the same letter (1 Corinthians 5:1), Paul uses the word
to describe an incestuous union between a man and his
step-mother.

Who then are the 'fornicators' (that is, the immoral

people) who, according to Paul, will not inherit the kingdom of God (1 Corinthians 6:9-10)?

The context suggests that Paul has in mind the specific case of fornication with prostitutes (v.15-16).

To the degrading union of a man with a prostitute, Paul opposes the Christian's union with Christ (v.17).

But, even if Paul might have had in mind the sin of fornication in general, it is worth noting that he is not content simply to issue a condemnation or deliver a prohibition.

He realised it was not enough to classify certain conduct as seriously sinful, but that it was much more important to present his readers positive motivation for doing good and avoiding evil.

Paul might well have stopped at verse 10. After all, the non-candidates for the Kingdom of God had been clearly identified. But he chose to add some 'padding' as well.

He speaks of the Christian's membership of the body of Christ, the indwelling presence of the Holy Spirit, and the destiny of the Christian to eternal union with Christ.

This is, in fact, Paul's approach in nearly all his letters. He doesn't moralise, that is, he doesn't attempt to give answers or solutions to moral problems without first theologising.

He always states the general theological principles first, then deduces from them the rules or guidelines for moral action.

I therefore find myself in agreement with the writer who recognises the futility of merely 'dishing out a load of "dos" and "don'ts",' but who sees the need for providing positive motivation for young people in the area of sexual behaviour.

Whether the precise terminology used by St Paul is the most effective means of doing this today might be open to debate, but certainly the principles which he lays down remain valid.

(See also Q63.)

Question 107:

The view expressed on premarital sex in 'Question Box' (Q104-6) saddened and depressed me. You state: 'There is certainly room for doubt about whether St Paul intended his condemnation (of fornication) to cover engaged couples, or

couples promised to marry,' and you go on to say, 'I there-
fore find myself in agreement with the writer who recognises
the futility of dishing out a load of "dos" and "don'ts".'
  I think God did just that when he gave Moses the Ten
Commandments. He said: 'Thou shalt not commit adul-
tery' and didn't add 'unless you are engaged or promised to
marry'.
  The views which you express are a watering-down of the
laws of God, a weak surrender to the permissive age, and
coming from a priest they are a sad and depressing thing.

Answer:
There is really nothing to be sad or depressed about. First, if
you read the relevant passage which I was commenting
upon, namely 1 Corinthians 6:9ff., it should be clear to you
why there is room for doubt about whether Paul was there
condemning sex between engaged couples. The context
clearly suggests the specific case of fornication with
prostitutes.
  I am *not* saying that he approved of sex between engaged
couples. I am simply saying that he does not seem to consider their case in 1 Corinthians chapter 6.
  I trust you did not deliberately omit an important word in
your quotation from my reply to Q104-6. The omission of
one word can change the sense of a whole sentence. You
quote me as saying: 'I therefore find myself in agreement
with the writer who recognises the futility of dishing out a
load of "dos" and "don'ts".'
  The missing word is 'merely' and that is a very significant
omission. I spoke of 'the futility of *merely* dishing out . . .'
  It is also important to read the rest of the paragraph which
states that such commands and prohibitions need to be
accompanied and supplemented by 'positive motivation for
young people in the area of sexual behaviour'.
  In the light of your selective reading of my reply, it would
seem that your sadness and depression are largely self-
inflicted.
  And since you raise the matter of the Ten Commandments, let us consider them at a little more depth.
  When God gave the law to Moses, he did not *merely* issue
a list of 'dos' and 'don'ts'. If the Ten Commandments were

just that, and were to be considered in isolation, they would amount to a very inferior system of moral conduct.

There is much more involved in doing God's will than not killing, not committing adultery, not stealing, not bearing false witness, not coveting . . .

The negative formulation of these commandments indicates that they are intended as no more than a minimal response to God's invitation to love and serve him. (Incidentally, the sin committed by unmarried people who have sexual intercourse is not the sin of adultery.)

This is the whole point of Jesus' moral teaching in the Sermon on the Mount (Matthew chs 5-7), especially in that section (5:21-48) where he contrasts the requirements of the commandments with the moral attitudes demanded of his disciples.

In this section and in the whole of the Sermon, Jesus' aim is to provide his disciples with positive motivation for doing good and avoiding evil.

His moral teaching is summed up in his reply to the man who asked him what was in fact the most important commandment.

His answer was: 'Love of God, and love of neighbour'. The Ten Commandments are ways of applying that twofold command (love of God and of neighbour) to concrete life situations.

As I said above, if the Ten Commandments were to be taken in isolation, and seen as merely a list of commands and prohibitions, they would amount to a less than adequate moral system.

But of course they were never intended to be taken in isolation or understood apart from their context. Their context is the whole pattern of call and response which runs throughout biblical revelation, God's call for a human response.

The Old Testament is the story of a God who took the loving initiative of choosing a people to be his own, of delivering them from a life of slavery and bringing them into a life of freedom, and of making a covenant with them.

His part of.the covenant was his promise to love them, care for them, protect them and be faithful to them.

They, for their part, were called upon to respond with love and gratitude to the God who loved them first by serving and obeying him. The Ten Commandments are a summary, but incomplete statement, of the kind of response that he demanded of them.

They are ten striking appeals, ten invitations to the people to walk in the ways of the God who had redeemed them. They are much, much, more than a list of 'dos' and 'don'ts'.

Question 108:

I agree with your reader (Q107) regarding sex before marriage. You state: 'The sin committed by unmarried people who have sexual intercourse is not the sin of adultery'. I maintain it is; if not, what on earth is it?

The Ten Commandments were given to us to be obeyed. 'Thou shalt not commit adultery' means just that, and should be taken seriously and obeyed by all.

I am 73 years of age and have kept the Commandments all my life, except for a few slight faults. Therefore, I maintain that if one can keep the Commandments, they can be obeyed by all who frequent the Sacraments, pray, and take up the Cross of Christ.

Answer:

The sin of adultery is the sin committed by a married person who has sexual relations with someone other than his or her marriage partner, or by an unmarried person with someone who is married.

Unmarried people who have sexual intercourse between themselves commit the sin of fornication, not the sin of adultery.

Adultery carries the added gravity of injustice against the other partner in the marriage, being a violation of that person's marital rights.

Certainly the Ten Commandments should be taken seriously and obeyed by all. The whole point of my answer was to establish the right context for such acceptance and obedience.

The Commandments are part of the loving response demanded from us by the God who chose us, calls us, loves us, and has made a covenant with us.

They are ways in which we demonstrate our love for and gratitude to the God who loved us first. They are not just a series of commands and prohibitions issued by a law-making God.

Question 109:

Can we have just one more word on fornication? In your reply (Q 104-6) you said a mouthful when you quoted the Church's teaching on this subject, namely, that on the objective level sexual intercourse before and outside marriage constitutes a serious sin.

You admitted that the Church has the power to give this teaching and you did not allow any exceptions. That is the objective statement.

Really what more need one know? We're not in the realm of making judgments, that's God's domain, but surely we can have a simple, direct objective teaching. When defining the law, surely the Church was aware of the porneia *of St Paul yet it did not make any exceptions. Objectively, every act of fornicating is sinful.*

Aren't we underrating our young when we say that 'dos' and 'don'ts' are futile? They accept these in every day life through a wide range of circumstances and, of course, they will do the same on the teaching of God.

I reckon our young are sick and tired of a watered-down religion. Maybe some now have a screwed-up conscience through wishy-washy teaching, but it's not our job to leave them in that state.

Let's be objective. Let's shout from the housetops that fornication is always objectively wrong and then, gradually, the misinformed consciences will be brought back to the straight and narrow.

If the Church can't exert that influence then we have failed lamentably. But before we admit our failure, let's back the faith of the young and spell out clearly a few 'dos' and 'don'ts'.

Answer:

I will not go into all the points that you raise, as it will only mean going over ground already covered. I should think that my answer to Q107 covers many of the comments you make.

After quoting what I said about the objective immorality of sexual intercourse before or outside of marriage, you ask:

'Really, what more need one know?'. I would suggest that there is a great deal more that people need to know.

They need to know the *reasons* for the church's teaching on the immorality of premarital and extra-marital sex. They need to know about the Church's teaching on marriage as a Sacrament. They need to know that when Christ gives two people to belong to each other in marriage, he gives them rights and privileges which it is morally wrong to anticipate.

They need to know that observance of the commandments of God and of the Church is part of the love response which a loving God calls forth from them. They need to know about the primacy of conscience and the relationship of conscience to the teaching authority of the Church.

You say that 'our young are sick and tired of a watered-down religion'. I submit that the most watered-down religion of all is one that claims to reduce morality to commands and prohibitions, rather than present its adherents with positive motivation for their behaviour.

Finally, I cannot help but note the significant fact that not one of the critical letters which I have received on this moral issue mentions the word 'love'.

This is a strange omission given that Jesus stated clearly on more than one occasion (and Paul repeated this teaching) that the whole moral law is ultimately reducible to love; love is the fulfilment of the law.

Question 110:
We have been following your articles with interest in the continuing debate over sexual relationships. The topics have swung from the original advice given to school children to pre-marital sex and to contraceptives.

It would appear that the whole issue is particularly sensitive, as it has no doubt always been, and I am surprised and pleased that the topics can be so easily discussed — even debated!

That the issues can be debated at all is what surprises me most. Please allow me to add to the debate with these comments.

I would have thought that cohabitation involving pre-marital sex would have been premeditated, cooperative, intrinsically self-damaging, and extremely poor exemplary behaviour.

Premeditated, because it obviously cannot be entered into without a great deal of organisation; cooperative, as it requires the consent of both people; intrinsically self-damaging, because the self-discipline required is the same as is required on many occasions during marriage.

I fail to see the distinction between the pre-marital and post-marital situation and cannot believe that the control required in the latter should have any less restriction in it than in the former.

Finally, the example set by such a couple irrespective of the state of their own consciences must surely weigh heavily in the debate.

Further, the couple would not enter such a situation with the intention of having children, and their lack of constraint being what it is, they would undoubtedly be practising contraception.

Surely no matter how valid an argument may be for contraception within marriage, that argument could not apply to pre-marital cohabitation.

Finally, the very fact that the issue can be subjected to debate is misleading and confusing for young people.

Would it not be better to say 'It is wrong!' — no qualifications! And anyone who is tempted, or is even already in the situation, then has no basis for rationalising it. Christ is the perfect forgiver. He will understand and welcome back.

Answer:

For the most part, I agree with your observations. If I have any reservations about your final paragraph, I think that what I have said in the answers to Q104-7 should be sufficient to indicate my mind and purpose.

Through this protracted debate there have been three main points which I have intended to emphasise:

(a) The objective immorality (of a serious nature) of sexual intercourse before and apart from marriage;

(b) The need for a positive presentation of the Church's teaching on the subject, and the inadequacy of unsubstantiated prohibitions, for example, 'it is wrong because the Church says so!'

(c) The need for compassion on the part of parents and others towards young people who have chosen a way which is at variance with the Church's teaching (which is not to condone their behaviour).

Purgatory

Question 111:

A friend of mine in the Uniting Church claims that there is no biblical basis for our belief in the state of Purgatory. How should I reply to this?

Answer:

The word *purgatory* is not found in the Bible, but the Christian Church from the beginning has believed in a state of purgation or purification after death, in which the dead could be helped by the prayers of those on earth.

In the pre-Christian era, the Jews had only a vague notion of this but there is evidence from the late Old Testament period that there was a belief that it was 'a holy and wholesome thought to pray for the dead, that they may be loosed from their sins' (2 Maccabees 12:46).

Unfortunately, 2 Maccabees is one of those seven Old Testament books which the Protestants do not accept as canonical and are therefore excluded from non-Catholic editions of the Bible — or at least included only in a separate section under the heading *Apocryphal Books*.

The quotation from Maccabees is therefore not of much help in discussion with Protestants on the subject of biblical justification for the Church's teaching on Purgatory.

There is a New Testament passage which I think has significance. I refer to the section of 1 Corinthians 3:10-15, in which Paul describes his ministry and the responsibility of all who will follow him and build upon the foundation he has laid. Among these ministers will be those (v.15) whose works will not stand up to the searching test of God's judgment. These will suffer a loss.

Like a person escaping from a burning house, these ministers will be saved, but their work and reward will be lost.

That these preachers of the Gospel will be saved indicates

that their faults are not serious enough to deserve condemnation, and they have not ruined the communities for which they were responsible.

The doctrine of Purgatory is not taught explicitly in this passage, but we can find a certain support for it. Paul's metaphor suggests a punishment for faults that indeed deserve punishment, but do not exclude from salvation. Of course, when he wrote 1 Corinthians, Paul still hoped for the second coming of Christ in his own lifetime. And so he situates this medicinal punishment at the Last Judgment.

The word 'purgatory' has been in common use in the Church only since the 13th century, but the belief goes back to the very early days of Christianity.

Archaeological excavations of primitive Christian cemeteries show that prayers for the dead were a part of early Christian spirituality. The most ancient liturgies known, from both East and West, contain Prayers for the Dead, just as does our Mass today.

Many early Christian writers mention this practice. St Cyprian (245 AD) says that such prayers had been said in all Churches since the time of the Apostles. And many will recall the beautiful passage from St Augustine's *Confessions* in which he tells us of his mother, Monica's dying request: 'Lay this body anywhere at all; the care of it must not trouble you. This only I ask of you, that wherever you are you remember me at the altar of the Lord' (Book 9, Ch.11).

Question 112:

Recently a friend of mine returned from a Requiem Mass in very high spirits. He had been told, I don't know by whom, that everybody who is buried with a Requiem Mass goes straight to Heaven.

I find this hard to accept, and at variance with current Church teaching on the need for purgation. It is only in the years since my retirement that I have come to terms with Purgatory; and with death not far away, I have come to look forward to being purged of all my imperfections to permit me to be absorbed finally into the Divinity.

Rather than the state of horror and torment that was regularly depicted on the third night of our annual parish mission during the 1940s and 1950s, I have come to see Purgatory as a state of joy and happiness in which we are perfected and prepared for final union with God.

Would you please comment on my friend's statement, and explain your belief in Purgatory?

Could you please also explain the Church's teaching on Limbo?

Answer:

The word 'Purgatory' comes from the Latin term meaning purification or cleansing. The official teaching of the Church is that there is a Purgatory, but the Church has nothing to say about its duration. Indeed, duration in Purgatory is difficult to conceive, because in the hereafter time no longer exists.

Certainly, we must not imagine Purgatory to be a kind of flaming concentration camp, or any sort of temporary hell. It is blasphemous to think of God as demanding his last pound of flesh. It seems preferable to think of Purgatory not in terms of time or place or punishment, but in terms of a purifying process. It is rather the painful aspect of the passage from this life into God's loving presence. One author has called it, 'our shattering meeting with God in the experience of death.'

At the moment of death we are suddenly confronted with God and his infinite love.

In the light of this, many of us — if not all of us — will painfully and shamefully become aware of our weakness and sinfulness. It is easy to imagine how, at this passover from death to life, we will have pass through the purifying fire of God's love.

The pain of Purgatory has nothing in common with the pain of Hell. It is rather the pain of wanting to be made totally worthy of union with God.

Purgatory, then, will be the experience of people who know they are saved and invited into God's presence, for all eternity, but who also know that for this step to be taken, they need to be purified by the power of God's love.

It is possible that some people are completely purified in this life. Our earthly existence is a form of Purgatory as we die daily to whatever is selfish, untrue and unChrist-like, and are daily being raised up by Christ to share more deeply in his life. For those who are fully open to Christ's purifying action in this life, Purgatory is already negotiated.

If we understand Purgatory not in terms of a time of detention, but in terms of passage from the sinfulness of this life to the presence of God, we might ask how our prayers can affect a process that has apparently taken place in a moment of time.

We do not know how our prayers benefit those who experience Purgatory. But we pray in faith, believing that somehow in God's goodness and in the mystery of eternity, our prayers have made their passage to God less painful.

Contrary to what many Catholics may think, there has never been any dogmatic statement by the Church about the existence of a state called 'Limbo'. Nor did Jesus himself make any pronouncement from which we can draw definite conclusions about its existence.

Limbo has never been more than a theological theory. Some theologians have thought that children who die not baptised go to a state of perfect 'natural' happiness, but are deprived of the far greater happiness of union with God.

What pastor would not assure the parents of a child who died without baptism that their child was with God? To say otherwise would be to impose limits on the love and mercy of God. God is not compelled to conform to our human reasoning.

For one who really believes in a loving and merciful God, it is hard to accept that he would penalise in any way those who through no fault of their own have been deprived of the sacrament of baptism.

This scepticism about the existence of Limbo is in no way intended as an argument against early infant baptism. In the sacrament of baptism, Christ welcomes a new member into his community, the Church; the baptised person becomes an adopted child of God, a member of the body of Christ, a temple of the Holy Spirit. No further justification for baptism should be needed.

Question 113:

There is one thing about our faith which puzzles me. We talk about the need for Purgatory where a soul has to be cleansed entirely of all stain of sin before entering God's presence. And yet we are permitted to approach and receive Christ in the Eucharist, although venial sin and even forgiven mortal sin leave us unworthy for such intimate contact with him. Is there not a contradiction here?

Answer:

I would like to refer you first of all to Q112 where I described Purgatory in terms of a purifying process, not in terms of a time or place of punishment. It is rather the painful aspect of the passage from this life into God's loving presence. Perhaps what I say about Purgatory might go some way towards answering your query.

There is a difference between the two situations which you raise. Paul describes the difference between this life and the next in these terms: *For now we see in a mirror dimly, but then face to face* (1 Corinthians 13:12).

In the hereafter, when we come face to face with the infinite holiness of God, we will experience the need to be completely purified by the fire of God's love, before we can enjoy his presence for eternity.

In this life we live by faith. Though as baptised Christians we are temples of the Holy Spirit, we can never be completely free from sin and its consequences. And after all, the Church on earth exists for sinners, not for the perfect. Jesus himself said: *I came not to call the righteous, but sinners* (Mark 2:17).

Question 114:

Further questions on the nature of Purgatory and the gravity of missing Sunday Mass, continue to appear. One reader finds it difficult to understand why Purgatory cannot be a physical place, or have a duration in time.

Metaphysical reasoning, he says, allows for the existence of time and place 'beyond the grave'. As for the question of an occasional failure in the obligation of attending Mass on Sunday, he finds my view 'both erroneous and damaging'.

I apologise for having to present the questions in this form because of their length, but I trust that their main point has been retained.

Answer:

Like every priest and every Catholic, I have thought a lot about Purgatory, its nature and function. I have come to my present understanding of Purgatory as a view which is compatible with the teaching of the Church — one that I have found in my pastoral experience makes more 'sense' to people, and one that I find personally satisfying.

Whatever the metaphysical reasoning concerning the existence of time and place outside of this earthly existence, I have serious difficulty in conceiving Purgatory as a place where a person is detained for an allotted time determined by God and then released when the process of purgation has been completed.

I prefer to think of Purgatory as the painful state or experience of encountering God after death, when we see him as we really are. Time and place are no longer part of my thinking on the subject.

As for the question of the gravity of the 'occasional' missing of Sunday Mass, I have attempted in my reply to Q149 to clarify the earlier reply.

I notice you do not use the word 'mortal' yourself to describe the sin of those who may occasionally disobey the Church's law in this matter. Perhaps this indicates that your thinking on the subject is not really far from my own.

I do not believe that the deliberate, conscious decision to miss Sunday Mass, even once, is a light matter. I certainly do not question the right of the Church to make precepts which bind its members. Perhaps it is a matter of terminology.

Is mortal sin, that is, sin that causes spiritual death, an apt way of describing the condition of the believing, loving Catholic who is guilty of occasional failure in this regard?

Reconciliation

Question 115:

In earlier issues of this newspaper, the benefits of Confession, especially the First Rite, were extolled rather extensively. When I was young, there was only one rite, as far as I can remember. Confessions were held before and after Mass whenever and wherever possible, and at schools every month or so.

Pius XII in his encyclical Mystici Corporis, *published in 1943, gives seven reasons for frequent Confession. These are: Christian humility grows, bad habits are corrected, spiritual neglect and lukewarmness are countered, conscience is purified, the will is strengthened, a salutary self-control is attained, and grace is increased by virtue of the Sacrament itself.*

Some even went so far as to advocate daily Confession in order to be 'more perfect'.

Would you say that Catholics on the whole became better and more practising Christians as a consequence of frequent Confession being encouraged? If not, could you state your reasons as to why this did not happen?

Could frequent Confession give people a 'guilt complex'? I presume that many would have developed one. In my opinion, unless it were approached in a very careful way, it could cause undue anxieties for persons not mature enough to handle problems of conscience because of their mental or emotional makeup, or because of their strict upbringing.

Otherwise, it would take a well-informed, balanced and well-adjusted person not to be disturbed in some way or another.

Could this drive for reconciliation be a result of ideologies — that sin (wrong) can only be done, when it goes against the directives of the State or society; that there is no such thing as sin or guilt — that it has been cleverly imposed on us by authority to manipulate and control those under them?

Answer:

You speak of a 'drive for reconciliation'. I presume you are referring to the increasing use of the term 'Reconciliation', in place of 'Penance' and 'Confession', as the Sacrament has previously been known.

Certainly 'reconciliation', the word and the idea, is not the product of any secular ideology, despite its welcome use by some Australian politicians recently. It is a term and concept with solid roots in the New Testament.

St Paul uses it to describe the life and work of Christ: 'God . . . through Christ reconciled us to himself and gave us (the Apostles) the ministry of reconciliation; that is, God was in Christ reconciling the world to himself . . . and entrusting to us the message of reconciliation . . . we beseech you, on behalf of Christ, to be reconciled to God' (1 Corinthians 5:18-20).

There is a definite advantage in describing the Sacrament as one of Reconciliation, rather than as Penance, or Confession. These terms place the emphasis on the action of the penitent; Confession — his confessing of his sins; Penance — his performance or saying of a penance imposed by the priest.

The term 'reconciliation' puts the emphasis where it should lie; on the action of Christ, who reconciles the repentant sinner with God, with the community and with himself. It also invites the penitent to approach the Sacrament more positively.

Instead of just asking 'What sins have I committed?', he is invited to ask the more fundamental question: 'What does Christ most want to heal in my life, here and now, through my reception of the Sacrament?'.

Reconciliation certainly does not imply that there is no such thing as sin or guilt. On the contrary, it presupposes sin and guilt. Sin is as much a reality as the air we breathe and the ground we walk on.

But sin is not just a matter of actions. Much more basically, it is a matter of attitudes and values. Our external actions are often only the symptoms and the end result of those interior attitudes which are most in need of Christ's healing.

Therefore, the most important question to ask in one's examination of conscience or review of life is not 'What have I done?' but 'What kind of person am I that makes me think and speak and act the way I do?'.

One of the main reasons for the scrupulosity, the anxiety and the guilt complex which many penitents experience, is that they have been instructed from childhood to ask the wrong question. Too much emphasis has been placed on *their* Confession and not enough on the forgiveness of Christ.

He is less interested in our miserable list of sins than he is in ourselves.

Pius XII's seven reasons for frequent confession constitute a strong argument for regular reception of the Sacrament. Daily sacramental Confession is unnecessary and undesirable.

In most cases, it would only serve to trivialise the Sacrament and encourage scrupulosity. Of course, Christ's forgiveness is by no means restricted to the Sacrament of Penance or Reconciliation. Daily acknowledgment of one's sinfulness and need for forgiveness is to be encouraged.

You ask whether Catholics in the past have become 'better Christians' as a consequence of frequent Confession, and then ask: 'If not, why not?'.

I suggest that if frequent confession did not lead in some cases to spiritual growth, it might have been because penitents continued to ask themselves the same questions in their examination of conscience and come up with the same answers — week after week, month after month.

Not surprisingly, they became bored with this routine and sterile recitation of the same faults. I believe this is the main reason for the decline in the number of people availing themselves of the Sacrament.

Probably the most important thing is to realise that the Sacrament of Penance or Reconciliation, like all the Sacraments, is a celebration.

In this case, the celebration of God's forgiveness, an occasion to thank and praise him because he is a God who takes delight in forgiving.

Question 116:

I received a tremendous amount of satisfaction from your reply regarding 'that new term Reconciliation' (Q115). I have been seeking to make the Sacrament more meaningful in my life to achieve the end results stated by Pius XII. Could you expand on your reply regarding what you think is reasonable, as to 'frequent' Confession, and also could you recommend a book that I could read for more enlightenment on this matter?

Answer:

I am pleased that you found my reply to the question on Reconciliation so helpful.

How often one should make use of the Sacrament depends to a large extent on the individual need. There are special circumstances and special times.

Someone might have committed some upsetting sin or series of sins, and wants to express his or her sorrow and be reconciled. Someone might feel a particular need for Christ's special help to do something about some sinful attitude, or one might experience the need to recommit oneself to a more fervent Christian life.

Most Catholics today are making use of private Confession (the First Rite of Reconciliation) less frequently than before. This may not be a bad thing in individual cases, though I fear that, in general, neglect of the Sacrament for prolonged periods has a detrimental effect on one's spiritual condition.

As a general rule, for a person seriously intent on deepening his or her relationship with God and other people, and appreciating the important help provided by the Sacrament of Reconciliation to achieve this aim, I would recommend monthly celebration of the Sacrament.

Unfortunately, only a small minority of Catholics now approach the Sacrament as frequently as that. On the other hand, it must be admitted that many who are confessing only once or twice yearly are making use of the Sacrament much more meaningfully than they did in the past. It is very difficult to lay down any hard and fast rule.

Of course, a person whose conscience informs him that he is in a state of serious sin should be reconciled as soon as possible, so that he can return to the Eucharist with a clear conscience.

A couple of books on the subject that you might find helpful are *Reconciling* by Fr J. Buckley and *The Sacrament of Reconciliation* by Fr Bernard Haring.

Question 117:

What is the teaching of the Church on Reconciliation? Does the division between venial and mortal sin still hold? May a person receive Communion before the Sacrament of Reconciliation, if guilty of mortal sin?

Answer:

The Sacrament of Penance or Reconciliation is one of the seven Sacraments of the Church; that is, one of those high points or peak moments in the life of a Catholic when the risen Christ, acting through his minister, the priest, forgives the sins of those who truly repent and sincerely seek his pardon.

As I have explained in a previous reply, the term 'Reconciliation' has an advantage over 'Penance' and 'Confession' because it places the emphasis on the action of Christ, where it should lie.

Both Penance and Confession describe an activity of the penitent, whereas Reconciliation describes the action of Christ who reconciles the sinner with God and with the Christian community.

This communal aspect of the Sacrament is important, because the priest, when administering the Sacrament, acts not only as the representative of the forgiving Christ, but also as the representative of the forgiving community.

This is important because every sin which we commit as members of Christ's body has an injurious effect on the body or community as a whole.

The Church's teaching remains that Catholics should avail themselves of this Sacrament at least once a year.

Those who are serious about growing in the spiritual life, seeking God's forgiveness and praising and thanking him for his gift of forgiveness, should make use of the Sacrament more frequently than that.

The division between mortal and venial sin does still hold. Many theologians today regard this as an inadequate division and suggest a threefold division of mortal, serious and venial sin.

The word 'mortal' describes the kind of sin which destines a person to eternal death and condemnation to Hell.

Perhaps this term is better applied to those who choose a way of life which is diametrically opposed to God's way and which implies a deliberate rejection of God's love and forgiveness.

Individual sinful acts of a grave nature, committed in weakness or passion but without the explicit intention of turning away from God, might be described as serious, rather than mortal.

As far as reception of the Eucharist is concerned, if a Catholic commits a sin which his/her conscience registers as mortal or serious, he/she is obliged to have recourse to the Sacrament of Reconciliation before presuming to receive Holy Communion.

Question 118:

An issue that I frequently hear discussed when the subject of Reconciliation is raised is the use of 'group Confession' or 'General Absolution' as an alternative to the Sacrament as it is celebrated on an individual basis. What does the modern Church see as the proper limits to the use of such 'group absolution'?

Question 119:

Is it enough for a Catholic to go to Reconciliation only according to the Third Rite? I have been a Catholic for only a few years and have been to the Third Rite several times. Although I have been to Reconciliation privately a couple of times, I am most uncomfortable with it and find I prefer the Third Rite. Could you please help me?

Answer:

The new Code of Canon Law has this to say about the celebration of the Sacrament of Penance or Reconciliation with General Absolution:

'General Absolution without prior individual Confession, cannot be given to a number of penitents together, unless: . . . there exists a grave necessity; that is, given the number of penitents, there are not enough confessors available to hear properly the individual Confessions within an appropriate time, so that without fault of their own the penitents are deprived of the sacramental Grace or of Holy Communion for a lengthy period of time.

'A sufficient necessity is not, however, considered to exist when confessors cannot be available merely because of a great gathering of penitents, such as can occur on some major feast day or pilgrimage.

'It is for the diocesan bishop to judge whether the above conditions are present. Mindful of the criteria agreed with the other members of the episcopal conference, he can determine the cases of such necessity' (Canon 961).

This legislation would seem to answer the question about 'the proper limits' which the Church sets to the use of General Absolution.

However, the final paragraph of the Canon explains the lack of a common policy throughout the Church, concerning the use of General Absolution. As far as Australia is concerned, the National Conference of Bishops has not as yet formally agreed on any definite criteria. In the interim, the bishops of individual dioceses have felt free to determine when a genuine case of necessity exists.

The practice in some dioceses is that priests are permitted to announce in their parishes a communal Rite of Reconciliation on special occasions. It is not permitted to announce the Third Rite, that is General Absolution, without prior individual Confession.

Should the number of priests be sufficient, in such circumstances the Sacrament should be celebrated according to the Second Rite, that is, with individual Confession for penitents in the context of a communal penitential service.

However, should the number of penitents make it impossible for the priests available to hear the individual Confessions, a case of necessity is adjudged to exist, and General Absolution may be given. In parishes in those dioceses which permit General Absolution under such conditions, the Sacrament is usually administered in this way once or twice a year, for example, prior to Easter and/or Christmas.

This restriction of General Absolution to one or two occasions each year is in itself an indication that it is *not* meant to be seen as an alternative to the First Rite of individual Confession.

Those whose conscience accuses them of serious sins receive forgiveness for those sins through General Absolution, provided the condition of true repentance is fulfilled.

However, the obligation remains with them to confess those sins privately at a later time.

For their own sake they need to complete the process of being reconciled with God and the Church by confessing their sins personally, really facing up to them, admitting them to a priest as a minister of Christ and representative of the community , and receiving from him an appropriate penance and whatever advice and guidance might be necessary.

Although those who are not conscious of serious sin, and have received General Absolution are not obliged to make an individual Confession, some of the reasons proposed in the previous paragraph might apply to them as well. It seems at least desirable for all to experience the Sacrament of Reconciliation according to both individual and communal rites.

The future of the Third Rite of Reconciliation with General Absolution remains somewhat uncertain. At the 1983 World Synod of Bishops in Rome, several bishops (including Australia's representatives) made a strong plea for its celebration to continue to be permitted in the kind of circumstances I have outlined above.

They would have included in their argument the fact that it has proved a most popular, moving and powerful liturgical rite in those dioceses where it has been approved. And on the evidence of many priests, they would have claimed with justification that, far from substituting for individual Confession, it has in many instances encouraged people to return to the First Rite, and brought people back to the Church.

As for the future, any criteria which the National Bishops' Conference agrees upon will depend on what the Pope decides following the recent Synod of Bishops.

Religion and Morality

Question 120:

In regard to the comment you made in answer to a previous question, I do not agree with you that the Church has the right to make moral laws to regulate the conduct of its members. I would love to know why the Church makes so many moral judgments on people.

I am a devoted Catholic myself, but I do not make moral judgments about what other people want to do. And as a student of philosophy at the University of Newcastle I do not make any form of judgment on anybody.

How are religion and morality related?

Answer:

I believe an answer to your question, 'How are religion and morality related?' can be found in the pages of Scripture. The Bible is the source book for two of the great world religions, Judaism and Christianity; and each of the Testaments, Old and New, contains a sizeable proportion of moral teaching and moral law.

The pattern we find running throughout the Bible to describe the way God deals with his people is one of call and response. In the Old Testament we are told that God chose a people to be his own, he delivered them from a life of slavery and brought them into freedom, and he entered into a covenant with them.

This covenant relationship was initiated and motivated solely by God's love. By it he undertook to love and protect the people he had chosen. For their part they were called to respond to the love which Yahweh, their God, had demonstrated in their regard. This loving response necessarily implied service and obedience — and the Ten Commandments are a summary of the kind of conduct their response should involve.

The moral law embodied in the Ten Commandments did not lose its force with the coming of Jesus Christ. In him God made a new covenant with the human race demonstrating his love more powerfully by sending his own son to offer himself as a sacrifice for sin. Again a human love response to God's saving action is demanded.

Jesus did not deny the enduring validity of the Ten Commandments, but he called on his followers to display a righteousness greater than that of the scribes and Pharisees (Matthew 5:17-20).

And so he refined, spiritualised and perfected the old moral law by the kind of moral teaching found, for example, in the Sermon on the Mount (Matthew 5-7). He taught his disciples that all morality can be reduced to love, love of God and love of neighbour (Mark 12:29-31 and elsewhere).

St Paul repeated this fundamental teaching of Jesus (Romans 13:8-10) but Paul, like Jesus himself, knew well that with our proneness to sin we need laws to serve as guidelines for putting into effect this double commandment of love.

The Church, the community which Christ established to continue his saving presence and activity in the world, would not be faithful to the intention of its founder if it did not put before its members laws of life to instruct and safeguard them in their moral conduct.

The Church's mandate for this is to be found in the very circumstances of its foundation, but specifically in such texts as: 'He who hears you (the disciples), hears me' (Luke 10:16) and 'whatever you bind on earth shall be bound in Heaven; and whatever you loose on earth shall be loosed in Heaven' (Matthew 16:19; 18:18).

There would appear to be confusion in your mind between moral law and moral judgment. The prohibition against judgment found in the Sermon on the Mount (Matthew 7:1) is directed at individual Christians, and concerns personal responsibility, not objective law. A better insight into the early Church's attitude to law might perhaps be found in a passage like Matthew 18:15-18.

As a Christian, I can hardly refrain from judging that actions like murder, theft, adultery and perjury are objectively evil. What Christ does ask me to refrain from passing judgment on is the personal responsibility of the one who performs such actions. Such judgments must be left to God.

So while it is true that laws should not be multiplied unnecessarily to become oppressive and burdensome, and thus interfere with that freedom which is the essence of the Christian vocation, the Church has indeed received from Christ the mandate to pronounce on questions of morality and to make laws for its members where necessary. In doing so, the criterion must always be how best can the Catholic be assisted to apply the divine commandment to love God and neighbour to his or her daily life situation.

Question 121:

I am disturbed by the number of individuals who seem able to lead adequate, positive, moral, balanced lives without any religious convictions, while others lead similar lives because of their religious convictions.

I cannot help wonder, sometimes, that religion (and Christianity in particular with its emphasis on love) is not something that affects people who have a deepseated psychological need and emotional dependence. They find this satisfied by accepting an invisible, all-powerful Father who is supported by a visible, organisational structure, the Church.

My wonder is reinforced by the apparent thriving of religion in times of adversity, and its weakness when human needs are satisfied in other ways.

Answer:

If you do not mind my saying so, I believe you are approaching things from the wrong direction. The Christian position is that people believe, and express that belief through affiliation with a visible, believing community, because God has called them to faith and to membership of the Church. This is a basic Christian premise: that faith is a gift from God.

God's call or invitation does demand a human response, of course — a response which can be positive or negative. It is when we come to consider the response of those who accept God's call that we can speculate on the human reasons why they do so. Not that I think there is much to be gained from such speculation.

Every person is an individual, and the human motivation

which leads people to accept God's offer of faith varies from person to person.

In his earthly ministry, Jesus ministered to the whole person, and the Church also exists for the whole person — intellect, will, emotions, and so on. If there are people who find their emotional and psychological needs satisfied by the Church, there is no reason to be concerned about that.

Whether that was the dominant factor in their acceptance of God's call is not for others to judge. Our discernment should be directed to the depth of our own commitment to Christ and his Church.

As for those who live good lives without apparent religious convictions, we do not know how God chooses to exercise his universal saving will in the case of particular individuals.

Certainly, salvation is possible outside the visible entity of the Church, and God's grace is operative in people's lives outside the structure of the Church.

The Church is a community called into existence by God to be a visible sign to the world of love, unity, reconciliation, and all those qualities which Christ intended his followers to display.

It is meant to be a living witness that this quality of life and love and truth is possible. That there are 'anonymous Christians' outside the visible Church is an undeniable fact of experience.

Your observation that religion often seems to thrive in times of adversity and wither in times of affluence is a sad, but true commentary on the fickleness and inconstancy of the human spirit.

Resurrection

Question 122:

My hope in persevering in this life is based on my faith in God and in Heaven. The question I put before you is very dear to me, but the Gospels seem to deny sex and marriage a place in the Kingdom of Heaven. Here is my question: When we meet in heaven, will my wife still regard me as her husband? My doubts are caused by Matthew 22:30.

Answer:

In his reply to the Saducees, Jesus is explaining in Matthew 22:29-32 the true nature of the Resurrection and the risen life. It is not a 'coming back' to earthly life; it is a going forward into a totally new form of life in God's presence.

The physical and sexual relationships of this world will have been transcended. Jesus does not mean that the saved will have no 'bodies'. The comparison which he makes with angels is meant to convey the idea of a new kind of bodily existence.

We have no blueprint of what form the risen body will take. In fact, Paul in 1 Corinthians 15:35 rejects the question asked of him about the nature of the resurrected body. The best description he could bring forward is that of a 'spiritual body' (1 Corinthians 15:44) which might seem like a contradiction in terms. Actually, what he means is a form of existence in which the person will be fully in possession of, or possessed by, the Holy Spirit.

In this heavenly spiritual existence, there can and will be no sex and marriage as they are experienced in this world. But eternal hapiness would seem to demand that we continue to know and love in a special way those whom we have known and loved on earth, and to be deeply conscious of their company.

It is unthinkable that we would be withdrawn from the

presence of those whom God has given us to love and care for in this life. Our loved ones in this world do not constitute an obstacle to our relationship with God; on the contrary, if the love is worthy and noble, our earthly relationships enhance and enrich our experience of God. So while it might be argued that the enjoyment of God's presence and the direct vision of him will be all we need to ensure our eternal happiness, I believe that the continuing enjoyment of the presence of those whom God has given us must be an integral part of our heavenly existence.

This is especially true of the married. In the Sacrament of Marriage, God gives two people who already belong to him by Baptism to belong in a special way to each other. It is as married people that they are called to holiness, and even given responsibility for each other's spiritual welfare.

Eternal life will be the crowning of our life in Christ which we live by faith in this world. When faith gives way to the vision of God, those who have walked with us and loved us on our pilgrimage must be with us to share the glory.

Question 123:

St Luke's Gospel (24:13-24) says that on the day of the Resurrection, Cleopas was one of the two disciples walking over the hills from Jerusalem to Emmaus when the risen Christ Jesus joined them, and they did not recognise him.

Who was the companion of Cleopas? I wonder why Luke of all people doesn't tell us. Have you discovered from your studies who he was? The relevant Gospel passage has always been a favourite of mine.

Answer:

I agree with you in your assessment of that passage from Luke's Gospel, describing the communication between the risen Lord and the two disciples on the way to Emmaus. It is one of my favourite passages too.

Unfortunately, I cannot answer your question about the identity of the second disciple, or why Luke suppressed his name, if he knew it. Some commentators suggest that Cleopas may have been Luke's source of information for the story.

Interestingly, there is an old tradition that Cleopas was the brother of Joseph, the foster-father of Jesus. But there is no biblical foundation for this tradition.

Question 124:

Over the years, I have recited the Creed concluding with the words 'I believe in the resurrection of the body and life everlasting'. I am now in my sixties, and I would appreciate your thoughts on what type of body I will have if I make it to Heaven.

Mary, the Mother of God, was given a great and singular honour of being taken to Heaven, body and soul. So it is logical to assume that we humans will not have the similar privilege of having this earthly body in Heaven.

If the body that one has in Heaven is not the same as the earthly one, then there can be no pleasure from the senses, as we experience them in this world.

A mother on her deathbed is often told not to sorrow, because she will see her loved ones in Heaven one day. If there is to be pleasure for a mother seeing her loved ones in Heaven, what about her not seeing a certain member of the family who does not make it to Heaven? My conclusion is: the happiness of Heaven is beyond our human comprehension.

Answer:

Your conclusion really answers most of your question. You have excellent support for your statement in the words of St Paul: 'Eye has not seen, ear has not heard, nor has it so much as dawned on man what God has prepared for those who love him' (1 Corinthians 2:9).

As for your question about the nature of the 'body' we shall have in the after-life, St Paul is not so helpful here. In the same letter (1 Corinthians 15:35), Paul says: 'Perhaps someone will say, "How are the dead to be raised up? What kind of body will they have?" A nonsensical question!' These are Paul's words, not mine.

In 1 Corinthians 15:44, he speaks of the risen body as a 'spiritual body'. This might seem to us a contradiction in terms, since in our experience the body is material, not spiritual. We have to remember, however, that Paul was thinking and writing in Jewish categories.

For the Jews, the 'body' was the equivalent of the 'person'. The Greeks thought of the human person as an incarnate soul, but the Jews thought in terms of an animated body.

Consequently, the Greeks, whose thought patterns we

have inherited, considered the after-life in terms of immortality of the soul; the Jews, on the other hand, thought in terms of the resurrection of the body. Because of their indentification of body and person, they could not conceive of any kind of life without a body.

When Paul speaks of a 'spiritual body', he simply means the human person fully possessed and penetrated by the Holy Spirit. As for the nature of that body, Paul categorically refuses to speculate.

Certainly, the 'body' we will have in heaven will not be the same as our earthly, physical, corruptible body. The risen Christ himself did not possess the same kind of body after his Resurrection as before. There was indeed identity between the Jesus who died on the Cross and the Christ who rose, but there was also change.

Your thinking on the Assumption of Mary seems to be astray. The dogma of the Assumption states that Mary, by reason of her privileged position as Mother of Jesus, already enjoys — in anticipation — the glorified state that we all hope ultimately to attain.

Mary's earthly body is not in Heaven. When you say that 'we humans' will not have the same privilege as she, you are forgetting the fact that Mary was no more or less human than you and I.

It would be against Catholic orthodoxy to attribute to her — greatest of the saints as she is — a kind of eternal life different from all who are united to Christ in faith and love.

Finally, you express your concern about the lack of any knowledge of pleasure of the senses in Heaven, because of the absence of an earthly body. It would seem to me that the kind of experience we will have of God will render any sense experience unnecessary.

Similarly, our 'seeing' and awareness of our loved ones will not require any physical vision or hearing or touch. We must not think of Heaven in physical or material terms.

Question 125:

You say (Q124) that 'Christ's earthly body is not in Heaven'. We are not told of the location where the body decayed, nor is any satisfactory explanation given as to why it was not found on the day of the Resurrection.

'If Christ be not risen', says St Paul, 'then our faith is in

*vain' (1 Corinthians 15). If you are right, then our faith is
certainly in vain. Thankfully, you are not right.*

*As a parent, I have a responsibility before God for my
children. I would think that you have a similar responsibility
to present Catholic teaching in a supposedly Catholic paper.*

Answer:

Your letter implies that you believe I deny the Resurrection
of Christ. If you still believe that, after reading the numerous
words on the subject which I have written, then I suppose
nothing I can say is going to change your mind. However, I
shall make one last effort.

By saying that Christ's earthly body is not in Heaven I do
not for a moment suggest that it remained buried or that it
decayed. It was transformed by the power of the Holy Spirit
so that it was changed from being his earthly, physical body
to a different state altogether — a risen, glorified body.

What was the composition of this new 'body' of Christ?
We do not know. How did it happen? We do not know. It is
a mystery of faith. What we do know is that the risen body
of Christ was, and is, no longer his earthly body.

The important thing which we must hold is that there is
an identity of person between the Jesus who died and rose,
but a transformation has taken place which results in a
completely new and different mode of existence . . .

This is just one of several letters which continue to appear
on the nature of the risen glorified body, whether that of
Christ, or of Mary, or of all believers at the general
resurrection.

Unless some new line of thought is put forward I do not
think there is any point in pursuing the subject further. I
believe that almost everything that can be said on the matter
has been said, and that just about every possible objection
has been raised. We are beginning to go round and round in
circles.

Perhaps we might let St Paul have the last word: 'Someone
may ask "how are the dead raised, and what sort of body do
they have when they come back", they are stupid questions'
(1 Corinthians 15:35; Jerusalem Bible translation).

Question 126:

Your answer to the question about the human body in

Heaven has me in a wee bit of a quandary. You say Christ's risen body was not the same as before, yet he invited the doubting Thomas to come and put his hand in his side, and feel the holes in his hands, the result of his Crucifixion.

Answer:

It is true that in John's Gospel, the risen Lord invites Thomas to put his finger in the wounds in his hands and side (John 20:27), indicating that Christ appeared to his disciples a week after his Resurrection in a form that showed the marks of the wounds inflicted in his crucifixion.

But this is only one side of the picture. The same Gospel tells us that Jesus was able to come and stand among his disciples, even though the doors of the room were locked (John 20:19).

Evidently, his risen body was not subject to the same restrictions as an earthly, physical body. He was apparently able to appear and disappear at will.

John also reports that Mary Magdalene failed to recognise Jesus after his Resurrection. When she saw Jesus, she did not know him, but supposed him to be the gardener (John 20:14-15). Again, Peter and the other disciples did not know Jesus when they saw him on the beach (John 21:4).

Moreover, Luke reports that the two disciples on the way to Emmaus walked and talked with Jesus for a long time without recognising him. It was only when he 'broke bread' that 'their eyes were opened and they recognised him; and he vanished out of their sight' (Luke 24:16, 30-31, 35).

Clearly, on weight of evidence, there was a difference between the earthly body and the risen body of Jesus.

What we must hold is the identity between the Jesus who died on the Cross and the Christ who rose from the dead, but at the same time acknowledge that there has been a transformation from his physical earthly body to his risen glorified body.

The Resurrection of Jesus was not just a resuscitation of a corpse, but a transition to a new mode of existence.

Question 127:

To judge from some of your answers to questions regarding the Easter texts in the Gospels, you seem to misinterpret some points.

As regards Christ's appearances, first to Mary Magdalene; why did she not recognise him at once? Common sense can give us the explanation. It was early morning.

His appearance must have changed after the ordeal of the Passion and Crucifixion and the tomb, followed by the transfiguration of the Resurrection, and finally she expected to find and to see a body, not the living Jesus. But she recognised his voice when he lovingly called her name.

Similar reasons explain the failure of the men on the road to Emmaus to recognise Jesus.

Although they had heard the tale of the Resurrection, their minds were not free yet to throw off the impact of the events of the past three days. And when Jesus joined them they barely looked up, still wrapped up in their misery.

Like Socrates, Christ simulated ignorance before he opened their minds and hearts and finally their eyes, so that they recognised him in the breaking of bread.

What a lesson, how to read and how to preach the word of God, so that hearts are burning and lifted up and able to recognise the Lord in the Eucharist!

Answer:

I find it difficult to accept your 'common sense' interpretation of the Gospel accounts of the appearances of the risen Christ.

The appearance of the risen Lord to Mary Magdalene is reported in John's Gospel. All the evangelists were theologians, but the fourth Gospel is the most theological of them all.

A close study of this Gospel reveals that its author does not operate along the lines you suggest. The kind of 'natural' and 'psychologising' explanation which you give of Mary's failure to recognise the risen Christ does not square with the approach adopted to the mystery of Christ throughout the Gospel.

Your explanation of the Emmaus story in Luke seems even less acceptable: that 'they barely looked up, still wrapped in their misery.'

And this, over a journey of probably many miles, during which this mysterious stranger took them through the whole of the Scriptures, explaining how the events of recent days had fulfilled God's plan!

We must be careful not to stop at interpretations of the Scriptures which may seem to satisfy the requirements of common sense, but may in fact be naive and superficial. Every Gospel passage must be considered in its context, and sometimes the context in question is nothing less than the entire Gospel.

Question 128:

It was with some interest that I followed your exposition of the nature of Christ's risen body. It would appear from the evidence of the Scriptures that Christ's risen body was indeed different from his earthly body.

This change can also be supported on the basis of reason, apart from the Scriptural evidence available. Unfortunately, however, it raises the question of the truth of the concept of transubstantiation, the change from bread and wine to the Body and Blood of Christ.

If the concept of transubstantiation were true, then it must follow that there was no need for any change in Christ's risen appearance from his earthly appearance, since transubstantiation teaches that an object may remain unchanged to the senses, yet at the same time be changed nevertheless.

My point is this: How can one believe in the difference in the appearance of Christ's risen body from that of his earthly body, and at the same time believe in the concept of transubstantiation, which maintains that a change can take place in an object without any indication to the senses that a change indeed has occurred?

Answer:

It appears that the matter of transubstantiation constitutes something of a problem for you in the area of faith.

For the uninitiated, transubstantiation was the name given by some mediaeval theologians, and subsequently adopted in official Church documents, to the process which occurs when bread and wine are changed in the Eucharist into the Body and Blood of Christ.

The word means that the substance of bread and wine has been changed, but their appearance, taste, feel, etc. remain as before.

I do not see the logic of the parallel which you draw

between the Eucharist and the transformation from the earthly to the glorified body of Christ. In the case of the Eucharist the bread and wine cease to be that and are really changed into Christ's body and blood.

In the case of the Resurrection, however, as well as transformation there remains a substantial or essential identity between the Jesus who dies and the Christ who rose.

The two cases are quite different.

Question 129:

In your answer to Q128 you state, 'In the case of the Eucharist, the bread and wine cease to be that and are really changed into Christ's body and blood'. To speak thus infers that the bread and wine are negated.

It makes the Catholic position on this Sacrament to be one of an impossible and mysterious dogma. The language expressed is out of date, is not correct, and has no part in a single reality.

Rather in this day and age of Einsteinian cosmology, we should be saying that Christ chooses to dwell in bread and wine as tangible communal love (containing sacrifice within himself) because the truth is, as long as that matter of bread and wine is just that, it is that and nothing else.

It does not disappear after the consecration, only is lived in by spirit. The Eucharist is even as we are — matter vivified by spirit, the Holy Spirit.

With all respect I believe it is time to throw out the anachronistic way of explaining this dogma. It is untruthful, and does not make for an intelligent Church.

Answer:

I make no apology for giving the impression that the Catholic position on the Sacrament of the Eucharist is 'mysterious'. Indeed it is. As for its being 'impossible', perhaps the words of the Lord in another context are relevant also at this point: 'With men this is impossible but with God all things are possible' (Matthew 19:26).

I subscribe fully to the view that the formulas used in defining dogmas of faith are time-conditioned, and that sometimes a reformulation and respresentation of doctrine is desirable and even necessary, if the Church's teaching is to have any relevance for, or impact on, contemporary man.

However, I cannot go along with those who would re-interpret the Church's dogmatic teachings to the extent that they are emptied of their original content, and change from their original purpose.

Whatever about 'Einsteinian cosmology', I feel that your plea for a re-statement of the Church's dogma of Christ's Eucharistic presence — the way his body and blood are present under the forms of bread and wine — falls into this latter category.

Your understanding of the Eucharist would appear to be an updated version of Luther's theory of 'consubstantiation' which has been condemned by the Church in a way that does not seem to allow for reformulation.

The Council of Trent stated: 'If anyone says that in the Sacrament of the Eucharist, the substance of bread and wine remains along with the body and blood of Our Lord Jesus Christ, and denies the complete change of the substance of bread to his body, and of the substance of wine into his blood, with only the appearances of bread and wine remaining, let him be an anathema (that is, excommunicated)'.

These are strong words, and it would seem to me that it leaves very little space for anyone to hold a view of the Eucharist such as the one you propose, and still claim to be faithful to the Catholic tradition.

Perhaps you should try to allow more for the 'mystery' element, and put more stress on the faith dimension rather than be striving for a satisfying intellectual comprehension of what is described after all in the Eucharistic prayers as 'this mystery of faith'.

Question 130:

What is the Catholic Church's teaching on reincarnation? Are Catholics free to believe in it? Are there any books printed about the subject?

Answer:

Belief in reincarnation is currently enjoying a period of popularity, mainly among those who have had some exposure to, or association with, eastern mystical religions. It is the belief that each human soul passes through several successive separate lives on this earth before being absorbed into the divinity.

Normally associated with this belief is the idea that each earthly existence represents an advance on the previous incarnation. It is believed that one lifetime is not sufficient to enable the human spirit to become worthy of eternal union with God, but that in each existence spiritual progress is made, and spiritual purification is taken a step further, until finally that state of perfection is reached which permits access into the company of God.

In a cruder form, some believers in reincarnation will allow even the dwelling of the Spirit in the bodies of animals at an early stage of the process.

There is no place for reincarnation in the Christian understanding of life, death, judgment and man's eternal destiny. It is unthinkable that Jesus himself, or the Bible as a whole would not have revealed such a fundamental fact about man's relationship with God, if it were true. The Bible is completely silent on the subject.

All the biblical teaching, and the teaching of Jesus, in particular, is rather to the effect that death is at once final and unique, and that after death comes the judgment which determines a person's eternal destiny.

The concept of reincarnation also clashes with the spirit of the Gospel, in that it suggests that man's attainment of eternal reward and happiness is the result of human effort and achievement.

The essence of Christ's message is that salvation is a pure gift which cannot be earned by human striving. The good we do is itself the result of God's gift of grace. Belief in reincarnation and the reasoning behind it clash with the concept of a God of infinite mercy.

Although there is no particular scriptural text which deals explicitly with the question of reincarnation (because the idea was simply not entertained) the following texts are significant:

● 2 Corinthians 5:10 'We must all appear before the judgment seat of Christ, so that each one may receive good or evil, according to what he has done in the body';

● Luke 16:19-31, the parable of the rich man and Lazarus, which teaches that one's eternal reward or punishment is the result of the works of a single life span;

● John 9:4: 'Night comes (that is, death) when no one

can work,' that is, there is no further time or opportunity available for any kind of merit;
● See also Galations 6:10.

The teaching of the Church has always been that immediately after death, each person experiences God's judgment, and the result of that judgement is to decide the fate of the person for eternity. The concept of reincarnation is therefore, as it always has been, totally incompatible with orthodox Christian faith.

You ask about books on the subject. I am sorry I do not know of any Catholic work which deals exclusively with this topic. I am sure you would find a number of works on the subject in a general book store.

My advice, if you are a practising Christian, is not to get too caught up in reincarnation, but to concentrate on the riches which are to be found in the pages of Scripture. Therein is contained all the truth which is necessary for the reception of God's gift of salvation.

Question 131:
Contained in the Conscience and Moral Truth *statement from the Australian Catholic bishops is this paragraph:*
'Pre-natal factors can profoundly and permanently influence post-natal life. In somewhat the same way practising righteousness in this life develops one's capacities for enjoyment in the next.'
On this model then, we are, in this life, embryos of our eternal selves.
Would you please comment on the second sentence?

Answer:
The passage from the Australian bishops' statement has a solid biblical foundation. The biblical authors often tend to anticipate events which normally are portrayed as future, and thus bring them back into the present experience of believers.

Biblical scholars and theologians use the phrase 'realised eschatology' to describe this phenomenon.

This technical expression means that many spiritual realities which are primarily associated with the future, and especially with the 'last things', are often referred to also as present possessions or experiences.

Our best biblical source for illustrating this viewpoint is the Gospel of St John. In the other Gospels, such concepts as judgment and eternal life are presented almost exclusively in future terms: the Last Judgment and life after death.

In John's Gospel, however, these realities are anticipated in the here and now. The future dimension is not ignored or rejected, but the emphasis falls on the present experience or enjoyment of these realities.

Thus in John 6:40 we read: 'Whoever sees the Son and believes in him *shall have* eternal life, and I shall raise him up on the last day'; but in 5:24 Jesus says: 'Whoever listens to my words and believes in the One who sent me, *has* eternal life . . . he has passed from death to life.'

In John 11:25, Jesus says: 'I am the Resurrection. If anyone believes in me, even though he dies, he *will live*.' While in 17:3 Jesus addresses his Father in these words: 'This *is* eternal life; to know you, the one true God, and Jesus Christ whom you have sent.'

These interchanges of present and future demonstrate that eternal life is not just a future reality, but something already present, actually in the possession of those who live by faith.

In the light of this evidence, your statement 'we (believers) in this life are embryos of our eternal selves' is an appropriate way of expressing the idea.

Sacraments

Question 132:

Some Leader *readers may have been perplexed or misled by your statement in 'Question Box' alleging there is no biblical evidence that Jesus instituted seven Sacraments.*

There is indeed such evidence in the following biblical texts which are some of those alluded to, or quoted by, the Council of Trent in the Catholic Church's response to similar allegations made by early Protestant teachers:

1. Baptism: *Matthew 28:19; John 3:5; Galatians 3:27.*
2. Confirmation: *Luke 24:19; Acts 1:8; 8:4-20; 19:1-7; Hebrews 6:1-6.*
3. Eucharist: *Luke 22:19-20; 1 Corinthians 11:23-25.*
4. Penance(Reconciliation): *John 20:22-23; Matthew 13:4; 16:19.*
5. Extreme Unction *(Anointing of the Sick): James 5:14-15; Mark 6:13.*
6. Orders: *Luke 22:19; 1 Corinthians 11:23-25; Hebrews 7:12; 2 Timothy 1:6; 1 Timothy 4:14.*
7. Matrimony: *Matthew 19:6; Mark 10:5-12; Ephesians 5:25-32.*

In the same article you state 'it might be an oversimplification to say the earthly Jesus instituted seven Sacraments'.

The teachings of the Catholic Church as clearly documented in the Council of Trent on the Sacraments, give an unambiguous condemnation of anyone who says either that the Sacraments were not all instituted by Jesus Christ or that there are more or less than seven.

Answer:

The point I was making was that the biblical evidence does not show that each of the seven Sacraments was instituted by the earthly Jesus.

It is not possible to answer your comments adequately in

the space which I have at my disposal. Readers might like to consult the multiplicity of biblical passages which you quote.

They will find, I am afraid, that most of them have nothing to do with Jesus 'instituting' anything.

The texts which you lump together are of unequal value in proving the thesis 'that Jesus instituted seven Sacraments'.

Certainly, the Fathers of the Council of Trent did not regard all of these passages as 'proof-texts' for that teaching of the Church. As you say, in some cases they are merely allusions.

For example, in the case of the Eucharist, the passages that you quote are indeed conclusive. We have clear biblical evidence that Jesus instituted the Eucharist at the Last Supper.

But when we look at the passages you bring forward concerning marriage, we find that the picture is not so clear.

In Matthew 19 and Mark 10, we read of Jesus strongly defending the indissolubility of the marriage bond, and condemning the practice of divorce and re-marriage.

In Ephesians 5 we have Paul's beautiful teaching on married love as a symbol of the union between Christ and the Church. But we find no reference at all to Jesus instituting a Sacrament of Marriage.

Many of your other references are still less clear. For example, I completely fail to see what Matthew 13:4 has to do with the Sacrament of Penance (or Reconciliation). Perhaps it is a misprint on your part.

One might ask if it is not an anachronism to seek biblical evidence for the institution of seven Sacraments by the historical Jesus.

Certainly there is no biblical record of Jesus telling his disciples that he was leaving them seven Sacraments to be celebrated in the Church. Nor is it possible to pinpoint the occasion on which he 'instituted' each of them or to prove from Scripture that he did so at all.

It is somewhat akin to a person trying to prove the authority of the Pope or papacy from Scripture.

The New Testament contains no direct reference to Pope or papacy. What we do find there is extensive evidence for the primacy of Peter among the 12 Apostles, and for the promises which Christ made to him.

This provides a solid, sound and legitimate foundation for later Church doctrine and practice.

What the texts included in your list from the Council of Trent show (most of them anyway) is that we can find a solid base in Scripture for the Church's sacramental teaching and practice.

Many of the texts show that the Church's teaching on the Sacraments is grounded in the life and ministry of Jesus himself, and that the Church's sacramental system is an extension of his own healing, saving and lifegiving activity.

It was, however, the Church which decided on the number 'seven', and it did so after lengthy theological reflection on the ministry of Jesus and the teachings of the New Testament.

Because the Risen Lord promised to remain with his Church always and to send the Holy Spirit to be its guide and teacher, it can indeed be said that Jesus Christ 'instituted seven Sacraments'.

Question 133:

Why would a priest object to my taking part in a Christian Outreach ceremony — Baptism by immersion? What does the Catholic Church think about Baptism by immersion?

I believe in my own Baptism in the Catholic Church. I know that I can receive the Sacrament of Baptism only once. My intention in taking part in the immersion in water was a symbolic act of renewed dedication to God.

Answer:

I can appreciate your priest's concern about your receiving Baptism at a Christian Outreach ceremony — whether by immersion or in any other form. His concern is that it would appear to be a statement on your part that you regard your Catholic sacramental Baptism as incomplete or inadequate.

You say in your letter that this is not the case, but that you see it as 'a symbolic act of renewed dedication to God.' I wonder whether the Christian Outreach people see it in the same light, or do they see it as your 'being born again of water and the Holy Spirit'?

If you were a parishioner of mine, I would be anxious also, because Christian Outreach — in this part of the world, at least — has the reputation of enticing people away from their own Churches.

Despite its claim to be non-denominational, my own experience is that it sees itself as a rival to the established Christian Churches, and especially to the Catholic Church. Because of this and its biblical fundamentalism, it is not a group to which I am well disposed.

I would certainly prefer to see Catholics renew their dedication to God in ways other than by Christian Outreach 'Baptism'.

To revert to 'symbolic' Baptism after having received sacramental Baptism in the Catholic Church would seem to me to be the equivalent of a disciple of Jesus returning to John the Baptist to experience his baptism of repentance. It is difficult not to see it as a form of regression.

Baptism by immersion is permitted and approved by the Catholic Church. In my own parish, parents who present children for Baptism are given the choice of Baptism by immersion or by the pouring of water.

Several choose immersion, and indeed this form of Baptism does fuller justice to the symbolism of participation in the death and Resurrection of Christ: dying to sin and rising to new life (Romans 6:3-4).

Question 134:
I should be very grateful if you would answer a few questions for me.

First I shall give a brief outline of the situation so that you may better understand what is worrying me.

My son, a practising Catholic, who attends Mass every Sunday, married a girl, an Anglican, who does not practise her faith. The only times I have known her to attend a Church service are when she has gone to Mass with my son.

However, when they were blessed with a child, she had it baptised in the Anglican Church, although she told her husband she had no objection to the child being brought up as a Catholic, if that is what he should want.

Now for the question:

1. The child is baptised as an Anglican. If, as we hope, it is brought up as a Catholic, what procedure must be taken when the time comes for it to receive the next Sacraments?

2. It is most likely the child will attend the State school.

*Can it be enrolled as a Catholic in order to attend classes
conducted by Catholic catechists although baptised in the
Anglican Church?*

*My only efforts so far have been prayer, as the family lives
in a distant parish, but when we say during the* Confiteor
*'and for what I have failed to do', I sometimes wonder to
what extent I could be guilty in that I have done nothing
more.*

*My son discussed the matter with his parish priest, who
told him that it was a matter for the parents of the child to
work out for themselves.*

Answer:

In my own pastoral experience, I have come across several
cases similar to the one you have mentioned concerning
your grandchild.

A typical case is that of a child of a mixed marriage
baptised in a Protestant church. The parents later decide to
send the child to a Catholic school and when the time comes
for First Confession and Holy Communion they express a
desire for the child to receive these Sacraments.

This indicates the intention of the parents that they want
their child to be brought up in the Catholic tradition, despite
his/her earlier Baptism in another Christian denomination.

In such a case, the child is not re-baptised, providing
documentary proof can be supplied concerning its Baptism.
The Catholic Church accepts as valid and sacramental the
Baptisms of other Churches, at least the mainline Christian
Churches.

However, before the child proceeds to the reception of the
Sacraments of First Reconciliation and Eucharist, there
should be a simple rite of reception into the Catholic
Church. This would take the form of an adaptation of the
rite of reception for baptised adults into the Church —
adapted that is to the child's capacity.

It would involve a profession of faith and a statement of
acceptance of the Church's teachings in words which the
child can understand.

Should the child attend a State school there is nothing to
prevent the parents requesting that the child attend religion
classes conducted by Catholic teachers. They need only
indicate their wish to the school Principal.

As for your 'negligence' in the matter and your guilt about your failure to do more, we are obviously dealing with a very sensitive area. How far you can go depends very much on your relationship with your daughter-in-law.

The interference of grandparents can often do more harm than good. I believe that in most cases, prayer, supported by your own example, is the best you can do, and the most you would be expected to do.

Question 135:

Would you please give me an explanation of the following, not only for my information, but also for others who cannot see the logic of it.

One of my sons was recently married and he obtained the baptismal certificate I received at the time of his Baptism. However, he was requested to obtain an updated copy of same.

Examination of the copy revealed exactly the same information as on the original. So what updating?

Would you kindly let me know the point of the exercise, so that I won't have to go through the same routine another 10 times not knowing why.

Answer:

The request which is made by a priest for a recent copy of a baptismal certificate at the time of a person's marriage is to guard against the danger of an invalid marriage on the grounds of the person having been married before.

When a priest has officiated at a marriage he is required by Church law to enter the details of the marriage against the name of the person in the church baptismal register.

If, as is very often the case, a person is married in a church or parish other than his or her place of Baptism, then the priest who performs the marriage should notify the priest of the parish where the person's Baptism took place, so that the marriage particulars can be entered into the baptismal register in that parish.

In the admittedly rare event of a person concealing a previous marriage, the obtaining of a recent copy of a baptismal certificate — provided the requirements of the law have been complied with — will reveal this impediment to the celebration of another marriage in the Church.

This would then be permissible only if the first marriage had been annulled by a Church court.

Question 136:

What is the Church's position regarding reception of the Sacraments for Catholics who are divorced and have remarried outside the Church?

Answer:

There is much that could be said on this matter, but because this particular question concerns just one aspect of the subject, I shall confine my comments to that.

The Church's position on the reception of the Sacraments for people in this category has not changed. Divorced Catholics who remarry outside the Church become ineligible to receive the Sacraments of the Church, except the Sacrament of Anointing of the Sick in a case of emergency.

The Church has come under strong criticism for maintaining this 'hard line' on the issue of divorce and remarriage. Its teaching and practice are based on the words of Jesus: 'What God has joined together, man must not divide' (Mark 10:9, Matthew 19:6).

Protestant Churches vary in their practice, but in general it can be said that they understand these words of Jesus as the statement of an ideal, which people should conscientiously strive to reach. If, however, people fail, and are repentant, they are prepared to allow them a second chance.

They argue that such an approach squares better with the compassion of Christ, as displayed in the Gospels.

The Catholic Church, on the other hand, feels compelled to maintain its position because it understands Jesus' words not merely as the expression of an ideal, but as a statement of law.

They do not appear to allow of any exception, but are rather an absolute statement about the permanence and indissolubility of Christian marriage. The Church does not feel free to change its legislation, in the light of Jesus' teaching.

Nor is the Church impressed by the argument that, because divorce is so prevalent in modern society it should modify its position to meet the new social circumstances.

Because marriage is under attack from so many quarters it

could likewise be argued that any relaxation by the Church of its law would be a further body-blow to the whole institution of marriage.

The Church sees itself as having a God-given mandate to protect the marriage bond. Sadly, but inevitably, some innocent people suffer as a result.

The Church's defence of the permanence of the marriage union is reinforced by its vision of marriage as a Sacrament.

It sees Christ as giving two people, who already belong to him through baptism, to belong to each other in an exclusive, life-long union. This gives added force to Jesus' words: 'What God has joined together, man must not divide.'

As the law of the Church stands, a divorced Catholic may not re-marry in the Church during the lifetime of his or her partner.

He or she would be free to do so, only if a Church court were to grant an annulment of the previous marriage. Without this, the divorced and re-married Catholic is entitled to the fullest possible pastoral care and support, but disqualifies himself or herself from participating in the Church's sacramental life.

Question 137:

My daughter married earlier this year, with a marriage celebrant officiating. This was not the sort of wedding she desired but there were several difficult circumstances and, after much heartache, she took the best course she could.

I have followed with interest the letters written to you about attending such weddings. (See Q 88-92.) When a dear child is involved, there are no 'cut and dried' answers. I went.

Now they have a daughter six weeks old.

When my daughter was just out of hospital, her husband made it plain that he would not tolerate a Catholic Baptism. She and the babe were coming to stay with me for a while, and I think he was afraid we would whisk the infant along to a 'Romish priest' on the quiet.

She was in no state for a bitter (and probably useless) argument. On my advice, she assured her husband that she would take no action without his consent and she and I agreed to pray about it and put the matter in God's hands.

And so it stands at present.

But I wonder, should I try and have a discussion with my son-in-law? We haven't much common ground. If he were a committed Christian we could work something out, but he has no apparent interest in religion. He is a nominal Presbyterian.

If he remains adamant, is it better to continue as we are, or to let him take the child along to a Presbyterian church for Baptism?

The infant is not very robust, and I am sure my daughter is distressing herself with the question: 'What if she should die without Baptism?'

I myself do not worry about that aspect; nevertheless I know she should be baptised.

I would appreciate your guidance.

Answer:

You make no mention in your letter of the parish priest in the town where your daughter lives. If the kind of situation which you describe were to exist in my own parish, I should like to be informed of it, so that I could explore some means of handling it.

I suggest therefore that you approach your daughter's priest and make him aware of the situation, if he is not already acquainted with it.

You might suggest to him that he call on your daughter, at first at a time when her husband is not at home, to discuss the matter with her.

Perhaps, as a result of this discussion, it might be decided that the priest could make a 'social call' when the husband is at home.

This could help to break down the prejudice which he has against the Church, and possibly convince him that the Church is not the threat which he obviously imagines it to be.

Whether this approach should be preceded by a discussion between yourself and your son-in-law is difficult for me to say, not knowing either of you personally or the relationship which you have with each other.

Reading between the lines of your letter, I suspect that it might be better to approach your daughter's priest first and obtain his advice.

Should your son-in-law remain obstinate, when all avenues have been explored, it would be preferable for the child to be baptised in another Christian Church rather than remain unbaptised.

Baptism in the other mainline Christian Churches is accepted as valid by the Catholic Church.

I have known of several cases where in the course of time the non-Catholic partner has had a change of heart and mind.

In these instances, even though the child has been baptised in another Church, he or she has subsequently received instruction in the Catholic faith, received the Sacraments of Reconciliation and the Eucharist, and been confirmed as a Catholic.

But first, I strongly suggest you investigate the possibilities I mentioned earlier.

Question 138:

Do you think 12 years of age is the most appropriate time for Confirmation? Can most children of this age truly appreciate the Sacrament?

Answer:

Your question about the most appropriate age for Confirmation highlights something of an anomaly in the Church's current sacramental practice. Baptism, Confirmation and Eucharist are commonly recognised as the three Sacraments of initiation into the Church.

In the early Church, most candidates for Baptism were adults. Immediately after Baptism, the bishop would impose hands on the newly baptised and pray for the gifts of the Holy Spirit. With sacred oil, he would make the sign of the Cross on the candidate's forehead while pronouncing the words, *I anoint you with the Holy Spirit*. The candidate was thus 'sealed' in the faith.

Only later, when entire countries became Christian and infant Baptism became the norm, did Confirmation become a separate event to be celebrated at a later date. It was about the fifth century when the laying on of hands, the anointing with oil, and the signing with the Cross came to be separated from Baptism, and the name 'Confirmation' was coined.

Although Confirmation has now been separated from Baptism, it continues to be seen as the completion of Baptism. Some branches of Christianity have retained the practice of infant Confirmation.

Strictly speaking, Confirmation should not be seen as the Sacrament of Christian Adulthood, or as the Sacrament which marks the transition from childhood to maturity. In our current Church practice it has come to be seen in this light. But although separated from Baptism by many years, the two Sacraments are closely connected in purpose and meaning.

It is not unlikely that in the years to come we may see a change in the Church's thinking and practice about Confirmation, especially now that the restored catechumenate has re-emphasised the close connection between Baptism, Confirmation and Eucharist as Sacraments of initiation.

Question 139:

Would you please explain the teaching of the Church concerning the sacrament which used to be called the Sacrament of Extreme Unction?

Answer:

The Sacrament of Anointing of the Sick was once referred to as 'Extreme Unction' (the final anointing), or the 'last rites'. The current Church teaching and practice, however, is not to defer the sacrament until a person is dangerously ill.

For example, elderly people in a weak condition may be anointed, even though there is no question of danger of death.

Through this sacrament, the Church communicates to the sick person the strength to bear suffering bravely and even to overcome it. There have been numerous instances of physical health being restored following the reception of the sacrament, or at least of a renewed peace and serenity. The sacrament ministers to the whole person.

The power of the sacrament to restore bodily health is sufficient reason for its not being delayed. There is no reason why a person may not receive the sacrament several times in the course of his or her life.

In case of serious illness, the family of the sick person should call the priest to celebrate the Sacrament of Anointing of the Sick. The sacrament may be validly given to people who have lost consciousness, or the use of reason.

In the case where a priest is called to a person who has already died, he does not administer the sacrament, but offers prayers that God will forgive the person's sins and receive him into the kingdom of heaven.

If there is doubt about whether or not the person is already dead, the priest administers the sacrament conditionally.

The revised forms for the celebration of the sacraments also allow for the communal anointing of the sick and the aged, preferably in the context of a Mass. As in the case of other sacraments, this practice highlights the communal dimension and expresses the concern of all members of the community for one another.

As one member suffers, all suffer; and as one member shares in the joy of the sacrament, all rejoice with him.

Question 140:

What are the rules regarding priests bringing Communion to the sick, aged, and housebound? If there are any rules, would three months and over be considered a norm?

Must these parishioners take Communion from a lay minister or nun if they are not happy with this arrangement?

Answer:

The frequency with which priests take Communion to the sick, aged and housebound is very much a matter that is left to the discretion of the parish clergy, after consultation with the people concerned.

There are no rules as such, but I should hardly think that three months and over would be considered a reasonable practice by pastors.

In most parishes monthly Communion at home for the sick etc would be considered a minimal responsibility. Weekly Communion at home is not exceptional.

Of course, the extension of the Eucharistic ministry to Religious and lay people makes it possible for the housebound to receive Holy Communion more frequently.

The problem you raise is that of elderly people who are unable to come to terms with receiving the Eucharist from anyone other than a priest.

This is a not uncommon problem because many sick and aged people would not have been in a position to hear the theology of the special Eucharistic ministry explained in the Church.

Lay ministers of the Eucharist should never be sent to the housebound without an explanation being given to the people concerned of the theology involved and without their permission being obtained.

Should they still be unwilling or unable to accept the explanation given, or be uncomfortable about receiving Communion from a Religious or lay minister, they should not be compelled to do so.

In such cases, their wishes should be respected and the priest should take the Sacrament to them.

Question 141:

What time is allowed to elapse before hosts reserved in the tabernacle are consumed or exchanged for new ones? (One week, two weeks, a month, three months?)

Answer:

I am not aware of any specific time laid down by Church law for the consuming of sacred bread reserved in the tabernacle. It is left to the discretion and devotion of the priest. I would imagine that most priests would replace the sacred bread every fortnight or perhaps monthly. Three months seems excessive.

But even if such an interval of time were allowed to elapse, it does not mean that the Eucharistic Body of Christ is no longer present.

Question 142:

I have difficulty in accepting the practice of the Church regarding Communion under both forms (bread and wine). The whole Christ must be present wherever his body or his blood is present. He is wholly present under every particle of the consecrated host.

Christ did command the Apostles who were his first priests to act in his name, and to be his instruments, and to administer the Sacrament as he did. This means that they must consecrate both bread and wine and receive Christ under both species.

Frankly, I see no reason for the laity to return to the practice of receiving both consecrated host and precious blood, as being important for ecumenism. Perhaps it might be conceded under the doctrine of the priesthood of all believers who are offering the sacrifice, but I would still think that the wisdom of the Church in having given the Sacrament under the species of bread is more likely to safeguard the great respect which is due to the blood of Christ.

Probably, one day I will be challenged on my decision not to participate in receiving the cup, but I have my answer ready.

Answer:

When the Vatican Council stated that 'the dogmatic principles recognised in the Council of Trent remain intact', it was referring to that Council's teaching that Christ is received whole and entire in a complete Sacrament, even when people communicate under one kind only, and they are not thereby deprived of any grace necessary for salvation. (Council of Trent, Session 21, *Decree on Communion*, C.1-3).

But as the quotation from *The General Instruction on the Roman Missal* (1969) indicates, the reception of Holy Communion under both forms does fuller justice to the sign which Jesus left us. 'When we eat this bread and drink this cup, we proclaim your death, Lord Jesus, until you come in glory' (Acclamation No. 3); 'By your Holy Spirit gather all who share this one bread and one cup into the one body of Christ' (Eucharistic prayer No. 4).

I do not really feel 'ecumenism' is a decisive factor behind the Church's restoration of this ancient practice. And I cannot quite follow your line of reasoning about respect for the blood of Christ.

Respect is due equally to the body and to the blood of Christ. Disrespect is certainly not shown by eating his body; why then should respect for his blood be endangered by drinking from the cup?

I hope you are not 'challenged' about your decision not to communicate by receiving the chalice. People's freedom should be respected as to whether they wish to receive Holy Communion under one or both kinds. As you say, Christ is wholly present under both forms. The important thing is to receive the Eucharist in the way with which you are comfortable whenever you are presented with the choice.

The Church's practice has not always been so. Back in the eighth century, Pope Gregory II (715-31), writing to Boniface, urged: 'One bread, one cup, if possible.' A couple of hundred years before, Pope St Gelasius I (492-96) was much more dogmatic. He said: 'If not under both species, don't go at all! You are dividing the species!'

This latter quotation does not represent present day Church policy or practice, but may be of interest to any one who imagines that there were no liturgical changes between the time of the Apostles and the Second Vatican Council.

Question 143:

The Second Vatican Council laid down 14 different celebrations where the blood of Christ is allowed to be received (Vatican II, p.187). Could you explain why in some churches the blood of Christ is received by the laity at all Masses?

Also, according to Vatican II, the doxology is reserved for the priest alone, with the laity responding with their 'Amen'. Why then is this not observed in all churches? Are we to believe that Vatican II is to be obeyed only by some churches, or are all churches bound to obey?

Answer:

It was not the Second Vatican Council which enumerated 14 different cases in which the blood of Christ is allowed to be received. The only directive about Communion under both kinds (bread and wine) which appears in the Council's *Constitution on the Sacred Liturgy* occurs in Chapter 2, paragraph 55, which states: 'The dogmatic principles which were laid down by the Council of Trent remaining intact, Communion under both kinds may be granted when the Bishops think fit, not only to clerics and Religious but also to the laity, in cases to be determined by the Apostolic See'.

The Council then gives three examples only (newly ordained priests, newly professed Religious, newly baptised Catholics). The directive to which you refer is from *The General Instruction on the Roman Missal*, promulgated by Pope Paul in 1969, four years after the Council ended. In this document, 14 categories of people are listed who may receive Communion with the chalice, 'with the Bishop's approval and after due instruction' (*Vatican Council II, Conciliar and Post-Conciliar Documents,* ed. A. Flannery, p.187).

This follows a statement of principles which represents a definite advance on Vatican II: 'The meaning of Communion is signified as clearly as possible when it is given under both kinds. In this form, the meal aspect of the Eucharist is more fully manifested, and Christ's intention that the new and eternal covenant should be ratified in his blood is better expressed.

'Also the connection between the eucharistic meal and the heavenly banquet in the Father's kingdom becomes easier to see . . . the faithful should be encouraged to desire Communion under both kinds, in which the meaning of the Eucharist is more fully signified.'

In June 1970, a further Instruction appeared from the Sacred Congregation of Doctrine and Worship, *On the extension of the faculty to administer Holy Communion under both kinds.*

It states: 'As time has gone on, it has been possible to witness an ever-increasing desire that the number of cases, in which it is possible to administer Communion under both kinds, should be further extended according to the needs of different regions and people.'

The same document does say that Bishops should not grant this concession indiscriminately; it urges that adequate instruction must be given to the people; and it demands that everything must be done 'in a way befitting the holiness of the Sacrament'.

Space does not permit me to quote from subsequent documentation on reforms in the liturgy. But summing up, it needs to be recognised that 20 years have now elapsed since the beginning of Vatican II which merely *began* the slow work of moving the Church closer to its ideals. The restoration of Communion under both forms is one area of renewal that has been moving gradually and slowly.

In the past two decades, we have seen a gradual increase in the use of the chalice. As parishes and communities have developed more experience with Communion from the cup in week day celebrations, they are ready to move to this practice on Sundays as well. In doing so, they would be acting in accordance with the spirit of the law: 'The faithful should be encouraged to desire Communion under both kinds.'

As for your query on the 'Amen' response to the doxology, 'Through him, with him, in him, etc.', again it is not the Council itself, but later documentation which specifies that the priest alone should recite the doxology, and that the people should restrict their participation to the response, 'Amen'.

This acclamation, called the 'Great Amen' is actually meant to be *sung* by all, especially in each Sunday celebration. Singing this acclamation is a strong form of participation by the community in the action of the eucharistic prayer.

Merely saying this acclamation understandably leaves a feeling of incompleteness and inadequate participation in the eucharistic action. Often the 'Great Amen' becomes a muffled and indistinct murmur as the people prepare to rise for the Lord's Prayer.

Consequently, congregations often feel the need to join in by saying the doxology with the priest. There is no need to be concerned that some parishes are doing this. Surely, it is a relatively minor 'misdemeanour', and one that is in keeping with the overall aim of greater lay participation in the liturgy of the Mass.

Question 144:

Canon 925 of the new Code of Canon Law, now in force, states: 'Holy Communion is to be given under the species of bread alone, or, in accordance with the liturgical laws, under both species, or in case of necessity, even under the species of wine alone'.

Is the giving of Holy Communion under both species at Sunday parish Masses in accordance with the liturgical laws?

Answer:

Statements emanating from Rome over the past 20 years on the subject of the giving of Communion under both species of bread and wine have left many of us confused.

There is a remarkable gulf between the ideals stated and the practice recommended.

A selection of extracts from these statements will illustrate what I mean.

The Second Vatican Council in *The Constitution on the Sacred Liturgy* (1963), had this to say:

'The dogmatic principles which were laid down by the Council of Trent remaining intact, Communion under both kinds may be granted when bishops think fit, not only to clerics and Religious, but also to the laity, in cases to be determined by the Apostolic See.

'For example, to the newly-ordained in the Mass of their ordination; to the newly-professed in the Mass of their Religious profession; to the newly-baptised in the Mass which follows their Baptism.'

In 1967 the Sacred Congregation of Rites issued an *Instruction on the Worship of the Eucharistic Mystery*.

In this instruction it is stated: 'Holy Communion, considered as a sign, has a fuller form when it is received under both kinds.

'For under this form (leaving intact the principles of the Council of Trent by which under either species or kind there is received the true Sacrament and Christ whole and entire), the sign of the eucharistic banquet appears more perfectly.

'Moreover, it is more clearly shown how the new and eternal covenant is ratified in the blood of the Lord, and it also expresses the relation of the eucharistic banquet to the eschatalogical banquet in the Kingdom of the Father (cf. Matthew 26:27-29).'

(There follows an extended list of cases when Communion under both kinds is permitted.)

The General Instruction on the Roman Missal appeared in 1969. It states: 'The meaning of Communion is signified as completely as possible when it is given under both kinds.

'In this form the meal aspect of the Eucharist is more fully manifested, and Christ's intention that the new and eternal covenant should be ratified in his blood is better expressed.

'Pastors of souls should therefore strive that the faithful who receive or see the reception of Communion under both kinds should be thoroughly instructed in the Catholic doctrines about Communion as expounded by the Council of Trent.

'First, they should be reminded that, according to the Catholic faith, Christ is received whole and entire in a complete Sacrament even when people communicate under one kind only, and they are not thereby deprived of any Grace necessary for salvation.

'Further it should be explained to them that the Church, when specifying how Sacraments are to be administered, has the power to make laws about Sacraments and to change these laws, so long as the changes do not affect the very nature of the Sacrament.

'The Church makes use of this power whenever she judges that reverence for the Sacrament or the spiritual good of the faithful requires changes in view of the particular circumstances of time and place.

'*The faithful also should be encouraged to desire Communion under both kinds, in which the meaning of the eucharistic banquet is more fully signified*' (italics mine).

(There follows a still fuller list of cases — 14 in all — when Communion under both kinds is permitted.)

In 1970 the Sacred Congregation for Divine Worship issued an instruction on the extension of the faculty to administer Holy Communion under both kinds. It states: 'In order that the fullness of sign in the eucharistic banquet may be seen more clearly by the faithful, the Second Vatican Council laid down that in certain cases — to be decided by the Holy See — the faithful should be able to receive Communion under both kinds . . .

'This desire of the Council has gradually been put into effect. The preparation of the faithful has accompanied this gradual development, so that from this change in ecclesiastical discipline there should come even more abundant fruits of devotion and spiritual growth.

'As time has gone on it has been possible to witness an ever-increasing desire that the number of cases in which it is possible to administer Communion under both kinds should be further expanded according to the needs of different regions and people . . .

'Moreover the [national] episcopal conferences may decide to what extent, for what motives, and in what conditions, ordinaries [bishops] may concede Communion under both kinds in other cases which have great importance for the spiritual life of the particular community or group of the faithful . . .

'This is on the condition, however, that the faculty should not be conceded indiscriminately . . .

'This faculty should not be granted on occasions when there are large numbers of communicants . . .

'. . . Before the faithful are to receive Communion under both kinds they should be adequately instructed on the significance of the rite.'

It needs to be noted, however, that this instruction was promulgated at a time when only priests were permitted to distribute Holy Communion.

It is understandable why the prohibition against distributing Communion under both kinds at Masses with large numbers of communicants should have been made at that time.

But in January 1973 there appeared a further instruction from Rome on Special Ministers of the Eucharist.

This document acknowledges that 'there are various circumstances in which a lack of supporting ministers for the distribution of Holy Communion can occur, for example, during Mass, because of the size of the congregation . . .'

This authorisation of lay people to distribute Holy Communion would seem to remove the grounds for the exclusion of Sunday Mass from those occasions when Communion could be distributed under both species.

But nothing new on the subject has come from Rome during the past 10 years.

It is also worth noting that the eucharistic prayers themselves seem to presume the reception of Holy Communion under both kinds.

For example, 'When we eat this bread and drink this cup, we proclaim your death Lord Jesus until you come in glory' (Acclamation No. 3); and 'All who share this bread and wine (or one bread and one cup)' (Eucharistic Prayer No. 4).

This, of course, is to say nothing of the injunction of Jesus repeated at every Mass that is celebrated: 'Take this [bread] all of you, and eat it . . . take this, all of you and drink from it, this is the cup of my blood.'

So while some confusion may remain about the letter of

the law on this matter, it would appear, in the light of the principles enunciated above, that the increasing number of parishes which are distributing Holy Communion under both forms (bread and wine) at Sunday Mass are certainly acting in accordance with the spirit of the liturgical laws.

Question 145:

It is difficult for me, even after 50 years as a Catholic, to understand how the instruction of Christ to 'Eat this bread and drink this cup' is left with only the bread being consumed. Is it a decision of the theologians that only the ordained may receive under both kinds? If so why then restrict the congregation to bread only?

It seems that the top billing, the punch line at the Last Supper proclaimed by Christ, is not enacted in most parishes. Very occasionally a priest at a weekday Mass will invite participation in both species but why only then? Did Christ intend only the apostles ordained by him to be the 'all of you'?

On the ecumenical level how does one explain to people of another Church their query: 'Why do you not take wine?'

Answer:

I refer you to my answers to Q142-4 on this matter of Communion under both kinds.

I am not sure when or why the restriction of Holy Communion to the form of bread alone came about in the Catholic Church. Certainly, Jesus did not intend his words at the Last Supper 'all of you', to be restricted to ordained ministers or priests.

In the early years of the Church, Christians celebrated the Eucharist by eating the body and drinking the blood of Christ — that is under both forms of bread and wine.

I presume that the restriction of Communion to the form of bread alone happened for practical reasons — such as pressure of numbers of communicants, hygiene, the danger of contracting illness from drinking from the same cup, danger of spillage of the blood of Christ, etc.

I say that it must have been for practical reasons because there is no theological reason why reception of the Eucharist should have been restricted to communicating under the form of bread alone.

Of course the whole Christ is present under the form of bread, so there is no question of any deprivation where Holy Communion is received under one species only.

In some parish churches the practice of distributing Holy Communion under both kinds has been restored. Careful and thoughtful planning has minimised the practical difficulties involved. In a recent answer in 'Question Box' I pointed out that there had been a gradual increase of cases in which distribution of Communion under both kinds is permitted.

I believe this is one of those areas where the *Consensus Fidelium* (the will of the Catholic people as a whole) will eventually see the full restoration of Communion under both kinds. This certainly does fuller justice to the sign value of the Sacrament of the Eucharist instituted by Christ.

Question 146:

I am submitting the following questions for your comment through 'Question Box'. The questions arose out of a challenge made by another Catholic. He wants to know:

(a) Why the words of the consecration in the Mass have been altered from Our Lord's own words 'Shall be shed for you and for many' to 'for ALL men'. He sees this as a departure from the decrees of the Council of Trent.

(b) Why is the Communion plate no longer used?

(c) Why have the altar rails been removed from the churches?

(d) He claims that there is no evidence of a papal document authorising the giving of Communion in the hands. He says that Pope Paul VI was pressured, mainly from Holland and Germany, to grant the concession.

Answer:

(a) The difference between the words of Jesus as reported in the Gospels and the words used in the formula of consecration in the Mass is only apparent, not real.

According to the Gospel accounts, Jesus at the Last Supper spoke of his blood being shed 'for the many'. In speaking thus he would have used the Hebrew word *rabbim*.   This Hebrew term denotes 'the many' in the sense of the whole, the totality. It does not mean 'many' in the sense of excluding some.

The fact is that Jesus gave his life for the sins of the whole human race, excluding no one. The universal salvific will of God is well expressed in the words of 1 Timothy 2:4, where it is said that God, Our Saviour, 'desires all men to be saved'.

The Eucharist is a re-presentation of the sacrifice which Christ offered once and for all on Calvary.

It is faithful to the intention of Jesus at the Last Supper and to the purpose of his death on Calvary, to translate his words to say that his blood is shed for *all* people, men and women.

To sum up, Our Lord's words have not really been altered at all. The English word 'all' is the more accurate translation of the Hebrew *rabbim*, the term which he actually used.

(b) The Communion plate generally is no longer used, though its use is not forbidden. In the great majority of parish churches, it is no longer used because it is considered unnecessary.

Use of the Communion plate represents an approach to the Eucharist which does not sit well with modern Eucharistic spirituality.

It reflects the view of the Real Presence of Christ in the Eucharist as of someone or something to be approached with exaggerated awe and even fear.

According to this view Christ was considered present in even the most minute particle of bread, hardly visible to the naked eye.

The accidental loss of such an infinitesimal particle was regarded as a risk to be avoided at all costs. Deliberate disregard for such a tiny particle was considered sacrilegious.

In fact, the body and blood of Christ are offered to us, and received by us, as food and drink. In no meaningful sense can a minute and hardly visible particle of bread be considered as food.

The body of Christ should not therefore be thought to be present in any real sense in such a tiny particle.

This is not to play down respect for the presence of Christ in the Eucharistic bread (and wine). It is simply to moderate this respect, which must always remain, with a little common sense.

(c) The same change of appreciation of the Eucharist and of the nature of the Mass as a community celebration explains the removal of altar rails from most parish churches.

The altar rails stood partly as a symbol of a separation of priest from people which is not in harmony with a true appreciation of the Eucharistic liturgy.

They reflected a theological approach to the Eucharist which saw the priest as the one who offered the Mass, and the 'faithful' as those who attended or 'heard' Mass.

Except for the altar servers, the sanctuary was the priest's domain. There were no lay readers or special ministers of the Eucharist.

In fact, the Mass or Eucharist is a community celebration in which both priest and laity (exercising their 'lay priesthood') are co-offerers of the sacrifice. Lay people are now encouraged to participate actively in the Eucharist, with the priest as president of the assembly.

In such a changed set of circumstances, altar rails as a dividing line between priest and laity are an anachronism.

(d) More than 10 years ago (25 January 1973), the Sacred Congregation for Divine Worship issued the Instruction *Immensae Caritatis*, approved by Pope Paul VI. I shall simply quote from this Instruction without further comment:

'Some episcopal conferences have sought the faculty from the Apostolic See to allow the minister of Holy Communion to place the Eucharistic species in the hands of the faithful . . . In this manner of receiving Holy Communion some points indicated by experience should be most carefully observed.

'Let the greatest diligence and care be taken particularly with regard to fragments which perhaps break off the hosts. This applies to the minister and to the recipient whenever the Sacred Host is placed in the hands of the communicant.

'Before initiating the practice of giving Holy Communion in the hand, suitable instruction and catechesis of Catholic doctrine is necessary concerning both the real and permanent presence of Christ under the Eucharistic species and the reverence due to this Sacrament.'

Sunday Mass and Work

Question 147:

My wife and I have tried to bring our children up to 'love, honour, and obey' both ourselves and the Church, and we have not had any real trouble. That is, until recently, when the newer approach of the clergy became more evident.

Our eldest daughter at home (15 years) did not want to go to Mass, as she was tired and had a lot of homework, always a good excuse. When questioned, she said, 'A priest told us we did have to go to Mass if we did not want to.'

Unfortunately, Father did say that, but did not clarify it and children are so keen to pick up all the wrong things.

This is my first question: What is the Church's ruling on Sunday Mass?

No frills, please, Father, as they tend to hinder, not help.

Also, some time ago, a priest started the sermon by saying 'abortion is an accepted fact of life'. He did not go on to explain the Church's attitude to abortion or contraception. And so my second question is What is the Church's teaching on abortion and contraception?

Answer:

The answers to the questions which you propose demand a certain amount of elaboration. But in response to your request, I shall try to keep my replies free from 'frills'.

The Church's ruling on Sunday Mass is that there is a serious obligation on Catholics to take part in offering the Eucharist with the community on Sunday, the Lord's day.

In the case of any law, there are circumstances which can exempt a person from the law's obligation, but I hardly think that the tiredness of a 15-year-old girl, or her volume of homework, add up to a valid reason for exemption from the Church's obligation.

Frankly, I do not understand what a priest might mean by

saying, 'we don't have to go to Mass if we don't want to.' At the very best, such a statement is unhelpful; it would be more accurate to call it wrong.

The Church condemns abortion because it takes away an innocent infant's right to life. Modern genetic evidence strongly indicates that the embryo and foetus are a full human person.

And even if the actual killing of an innocent person were not involved, there is still at least a willingness to destroy an innocent human life, and therefore a grave moral evil.

The Church teaches that contraceptive birth control as a means of preventing the generation of children is morally wrong in normal circumstances. The Church bases its teaching on its regard for marriage and the sacredness of human life.

One of the main purposes of the sexual act is to bring into existence new human persons destined for eternal life. Artificial means of contraception have the effect of preventing life in an act intended to give life.

As I have said, much more could be said on these three issues; but you asked for brief, direct answers. 'Frills' will be supplied on request.

Question 148:

From different people studying adult faith education programmes, I have been told that the teaching of the Church has changed with regard to the Sunday Mass obligation. Would you please enlighten me?

Answer:

You have been misinformed. The Church has not changed its teaching with regard to the Sunday Mass obligation. Some theologians may be proposing views which conflict with the Church's official teaching, or speculating about possible changes in that teaching — but that is not the same thing.

Then again, you may have received a garbled version of what some lecturer actually said.

While the Church's teaching has not changed, the way that teaching is presented may have changed — and that might not be a bad thing.

Some of us will recall 'horror stories' which were often

preached at parish missions. We were told, for example, of the young man who had never missed Sunday Mass in his life, but decided to go the beach one weekend instead of attending Mass. He was killed in a car accident on the way home, and was doomed to hell for all eternity.

I do not accept that. Nor as a confessor am I unduly concerned about the spiritual welfare of the person who confesses to missing Sunday Mass on the odd occasion. Probably this assessment is due to a better understanding of what constitutes 'mortal' sin, that is, of sin which leads to spiritual and eternal death. Like most confessors, I am not as confident about categorising mortal sin and venial sin as the moral theologians once were.

Mortal sin is a fundamental rejection of God's love, which drives his grace-presence from us. It is mortal or deadly in that it kills the divine life within us. For a sin to fall into the category of mortal, the offence must be serious in itself, the sinner must fully realise its seriousness, and must deliberately choose his way rather than God's. The mortal sinner is prepared to repudiate his friendship with God by the choice he makes.

Perhaps mortal sin might best be described as the choice of a way of life contrary to God's way, which is knowingly and deliberately chosen. The person who misses Sunday Mass occasionally does not necessarily fall into this category. In fact, a particular failure, if it is not his normal way of life, certainly does not put him in this category.

When all this has been said, it remains true that the Church's teaching about the obligation of Catholics to attend Sunday Mass has not changed. Participation with the believing community in the celebration of the Eucharist is an integral part of being a Catholic Christian.

Question 149:

It is known that in some quarters there has been confusion among Catholics, especially children, regarding Sunday Mass obligation. This confusion is highlighted by a statement in The Catholic Leader *in which you intimated, in reply to a question, that it is not mortally sinful to miss Mass on Sunday, occasionally (Q 148). If I have gained the wrong impression I trust that you will clarify the issue, as untold damage may already have been done to simple minds.*

Answer:

The obligation on Catholics to come together on Sunday (the Lord's day) to celebrate the Eucharist as a community is a serious one. It follows that to neglect this obligation, and miss Mass without sufficient reason, is a serious matter.

I put to you a hypothetical case, the case of a person who has obeyed the Commandments of God and the Church, and has done his best with the help of God's grace to live as a Christian or a Catholic should, but then for no real reason decides on a particular Sunday not to attend Mass.

Has he committed mortal sin, or is he in the state of mortal sin? In other words, has this single act (or omission) killed the divine life within him, the life of grace? For that is what mortal sin means: sin that is deadly or death-causing, bringing about a state of spiritual death, and, if unrepented, ultimately eternal death, the loss of eternal life.

It is difficult for me to assign the person mentioned in the hypothetical case above to that category. The mortal sinner is one who deliberately and knowingly rejects God's way and chooses his instead. Is that the situation in the case which I have described?

Many theologians are now arguing for an extension of our traditional division of sin into mortal and venial, to a three-fold division, of mortal, serious, and venial. According to this classification an occasional failure in the matter of attending Sunday Mass would be a serious, but not mortal sin.

This is not the Church's official teaching on the subject, but is a view that is gaining wider acceptance.

Mortal sin is a fundamental rejection of God's love which drives the grace-life from us. The mortal sinner is prepared to repudiate his friendship with God over the choice he makes. Only God himself can know who is in this condition.

Question 150:

Let's face it. The Mass is meaningless to 99 per cent of the under-25s, and mumbo jumbo to 99 per cent of the 25-40s. Only in the over-40s does there develop any real understanding of the symbolism of the Mass. Why have a liturgy that makes some sense only in the second half of one's life? Please do not devote your reply to a criticism of the percentage generalisations.

Answer:

I have to say that your comments do contain some rather sweeping generalisations. I am not prepared to accept them entirely, for they contradict my own experience. I know that a high proportion of the under-25s do not regularly attend Mass, but I do not believe the main reason is their inability to understand the symbolism of the Eucharist. People in this age bracket do often complain that they find the liturgy boring or too formalised. But as for the understanding of the 'symbols' involved, it seems to me that these can be and, indeed, are understood not only by under-25s but even by under-14s.

In many parishes children are given a thorough preparation for school class Masses and much of this preparation involves a detailed explanation of the symbols and structure of the celebration. By the way they participate, the children show that, by and large, they absorb their lessons well.

Masses prepared and celebrated specifically for youth, for example in the context of weekend retreats or camps, can also serve to give young people a greater awareness of the meaning of the Mass. Some parishes have special children's liturgies on Sundays, with the children of different age groups celebrating their own liturgy of the Word at their own level of understanding, and then joining their families for the liturgy of the Eucharist.

Another means of instructing people in the meaning of the Mass is to have a parish education night in which one priest celebrates Mass in 'slow motion', with another explaining the celebration — step by step — as it proceeds. The Mass is a mystery of faith, but it is also basically a very simple celebration.

I cannot fully accept your assessment of the situation. But if it were true, I dread to think what would be your evaluation of things if we were still celebrating Mass in the Old Latin rite. The new order of the Mass is the result of a serious effort to make the Eucharist more relevant and meaningful for today's Catholics. For the most part I believe it has been a success.

Question 151:

Confessors in the past have told me that I committed a mortal *sin for missing Mass on Sunday, although they had the knowledge that I was a daily communicant at the time. I now feel that I appreciate daily Mass more than I do Sunday Mass. So if I had a choice I would attend Mass every day of the week except Sunday. Because of my thoughts am I sinful and is it wrong even to suggest such a thing?*

I had the privilege of hearing Fr Gerry Austin at Banyo Seminary (July 1982) and he was saying that the Church may replace the magic number of seven and proclaim more Sacraments.

This was acceptable to my thinking as I have attended many Church occasions where I felt there was a great outpouring of God's grace, although no Sacrament was involved.

Should not his ideas on the subject be given more prominence? It would then not come as such a shock to Catholics when they hear that there may be change.

Answer:

Your preference for weekday Mass is no doubt a matter of temperament and personal spirituality: your preference for participation in a quieter and simpler form of worship.

It is certainly not wrong to feel this way, but the Sunday liturgy has an added dimension which goes beyond personal devotion and is a fuller expression of our identity as Church. Besides, the divine commandment to keep the Lord's Day holy is best fulfilled by participation in the Eucharist.

On the matter of the Sacraments and their number, I believe there is no chance that the Church will change the number, seven — which is such an integral part of our Catholic tradition.

In the early days of the Church, before the number seven was settled upon, there were other candidates for admission to the Church's list of Sacraments. But the enumeration of seven Sacraments is now part of the Deposit of Faith. There is nothing 'magic' about the number, seven — although, in the Bible, seven is the number which symbolises totality and perfection.

Nor is the restriction of the number of Sacraments to seven meant to suggest that there are not other powerful avenues of God's grace available to us.

The Sacraments are important occasions in our lives

when Christ encounters us in a special way, but his contact with us is by no means limited to these moments.

It may well happen that a person may have a deep experience of God's grace-filled presence in such devotions as paraliturgies, communal blessings of the sick, penitential services, the Way of the Cross, or Benediction of the Blessed Sacrament — or even in some person or event that we experience outside the strictly 'Church' environment.

All of these meetings with Christ are 'sacraments' in a broad sense, that is, signs of his presence and activity in our midst.

Question 152:

Catholics believe in God. They believe that worship and public acknowledgement are due to God in strict justice. Being Christians, they believe that Jesus Christ, the God-Man, has taught us how to worship God, principally by assisting at the Sacrifice of the Mass, as far as public worship is concerned.

They believe that Jesus Christ established the Catholic Church which speaks with his authority. When the Church decrees that all Catholics must fulfil their duty of worshipping God by attending Mass on Sundays, Catholics all over the world do so in a spirit of obedience to the authority of the Christ in whom they believe.

They attend Mass because they owe this service to God. As they know it is a sin to refuse to pay what they owe to the baker for the bread with which they nourish their lives, so they know it is a greater sin to refuse to pay what they owe to God for the life that bread nourishes.

And since God is God, they go to Mass whether they feel like it or not. Such reasons apply to priests, Religious and laity alike.

Answer:

On more than one occasion Jesus taught that the whole moral law rests on the twofold commandment of love of God and love of neighbour (Matthew 22:36-40; Mark 12:28-31; Luke 10:25-28). This is the essence of the whole moral teaching of Jesus. The presence of this teaching in all three synoptic Gospels underlines its importance. John's

Gospel has the same message: 'If you love me, you will keep my commandments' (14:15).

In the light of this, it is surprising that anyone should write at length about the observance of *any* moral law mentioning strict justice, authority, obedience and sin — and yet not once mention the word 'love'.

I am not questioning what you say about justice, authority and obedience, but unless these notions are discussed within the context of love, then we finish with a distorted picture.

Question 153:

A priest asks whether I am 'pushing' the theory of the distinction between mortal, serious, and venial sin for some bright seminary 'experts', or other 'neo-modernists' whose aim is to explain away the notion of sin.

Another reader expresses his surprise that no one in authority has corrected my views about the spiritual condition of those who acknowledge the Sunday Mass obligation, but who 'occasionally' fail (see Q 148).

He asks whether the same line of reasoning might not be applied to those who murder, commit adultery, or rob a bank. He believes that those attitudes are responsible for 'thousands of our young people leaving the Church'.

Answer:

I must confess that I am surprised at the reaction to my views about the gravity of the sin of missing Sunday Mass. I would like to give an assurance that I am not acting as a 'front man' for anyone.

There is really nothing more I can say on the subject except to quote from a recent book, *In His Light*, by Rev William Anderson, a publication which comes complete with 'Nihil Obstat' and 'Imprimatur' — an assessment by a person in authority that the work contains nothing contrary to Catholic faith or morality: 'When a person consciously decides to follow one's own will in life, this person rejects God and commits a mortal sin. This is a continual way of thinking, a "fundamental option" to choose oneself over God. Just as we cannot say that one act of love makes a person a loving person (although there are cases where this does happen), we cannot say that one non-loving act can make a person an unloving person.

'In this way, the seriousness of a sin can be determined by the fundamental way of thinking of an individual. If one unloving act can change a person's whole direction of thought, then that person commits a mortal sin. Ordinarily this does not happen.'

Question 154:

Many people go to Sunday Mass with all the right motives — love of the Mass, desire to fulfil an obligation that is grave, desire to get to heaven and avoid eternal punishment — simply because they have been trained by good parents and teachers in positive Christian discipline.

One cannot really separate the motives of love, sense of obligation, carefully formed habits, fear of the loss of God and of eternal punishment in hell, in leading the Christian life. They all play their part in leading us to God.

Answer:

It cannot be denied that many Catholics attend Sunday Mass with mixed motives. But I strongly disagree with the statement that it is not possible to separate such diverse motives as love of God, habit, and fear of eternal punishment in hell.

They are certainly separate in my own spirituality; and I should be very surprised and disappointed to think that they are not clearly distinguished in the minds of most Catholics in the performance of any good works they do — including attendance at Sunday Mass.

Question 155:

I have two questions:

1. What is the aim (aims) of a Catholic Mass?

2. What distinction is there between a week-day and a Sunday Mass?

We are looking at ways of improving our parish Masses. As a youth group we are looking for as simple as possible a direction to move.

Answer:

The 'aim' of the Mass, or Eucharist, is to enable members of

the Catholic community to come together to praise and
worship God in the best possible way.

This statement is based on a number of principles which
have their foundation in the Scriptures.

The first is that Jesus' clear intention was to establish a
community. For this purpose he chose and trained 12 disciples to be the nucleus, or core group, of such a community
— a community which soon came to be designated as
Church.

On the night before his death in very solemn circumstances Jesus instituted the Eucharist, and commanded the
disciples to 'do this' in memory of him, that is, to reproduce
in their subsequent community gatherings the action which
he performed at this farewell meal with them.

This separation of his body and blood, under the forms of
bread and wine, anticipated the sacrifice which he offered of
himself to his Father the following day on Calvary.

He thus made provision for his followers to be able to
unite themselves with him, and re-present his perfect act of
sacrifice to the Father, and so to take part directly in its
saving effects.

Thus it is that we Catholics are enabled (in union with
Christ) to offer to God the greatest possible act of worship,
of which the main elements are praise and thanksgiving.

At the same time, when we share in the same body and
blood of Christ by our reception of Holy Communion, we
celebrate and reinforce our unity with one another.

The Eucharist is the principal means of building up the
Body of Christ, which is Paul's phrase to describe the
Church.

The Eucharist has been called 'the summit and source' of
Christian life and activity.

What I have said earlier explains why it is the summit of
Catholic life. But it is also meant to be the source of the life
of love and service which Christ demands of his disciples.

I think this aspect of the Eucharist is beautifully illustrated
in the 13th chapter of St John's Gospel.

John doesn't actually describe the institution of the
Eucharist at the Last Supper. He has already said all that
needs to be said about the Eucharist back in chapter six.

Instead he describes Jesus' humble act of service in washing his Disciples' feet, and reports how on several occasions Jesus urged them to love one another.

John knew well that Jesus in fact instituted the Eucharist on this occasion. By telling us that he preceded the Eucharistic action by washing their feet, and that he surrounded it by repeated demands on them to love one another, John shows us that the Eucharist which we celebrate in church is meant to flow over into our daily relationships.

Any liturgy-minded group seeking to 'improve' their parish Mass should therefore be looking at ways and means to inspire the parish community to more enthusiastic praise and worship of God, to make them more aware of the unity that binds them together, and to motivate them to go out in love and service to their brothers and sisters.

In terms of what is celebrated, there is no distinction at all between Sunday and weekday Masses.

One of the Ten Commandments, however, was to keep the Sabbath Day (the Lord's Day) holy.

For reasons which we will not go into here, the first Christians chose to change the Lord's Day from the Jewish Sabbath to the first day of the week, or Sunday.

In the book of the *Acts of the Apostles*, there is mention of the Christians coming together to worship on the first day of the week.

Elsewhere it is said that their practice was to sing hymns, to pray, to hear the word of God read and explained, and to break bread together (that is, celebrate the Eucharist).

Herein are contained all the essential elements of our Mass.

Question 156:

I think people who ask questions want a straightforward answer. For example, 'Is it a mortal sin to miss Mass on Sunday without a reasonable excuse?' Answer: 'Yes, it is.'

The pros and cons of whether one would be punished if death occurred with this sin on one's soul is up to God, surely, who is the supreme judge of all, who knows everyone's motivations and dispositions at all times. Those who are concerned for souls know that prayer and lots of it is the answer.

The other question, 'What work would constitute a mor-

tal sin if done on the Lord's Day?', needs a more positive answer. Go to Mass, yes — to give glory to God, but don't let the Lord's Day finish there. Do what has to be done: cook the dinner, make the beds, tidy the house, water the plants, but (even though very little daily work is servile in this technological age) is there any need to do things like washing, ironing, scrubbing the floor, cleaning the windows, on this day?

Couldn't the family benefit from a more relaxed atmosphere — a day with the children, a visit to friends, an inspiring book, a musical interlude — all done for the glory of God?

In this day and age a more positive approach is needed: our example, prayers, going to Mass, talking unashamedly about God, discussing modesty and behaviour with our children, saying the Rosary with a friend. It is easy enough to say, but it needs an effort to put into practice.

Be calm, hopeful and full of love at all times. This is my prayer for mankind and I hope it is mankind's prayer for me today.

Answer:

Let me take first your comments on Sunday observance in the matter of work. I am in full agreement with the proposals you put forward about how the Lord's Day might ideally be observed. In fact, there are many Catholic people, and Christian people in general, who approach their Sundays in the spirit which you advocate.

Unfortunately, in the society in which we live, a growing number of families are unable to attain the ideal. The man of the house works five days a week, from early morning to late afternoon. In an increasing number of households, perhaps by choice, but often out of economic necessity, the wife is also part of the workforce.

In the case of young families, Saturdays are often taken up with transporting children to and from sporting events in which they are involved. Which leaves only Sunday for work which may be 'servile', but is not, in the circumstances, 'unnecessary'. Improvement and maintenance of home and grounds might not be the way people would choose to spend their Sunday, but often they have no real choice.

In such cases, I believe they can 'sanctify' the Lord's Day and obey the divine commandment by their community worship, and by doing their best to observe the spirit of the day even though circumstances might not allow them the luxury of abstaining from hard work.

Life was much simpler when the 10 Commandments were promulgated. It is because of these changed circumstances that I believe the Church has wisely chosen to be non-directive in the matter.

As for the gravity of the matter of the Sunday Mass obligation, is it too much to hope that we might cease to think in terms of 'obligation' and 'mortal sin' when this question is raised? I believe this puts the whole matter of our worship in a false perspective. If the teaching Church were to declare tomorrow that Catholics were no longer obliged to attend Sunday Mass, what would be the result?

Would there be a sudden and dramatic decline in the numbers attending? I would like to think not, but perhaps I am over-optimistic. Certainly such a relaxation of Church law (which I am not advocating) would clearly distinguish between those who attend Mass out of a sense of obligation and the fear of committing sin, and those who do so out of love of God.

St Paul's letter to the Galatians is most instructive on this point. The main theme of this letter is that the Christian vocation is a call to freedom: 'for you were called to freedom, brethren' (5:13); 'but if you are led by the Spirit, you are no longer under the law' (5:18).

Paul acknowledged the need for law because he was aware of our sinful human nature. Because we are all sinners to a greater or lesser extent, we need a code of laws to help us to distinguish between 'the works of the flesh' (5:19-21) and 'the fruit of the Spirit' (5:22-23).

Paul himself frequently laid down rules of conduct and delivered moral exhortations. But he saw these precepts simply as applications of the law of love. 'The whole law is fulfilled in one word: you shall love your neighbour as yourself' (5:13-14).

Paul would have been horrified at any suggestion that external laws should be seen as the dynamic principle of Christian living.

It follows that any observance of law which is not motivated by love is useless. External laws derive whatever value they have from the law of the Spirit or the law of love. Mere observance which is empty of love is not an exercise of Christian freedom. On the contrary, the Christian who makes law the dominant element in his life renounces his freedom and becomes a slave to the law.

The person who thinks of celebrating the Eucharist with the rest of the community on the Lord's Day primarily in terms of obligation, or of avoiding mortal sin, is a poor apology for a Catholic Christian.

As St Augustine said: 'The person who avoids evil, not because it is wrong, but because of a commandment, is not a free person. The free person is the one who avoids evil because it is evil' (and who does good, because it is good).

Question 157:

Could you please outline the cold, hard basic facts about what work a person is allowed to do on Sundays around his house and yard and with his car, without breaking the Sabbath Day moral law?

Answer:

It is not easy to give 'cold hard basic facts' about this matter, because it is an area where the Church largely leaves it to the conscience of the individual person.

The word 'Sabbath' comes from the Hebrew verb *Shabat*, which means to cease work, to rest from work. Among the Ten Commandments given by God to Israel was, 'To keep the Sabbath Day holy', that is, to reserve it in a special way for the Lord.

In the Book of Exodus (20:2-7), the motivation given for the observance of the Sabbath (for the Jews, the seventh day of the week) was that God rested from his creative activity on the seventh day, and that man should do likewise in imitation of him.

Much later, the Scribes and Pharisees devised a complex set of rules about the extent of activity which was permissible on the Lord's day. This legalistic approach got out of hand, to the point that 39 ways of breaking the Sabbath were enumerated.

Jesus pointed out the absurdity of these man-made regulations, which led the Jewish leaders to be critical of him even when he healed the sick on the Sabbath day.

In the early days of Christianity the day set aside for the Lord was changed from the seventh to the first day of the week, partly in honour of the Lord's Resurrection on that day, partly to distinguish the Church from Judaism. The Jewish rules about Sabbath observance were discarded.

Obviously, the first and most important way of keeping the Lord's day holy is to join with the rest of the believing community to praise, honour and worship him. This Catholics are obliged to do by celebrating the Eucharist, the highest point of our Christian life and activity.

As for manual work, the Church has seen fit to allow people a considerable freedom. The old catechism spoke in terms of 'unnecessary servile work' without attempting to define that any further.

My own view is that people who have put aside the hour to worship God by attending Mass should have no worries about any work they feel needs to be done.

Usury

Question 158:

Have the Church's teachings on usury been changed, and if so, where are these changes documented? My question is prompted by the high interest rates charged on housing loans — for example, a $30,000 loan over 25 years at 14.5 per cent requires a total payment of $111,780, which is 3.7 times the original $30,000.

Answer:

Yes, the Church has changed its teaching on usury, which is basically the premium paid for a pure loan.

The Church in earlier days based its condemnation of the practice on biblical texts like Leviticus 25:35-37 and Exodus 22:25. Early Church writers argued that the charging of interest was contrary to divine law.

The Council of Nicea in 325 AD decreed that the just man 'does not take interest on loans' and quoted Psalm 15:5. This became the favourite text in the early Middle Ages against the demanding premium on a pure loan. Until the 11th century, at least, the practice of usury was treated as a form of avarice and as a serious sin against charity.

Indeed, the Council of Vienne in 1314 declared that anyone who claimed that taking a premium on a pure loan was no sin, was to be punished as a heretic!

The great Thomas Aquinas held the view that money was a 'sterile' commodity. Lending money was like lending a cup of sugar, a neat exchange of a consumable item. Thomas, however, did hold that in the cases of the loan of a house or a horse, a service fee for the usefulness of what was lent could be lawfully accepted.

Since then, of course, money has taken on the character of a 'fruitful', as opposed to 'sterile', commodity. In a changing economic system, it began to be recognised that money gives to the borrower more than the substance of the loan.

Usury began to be understood as excessive and unjust interest. The old condemnations came to be considered obsolete.

Coming down to more modern times, Pope Leo XIII, in his encyclical *Rerum Novarum* (1891), condemned the exploitation of workers and cited 'rapacious usury' as an instance of injustice even in modern economic conditions.

The old Code of Canon Law promulgated in 1917 also has relevance in the present climate of high interest rates placed on essential loans, for example, for housing and other developments in accord with basic human needs.

Canon 1543 says, in part, that in lending money 'it is not itself unlawful to contract for payment of profit allocated by law, *unless it is clear that this is excessive,* or even for a higher profit, if just and adequate titles are present.'

Such 'titles' include: actual damage, loss of profit, risk to the amount lent and danger from delay in returning what was lent. Only such titles justify the right to claim and the duty to pay a just rate of interest on money lent.

The change in the Church's teaching on usury can be explained by the change in the economic system from feudalism, which was when the absolute prohibitions were delivered, to capitalism which is a completely different ball game.

At the same time, my own opinion — for what it is worth — is that figures such as those you quote illustrate that current interest rates are excessive, unjustified and immoral. Perhaps the Church should be more outspoken about the immorality of the situation.

Question 159:

Your question and answer on usury (Q 158) reveal a lack of appreciation of economic matters that is greatly to be deplored.

At the present rate of inflation my September 1982 dollar will have, in September 1983, the purchasing power of 90 cents in terms of present money.

If I lend $30,000 in September 1982, it is worth $3,000 less in 1982 dollars in September 1983. At a 14.5 per cent

*interest rate I would receive $4350 interest in that one year
and pay tax on this amount at (say) 46 cents in the dollar,
that is $2001. The difference between $4350 (received) and
$2001 (tax) is 2349 in 1983 dollars.*

*I have already lost about $3000 due to inflation, so my
overall loss in purchasing power is $3000 minus $2349, that
is $651. Would I not then be a Good Samaritan to the
borrower? Certainly, I would not be making excessive,
unjustified and immoral demands as you claim.*

Question 160:

*In replying to a question on the Church's current teaching
on usury, you concluded your reply by stating that current
interest rates are 'excessive, unjustified and immoral.'*

*Having regard to all the circumstances, I believe that any
commentary on usury as such should have been made in
relation to all associated facts. If the rates are 'excessive' and
'immoral', surely the rates of interest paid to depositors are
also excessive and immoral, as there is a direct relationship.*

*Money is a commodity, subject to supply and demand. If
banks and building societies do not pay high interest rates to
their depositors, funds flow to other areas, and it is these
funds which are the main basis of housing loans.*

*I believe that society as a whole contributes more than
any other factor to high interest rates.*

*People complain about paying high rates, but they have
hesitation in moving their funds to where they get the best
rate. Unions clamour for higher wages; others for higher
prices; and sectional groups seek greater volumes of government funds into a variety of areas far removed from
government housing projects.*

*The subject requires and provides a far greater scope for
objective discussion than considering a 1982 problem in the
light of an 1891 encyclical. One may be pardoned for won-
dering if the directors of the Vatican Bank have read and
implemented the tenets of* Rerum Novarum.

Answer:

To the charge that my appreciation of economic matters is
deplorable, I can only plead 'guilty'. The original question
was whether the Church has changed its teaching on usury

or interest-taking. The main thrust of my answer dealt with that limited area, in which I have a certain competence: in matters economic, I have virtually nil.

I did say, by way of an appendix to my answer, that current interest rates seem to be 'excessive, unjustified and immoral'. I agree with the comment that 'society as a whole contributes more than any other factor to high interest rates'. I did not intend to isolate any section of society as the sole guilty party.

In other words, the 'immorality' is an inbuilt part of the system.

I do not agree, however, that it is irrelevant to consider a 1982 problem in the light of an 1891 encyclical like Leo XIII's *Rerum Novarum,* and the principles which it lays down. If those principles were true then, they are true now. As for the familiarity of the directors of the Vatican Bank with these principles, I would prefer not to comment.

But because this issue is such a timely one, and one that is likely to figure even more prominently in people's thinking in the months and years ahead, I should like to offer a few further thoughts on the question of usury.

Until comparatively recent times, the word 'usury' had a very specific connotation. In its primary sense, it denotes a charge made for the use of something which has no value except in its use.

If I were to lend a box of matches and charge something for the use of the matches over and above their value, I would be guilty of usury. The matches have no value except in their use. Therefore, to demand in return for the loan an equivalent box of matches, *plus* something for their use, is to be guilty of usury in its primary sense.

It is only in more recent years that people have tended to see usury as *exorbitant* interest charged on loans. Originally usury was the charging of any interest at all.

Philosophers, theologians and canonists of the Middle Ages recognised every loan of money in this light.

St Thomas Aquinas, arguably the greatest of Church theologians next to the New Testament authors, is most explicit. In his celebrated *Summa Theologiae,* he says: 'The proper and principal use of money is its consumption or spending . . . For this reason, it is by its very nature unlawful to take payment for the use of money lent. Such payment is called usury. And just as a man is bound to restore other ill-gotten goods, so he is bound to restore the money which he has taken as usury.'

Of course, it was always recognised that there were certain *external* claims to interest on a monetary loan (for example, risk, personal loss, etc.), but the current question is about a title to interest by reason of nothing more than the very loan itself.

The common modern approach of moralists to this matter is along the lines of the view expressed by the reader who argues that the nature of money has changed . . . 'Money is not now merely a medium of exchange, but an instrument of production: so, just as money may be charged for the use of land, or of a house, so money may be charged for the use of money.

'Money now has its fair and reasonable price like any other commodity, and the sin of usury is committed not by taking a fair and reasonable interest for a loan, but by taking excessive interest.'

There is, however, another possible approach to the question. Nearly 40 years ago, John P. Kelly, a Brisbane solicitor, delivered the annual Aquinas lecture, which was subsequently published under the title, *Aquinas and Modern Practices of Interest Taking.* He maintained that St Thomas Aquinas foresaw the disastrous consequences that would follow if money — then as now a means of exchange — were allowed to assume the stature of productive capital.

The introduction to Mr Kelly's thesis was written by the highly respected economist, Colin Clark. Dr Clark wrote: 'It is quite wrong to suppose that St Thomas Aquinas wrote only for a simple rural community, and took no account of the problems and complexities of modern finance . . . He faced in essence exactly the same problems that we have to face, and his conclusions only need translating into modern language.

'So translated, they show that any interest on loans, back deposits, government bonds, mortages, debentures, outstanding accounts, etc, is an offence against morality . . . At the heart of the great structure of present day usury lie what are called "national debts". . . .

'I think that I am on safe ground in predicting that during the next few years the budgeting problems posed by huge national debt interest payments will provoke, in every country of the world, a close study of the ethics of usury . . . There is no escape from the conclusion that government loans must be interest free . . .'

As we have said earlier, the basic argument used by those who justify interest-taking on a loan seems to be that money now is not the same as money was in the time of Thomas Aquinas. In other words, it has become 'virtually productive'! This argument has been accepted by most Catholic moralists.

But does this beg the question? Even today, can money be actually productive unless it is spent or consumed, just as it had to be in the 13th century, the time of Aquinas?

Are not usury received and usury exacted both unjust? Does inflation justify usury? Perhaps they explain and support each other, but are they justified? Society might seem to be paying a terribly dear price for its changed approach to the matter of usury.

And how true is it to say that the Church has changed its teaching on usury?

In the present social and economic climate, such questions might seem to be Utopian and unreal.

But one of the roles of the Church is to be a constant constructive critic of society, and not just an acceptor of the *status quo*. So while I admit to a deplorable lack of expertise on economic matters. I feel justified in submitting these questions for people's consideration.

Top religious titles from Dove Communications

JOHN XXIII: Pope of the Council
Peter Hebblethwaite
$19.95 (Cloth)
30 b & w photographs, many previously unpublished
In the few years of his reign, Pope John XXIII transformed the Roman Catholic Church and the image of the papacy. He called the Second Vatical Council and gave it a vision for the future. He mediated in the Cuban missile crisis and promoted dialogue between East and West, and understanding between Catholic and non-Catholic. When he was elected at the age of 78 he was called the stop-gap pope; when he died he was mourned by the whole world.

In this definitive biography, Peter Hebblethwaite uses important new evidence from ecclesiastic and diplomatic sources to examine the life and beliefs of John XXIII. He provides an outstanding contribution to the history of the Catholic Church and the world in the 20th century, together with a moving account of a man with human failings and doubts who became the pope 'in whom the Church and the world were prodigiously blessed'.
(January)

RELUCTANT CONSCIENCE: Closing the Gap between
the Gospel and Reality in Australia
Alan Nichols
$8.95
'It is very worrying to see the Church at a loss for words in applying the Gospel to secular Australia, to see church leaders reluctant to criticise government policies, or if they do, only the moral ones and not the economic or social policies'.

Alan Nichols, Director of the Mission of St James and St John, Melbourne, provides the Christian reader with a stronger motivation for engaging in a personal ministry of social justice. At the same time he seeks to challenge the Church's reluctant conscience to do this corporately.

A major achievement is his theological analysis of thinking within the evangelical tradition and his suggestions for meeting-points for Catholic and Protestant writers on justice issues.

MARRIAGE, DIVORCE AND NULLITY: A Guide to the Annulment Process in the Catholic Church
Geoffrey Robinson
$7.95
Australian canon lawyer, Bishop Geoffrey Robinson from Sydney provides a helpful and compassionate guide to marriage, divorce and the annulment process in the Catholic Church. His book addresses those Catholics who believe that marriage blessed by the Church is for ever, as well as those who believe the Church should recognise civil divorce and allow Catholics to remarry without further ado.

Marriage, Divorce and Nullity is the first book to relate the new Canon Law to the annulment process.

SEASONS OF HOPE: Christian Issues in the Modern World
Anthony Kelly CSSR
$7.59
What can the Gospel mean for us in Australia today? In our country Easter falls at the time of mellowing autumn, Christmas at the height of summer. Our seasons cause us to reinterpret many of the traditional scriptural messages. In a similar way we face the challenge of reshaping the whole Christian vision in a way that will be credible and responsible.

Tony Kelly, the President of Yarra Theological Union, Melbourne, responds to this challenge in these essays. He covers a wide spectrum of topics, always with a freshness of approach, a lack of glib answers. He writes for a new generation of Christians who see themselves as a pilgrim people with a crucial role to play in a changing world.

WOMAN: FIRST AMONG THE FAITHFUL
Frank Moloney SDB
$8.95
This book attempts to show that Jesus of Nazareth established a new reign of God where all accepted fears, taboos, distinctions and divisions between male and female had been wiped away. Father Moloney contends that all the major writings of the earliest Church are at one in presenting women as often the first to come to faith, and their faith is often used either in contrast to the littleness of the faith of others or to show the way to true faith.

Father Moloney is an internationally recognised scholar of the New Testament.
(March)

HEAVEN'S BACKYARD
David Lander
$7.95
In David Lander's poems God is amazed by, and is at the mercy of, the universe that he himself has made. He is a casual, gentle and domestic creator. Mishaps, blunders, deceits, affection, discovery, surprise and whimsy abound in these interactions between a very human God and his teeming, unpredictable backyard.

Published with the assistance of the Literature Board. First in Dove's new series of Australian religious poetry.